The Simpsons in
the Classroom

The Simpsons in the Classroom

Embiggening the Learning Experience with the Wisdom of Springfield

KARMA WALTONEN
and DENISE DU VERNAY

McFarland & Company, Inc., Publishers
Jefferson, North Carolina, and London

LIBRARY OF CONGRESS CATALOGUING-IN-PUBLICATION DATA

Waltonen, Karma, 1975–
    The Simpsons in the classroom : embiggening the learning
experience with the wisdom of Springfield / Karma Waltonen
and Denise Du Vernay.
        p.   cm.
    Includes bibliographical references and index.

    ISBN 978-0-7864-4490-8
    softcover : 50# alkaline paper ∞

    1. Simpsons (Television program)   I. Du Vernay, Denise,
1973–   II. Title.
PN1992.77.S58W35   2010
791.45'72 — dc22   2010008145

British Library cataloguing data are available

Cover images ©2010 Shutterstock

Manufactured in the United States of America

McFarland & Company, Inc., Publishers
    Box 611, Jefferson, North Carolina 28640
    www.mcfarlandpub.com

Karma dedicates this book to Alexander,
her special little guy.

Table of Contents

Acknowledgments

The authors would like to thank David Silverman, Dana Gould, Denise Sirkot, Sergio Guerra, Rick Miller, Jouni Paakkinen, Tammy Hocking, Deborah Coxwell-Teague, and Al Yankovic. We'd also like to thank our interns, Alan Eng, Minh Nguyen, and Brian To. Special thanks to Alexander Waltonen, who contributed and fact-checked even though he probably had better things to do. Thanks also goes out to Susan Wolfe, who quickly answered emails with linguistic inquiries; Roberto Delgadillo, who found secondary sources for us; Margaret Mercer, who checked our French; Elizabeth Lanceman, who checked our British English; and Kurt and Kelly Kramer, who helped us uncover the mysteries of Word 2007. Also, we can't forget Mignon Fogarty (aka "Grammar-Girl"), who, through the magic of Twitter, answered punctuation questions on the fly. Thank you to everyone who talked *Simpsons* with us over the years and to our students for inspiring us and for putting up with our (mostly) perfectly cromulent teaching. Finally, thank you to *The Simpsons* for embiggening our lives.

In addition to acknowledging her wonderful friends, family, and colleagues, Karma would like to specifically thank the Margaret Atwood Book Club of Davis, Ken Freeman, and Rae Gouirand for their support; Heather Watne for physical health; Mitchel Adler for mental health; and Jim Bradley for the most extraordinary writer's retreat imaginable. Denise, I have just three words for you: Best. Friend. Ever.

Denise would like to thank her sometimes skeptical but always supportive family, the wonderful teachers she's learned from and worked with over the years, especially John O'Brien, Joe Basile, Ed Allen, Bonnie Braendlin, Tonia Hoffman, and, of course, the lovely and brilliant Karma Waltonen, without whom life is unimaginable. Thanks to my loved ones who've encouraged my writing and Simpsonology over the years, especially Joe Vince for keeping me in pizza and Diet Coke (not to mention lending swift Google-Fu skills), TJ Young, Jeff Du Vernay, Amy Deuchler, Justin Shady, Katherine Bryja, Carrie Antlfinger and the rest of the food night group, the Harrisons, and Reed Bender (you're the coolest).

Preface

The Simpsons has been the deserving object of attention, debate, and scholarship since its start more than 20 years ago. We have been part of the discussion in classrooms, conferences, and the occasional brewpub; we have collected what we've learned about teaching *The Simpsons* in this book.

There are many secondary texts that deal with *The Simpsons*, and while some of them do focus on education, there is currently no pedagogy text. We have written that pedagogy text. This book aims to help high school and college teachers integrate *The Simpsons* into lessons smoothly, whether the course's focus is composition, literature, linguistics, theater or film studies, or any humanities discipline. The book also offers ideas on how to teach a full *Simpsons* course. We share the exercises, prompts, and even syllabi that we use in our own classrooms. Because we have been teaching *The Simpsons* since 1999, we are sharing our most successful assignments (sparing teachers the need to start from scratch) and we're happy to do it!

There are many benefits to using *The Simpsons* in classes. The most obvious is that it's funny: Laughing students are not sleeping students. The fact that the students will already know the show — and that we can then use the show as a jumping-off point for their lessons — is beyond helpful. Students may at first be resistant to seeing the familiar as strange, which is required for critical thinking, but they soon become engaged when they are able to use their familiarity with a subject as knowledge. They are already experts on their culture; why not let them use their strengths as we take them into unfamiliar realms of discourse?

I'm Learnding!: An Introduction to Simpsonology

I believe that fiction writing is the guardian of the moral and ethical sense of the community. Especially now that organized religion is scattered and in disarray, and politicians have, Lord knows, lost their credibility, fiction is one of the few forms left through which we may examine our society not in its particular but in its typical aspects; through which we can see ourselves and the ways in which we behave towards each other, through which we can see others and judge them and ourselves. — Margaret Atwood

And how is education supposed to make me feel smarter? Besides, every time I learn something new, it pushes some old stuff out of my brain. Remember when I took that home winemaking course and I forgot how to drive? — Homer Simpson

Why The Simpsons?

In "Little Girl in the Big Ten," Lisa Simpson attends a class at the local university — "Anthropology 101: Passive Analysis of Visual Iconography." After watching the usual bloody *Itchy & Scratchy* fare, the following discussion takes place.

> **Professor:** So what does this cartoon mean?
> **Tina** (a student): It shows how the depletion of our natural resources has pitted our small farmers against each other.
> **Professor:** Yes, and birds go "tweet." What else?

The Simpsons is mocking teachers like us!

It's not the first time, actually. We both attended and taught at Florida State University. Shortly thereafter, in the episode "Smart and Smarter," a character played by Simon Cowell said of Maggie, "Your baby is brilliant. Why, she could already teach at Florida State." As Maggie is an undiscovered genius, we don't mind. We wouldn't anyway. It's high praise even to be noticed by the show that called Princeton a clown college.

Karma shows the clip of "Passive Analysis of Visual Iconography" on the first day of her *Simpsons* class as a way to address the elephant in the room ("What are we doing here?") by letting the show itself pose the question.

Many people out there use *The Simpsons* in their classrooms. The classes are more varied than one might think — American studies, women's studies, literature, composition, science, psychology, sociology, religion, political science, and even math.[1]

There are many reasons for this:

1. As of 2007, there were no 18-year-old students entering college who had grown up without *The Simpsons* as a part of the world around them.

2. *The Simpsons* permeates our culture. It is referenced in and has influenced many other media. *South Park*, exhibiting what Harold Bloom might call the anxiety of influence, even had an episode about how difficult it is to obtain originality when confronted with the *Simpsons* oeuvre: "*Simpsons* Already Did It." The Simpsons have a star on the Hollywood Walk of Fame. The former prime minister of England and every Beatle except John Lennon has guest starred on the show. Pollsters consistently report that people can name the characters in *The Simpsons* more easily than they can remember aspects of politics and history. "D'oh" is now in *The Oxford English Dictionary*. In 1992, President George H. W. Bush used *The Simpsons* as a benchmark with which to measure family functionality (though the reference was meant as an insult).

3. Thus, those who ignore *The Simpsons* are in danger of being culturally illiterate. What used to be oral stories and popular entertainment (Greek myths and Shakespeare's plays, respectively) became necessary reading for those who wanted to understand allusions and revisions in later art and literature. *The Simpsons* is a necessity for those who wish to stay on the pulse of contemporary culture. (The fact that you need to understand Greek myths and Shakespeare to understand some of *The Simpsons* should not be overlooked.)

4. One mark of superior cultural literacy is to be able to compre-

hend and appreciate a culture's sense of humor. Unfortunately, humor is a devalued aspect of culture. As Helle Klem Thomsen and Jacob David Eichler, editors of a Copenhagen Business School Press anthology of American humor, explain, it is as if "a text must be serious in order to be relevant and meaningful" (7). Their anthology was created, however, to further international understanding: "One touchstone of really understanding a foreign culture and language is [the ability to] appreciate their humor" (9).

The Simpsons is our text of choice because it captures our zeitgeist. What other show so perfectly captures America while satirizing it at every turn? As Duane Dudek of the *Milwaukee Journal Sentinel* maintains, "If television stirs primal memories of ancient communal campfires, then *The Simpsons* are [sic] the cave paintings for our times." We are social anthropologists, exploring the cave paintings to understand what they reveal about our culture.

If you're reading this book with an eye to using *The Simpsons* in your classroom, we don't need to convince you that this is more than *just a show*, more than *just a cartoon*. We'll list articles and books in Chapter 1 that do make this argument, however, in case you need them in your arsenal. However, if you are reading this book simply because you're a *Simpsons* fanatic, we do not mean to alienate you by constantly talking to you like you're a teacher. Thank you for reading the book!

While there are many secondary texts that deal with *The Simpsons*, and while some of them do focus on education, there is as yet no pedagogy text. With this book, we aim to help you integrate *The Simpsons* into your lessons smoothly. We will also give you ideas on how to teach a full *Simpsons* course, sharing the exercises and prompts we use. We will also update our webpage www.simpsonology.com as new episodes appear, as new sources appear, and as new resources are found.

There are both superficial and more thoughtful benefits to using *The Simpsons* in class. On the surface, attendance is not only improved, it is enthusiastic. Students are often more inclined to participate in class discussions when they think they're discussing an entertaining TV show with which they are often already intimately familiar. When the lessons shift to topics that are less familiar, the students are already engaged and have gained confidence. As Robert J. Thompson explains: "The genius of using *The Simpsons* [in classrooms] is taking difficult concepts and using something students know intimately. *The Simpsons* is like a Trojan horse and is a useful tool in getting students to learn" (quoted in Keslowitz 6).

One of the best examples of this is seen by posing the following question at the beginning of an integration of *The Simpsons*: Were any of you NOT allowed to watch this show? Students launch into a discussion of parental techniques, censorship, and media. This show often inspires even the shyest of students into talking.

There are disadvantages to using *The Simpsons*, however. Some students may have been sheltered from *The Simpsons* or may have been raised in one of the countries where it wasn't as invasive as in our own. However, we have never known a medium so useful in facilitating cultural literacy for these types of students.

Some students, when they hear *The Simpsons* is on a syllabus, assume they will be in for an easy class and an easy A. Occasionally, students choose a time slot, and not necessarily a class, and may not take the subject matter seriously. These students will be insolent when asked to start paying active attention to the show and the class. We advise attempting to weed out these students early. If they manage to stay in the class, they might need to be reminded that Shakespeare was once "popular culture," too. (These students might also be seen as your great challenge of the term — if you can get them thinking critically, you will have scored a point for the side of light.)

We must sometimes defend ourselves against parents, students, and colleagues who keep saying the word "cartoon" as if it's the ketchup you've just offered them for their filet mignon. Most of these people haven't watched the show. They often quiet down once you tell them that the vast majority of the show's writers are from the Ivy League; some require a reason to be impressed before they can accept something as college material. These sorts of people have existed throughout history, declaring themselves critics — whenever anything is popular or belongs to a relatively new genre, they cry foul.

One of the reasons why watching and teaching *The Simpsons* is rewarding is that it's a text that invites critical thinking. Theorists have been classifying texts along the critical thinking spectrum for a long time. Roland Barthes divides texts into *readerly* and *writerly*. *Readerly* texts are not challenging for the reader, while *writerly* texts disturb expectations and call attention to the act of reading or viewing. The latter texts reward those who return to the text after the first read. Stanley Fish discusses texts in much the same way, but he uses the terms *rhetorical* and *dialectical*. The *dialectical* (writerly) text "is didactic in a special sense; it does not preach the truth, but asks its readers to discover the truth for themselves, and this discovery is often made at the expense not only of a reader's opinions and values, but of his self-esteem" (quoted in Freund 98).[2]

Both reader-response and reception theorists would agree with Margaret Atwood that every reader is different, as every reader comes to a text with a distinct history — including a unique reading and viewing history. Each experience changes a person further: "Reading is also a process and it also changes you. You aren't the same person after you've read a particular book as you were before, and you will read the next book, unless both are Harlequin Romances, in a slightly different way" (Atwood, *Second Words* 345).

Jamey Heit reminds us that, "[a]s a postmodern show, *The Simpsons* relies in part on its viewers to generate meaning" (12). While some believe that the show has radical ideas (others claim that it's evenhanded), whatever meaning that is taken from the show comes from an interplay of many factors, including an audience trained in a certain level of cultural and teleliteracy: "Meaning must grow out of *The Simpsons* interacting with, not dictating to, its audience" (13).

Of course, to get the most out of an experience, it is necessary to participate actively rather than passively. Unlike the professor in *The Simpsons*, we discourage "*passive* viewing of visual iconography." Passive viewing may be what some students expect in the beginning, but active viewing is what must be nurtured and demanded. The active viewer asks questions and makes connections. A writerly text of this stature deserves nothing less.

He's Bart Simpson; Who the Hell Are We?

Karma has been watching *The Simpsons* from the beginning — the very beginning, when they were only animated shorts on *The Tracey Ullman Show*. Karma has always had a penchant for comedy and saw Ullman as a successor to another of her heroes, Carol Burnett. When she heard that there would be a *Simpsons* Christmas special, she and her mom set up the VCR. Karma's mother, unlike Karma's grandmother, found the show endearing rather than a promotion of bad behavior. Karma tape-recorded every episode and became one of those annoying people who can find a *Simpsons* quote for every occasion.

She met Denise in graduate school, as Karma was setting up her first *Simpsons* course. Karma has taught *The Simpsons* at Florida State University and now teaches courses on the show at the University of California, Davis.

Denise, too, discovered and loved *The Simpsons* from the beginning. She taught *The Simpsons* at Florida State University and currently teaches communications and humanities courses at Milwaukee School of Engineering, working *The Simpsons* into her course plans frequently. Once, after a week in a cabin on an island in a northern Minnesota lake (without indoor plumbing), her friend asked if she was looking forward to getting home. "Well, I do miss Bart," was all she said.

What We Won't Do

While we would love to really show off our geekiness by referencing everything that can possibly be referenced in this show, we simply cannot discuss every *Simpsons* moment and episode that strikes our fancy. We're very sorry if we didn't get to share your favorite joke with you.

We will try not to repeat the mistakes that some books and articles have made in the past. We are Simpsonologists[3] and take the name seriously. Thus, we are not passing fans who may have seen a few episodes and have decided that we can write about the life of the show. We are not trying to sell a book about a particular *Simpsons* topic after having rather randomly picked this show as our medium. We may make mistakes, but not because we aren't familiar with the canon; it will be because people make mistakes. In practical terms, this means that we won't treat "Treehouse of Horror" (Halloween) episodes as part of the "realistic" canon. We also won't say silly things like Maggie has never spoken, when in fact Elizabeth Taylor voiced her first word.[4] As the show is still in production, we will potentially fall victim to a temporal problem — that is, we might make a generalization or draw a conclusion that is disputed by shows yet to come.

We will not be devoting time to a history of the show or the characters. Most secondary sources do this. Presumably, if you're reading this, you know who the family members are, what the name of their town is, and other basic information. If you need a good overview of the early history of the show, we recommend Chris Turner's *Planet Simpson*. We, unfortunately, will also refrain from constantly inserting *Simpsons* jokes and quick references. (We cannot make the same promise on the website!)

We will not attempt to talk about subjects that we don't know much about. Thus, this book is geared toward the humanities. While we can talk about philosophies of learning and Marxist theory, we can't be that helpful with physics and economics. The ways in which other authors have discussed how *The Simpsons* intersects with these ideas is covered in Chapter 1.

Finally, we will not throw a lot of theory at you, nor will we seek to render unintelligible the information related here via jargon, syntax, or pretentious diction — except right there. When theory is mentioned, it will be referenced for those who aren't familiar with it. We prefer practicality to theory. We also prefer clarity and being readable over ambiguity and being undecipherable.

What We Will Do

The remainder of this chapter will give a timeline of the show, highlighting important moments both within the world of the show and within the wider contextual and pop-cultural world. We hope this is useful to people who need to brush up on their *Simpsons* history or who want to be able to discuss the show within the broader culture. We will conclude this chapter with an episode guide, geared to allow teachers to find the *Simpsons* episode that fits the topic they're interested in.

Chapter 1 is an overview of secondary sources on *The Simpsons*, including books, Internet resources, and significant articles. Consider this an annotated bibliography.

Chapter 2 discusses the use of *The Simpsons* in composition classrooms, reviewing critical thinking and argument terms before launching into activities and paper assignments related to argument, logic, and style, and editing.

Chapter 3 deals with linguistics. This chapter discusses many of the subfields within linguistics (phonology, morphology, language acquisition, etc.) and gives examples, not just of how *The Simpsons* has interacted with these subfields, but in the case of morphology, how *The*

Simpsons has actually affected language. The chapter closes with some activities and assignments suitable for students taking introductory linguistics.

Chapter 4 details how *The Simpsons* intersects with literature, including poetry, fiction, drama, and film. While many of the assignments from Chapter 2 would be appropriate in a literature classroom, this chapter ends with a general discussion of literature with targeted paper assignments.

Chapter 5 is concerned with how *The Simpsons* intersects with cultural literacy, including popular culture, social issues, and cultural issues and shifts. Particular attention is paid to using *The Simpsons* in humanities classes.

Chapter 6 discusses the show as a piece of art in and of itself. Its genre and methods (postmodern satire, parody, etc.) will be discussed, before moving on to activities and a sample syllabus. Due to the problems of defining postmodernism, parody, and other relevant terms, this chapter is the most theory-laden.

We do not intend this book to be the end-all and be-all for teaching *The Simpsons*, but we hope it provides useful information and ideas and continues the pedagogical conversation.

The Simpsons *Timeline (Forever Incomplete)*

April 5, 1987 — *Married with Children* premieres. It is the first prime-time series to air on Fox. *The Tracey Ullman Show* airs immediately thereafter.

April 19, 1987 — The Simpson family appears in an animated short on *The Tracey Ullman Show*.

[January 20, 1989 — George H. W. Bush takes office.]

[July 5, 1989 — *Seinfeld* premieres on NBC.]

[November 9, 1989 — Crowds dismantle the Berlin Wall.]

December 17, 1989 — "Simpsons Roasting on an Open Fire" — first full-length episode — premieres.

January 14, 1990 — "Bart the Genius" premieres with the classic opening credits, including the first couch gag and the first chalkboard gag ("I will not waste chalk").

[February 11, 1990 — Nelson Mandela released from jail.]

[August 2, 1990—Gulf War begins.]

October 11, 1990—The first episode in Season 2, "Bart Gets an *F*," pits *The Simpsons* against the most popular sitcom of the time, *The Cosby Show.*

October 25, 1990—The first "Treehouse of Horror" airs.

November 8, 1990—In "Dancin' Homer," Tony Bennett appears as himself, the first guest star on the show to do so (other guest stars voiced characters).

November 20, 1990—"Do the Bartman" video premieres around the world. The single was #1 in many countries. Michael Jackson was a coauthor, although contractually he could not receive credit.

[February 28, 1991—Gulf War ends.]

[August 6, 1991—The World Wide Web is publicly available.]

January 27, 1992—President George H. W. Bush, campaigning for reelection, says: "We're going to strengthen the American family to make them more like the Waltons and less like the Simpsons." (Note that this line recurred in slightly different wording in several of his speeches around this time.)

January 30, 1992—A rerun of "Stark Raving Dad" has a short new opening, in which Bush's comments about the Simpsons is aired. Bart, who is watching him on television, retorts, "We're just like the Waltons—we're praying for an end to the Depression, too."

February 20, 1992—"Homer at the Bat" is the first episode to beat *The Cosby Show* in the ratings.

March 26, 1992—"Colonel Homer" airs. It is the last episode to air opposite *The Cosby Show.* This is the only episode with Matt Groening listed as principal writer.

April 30, 1992—*The Cosby Show*, which had been up against *The Simpsons* on Thursday night for years, goes off the air.

June 25, 1992—The blackboard gag in a rerun is changed so that Bart writes "It's potato, not potatoe," mocking Vice President Dan Quayle's inability to spell the word during an elementary school visit. Episode: "Two Cars in Every Garage and Three Eyes on Every Fish."

October 1992—Tracey Ullman sues for some *Simpsons* money. She loses her suit.

October 1, 1992—"A Streetcar Named Marge" offends some people in New Orleans.

October 8, 1992—The chalkboard in "Homer the Heretic" reads "I will not defame New Orleans."

[January 20, 1993 — President Bill Clinton takes office.]

[April 5, 1994 — Kurt Cobain dies.]

April 29, 1994 — The 100th episode airs. "Sweet Seymour Skinner's Baadasssss Song" has Bart write "I will not celebrate meaningless milestones" on the chalkboard.

March 5, 1995 — Matt Groening takes his name off the credits for "A Star Is Burns," as he feels the episode is an ad for another Fox show, *The Critic*.

April 30, 1995 — Willie calls the French "cheese-eating surrender monkeys" in "'Round Springfield."

May 21, 1995 — The first part of "Who Shot Mr. Burns?" airs, marking the end of the sixth season, the beginning of a contest to solve the mystery, and the only two-part *Simpsons* episode (to date).

January 14, 1996 — "Two Bad Neighbors" allows Homer a fistfight with George H. W. Bush (not playing himself). The DVD feature shows an exchange of letters between Barbara Bush and the staff, after she had said the show was dumb.

February 18, 1996 — "Cromulent" is invented in "Lisa the Iconoclast"; it is now found in *Webster's New Millennium Dictionary of English*. ("Embiggen" also appears in the episode.)

[January 12, 1997 — *King of the Hill* debuts on Fox. The show is created by *Beavis and Butthead*'s Mike Judge and *Simpsons* writer Greg Daniels. (Daniels will go on to create *The Office* for American television.)]

February 9, 1997 — "The Itchy & Scratchy & Poochie Show" episode marks *The Simpsons* overtaking *The Flintstones* as the longest-running prime-time animated series. (Krusty refers to television history within the episode.) Comic Book Guy declares the *Itchy & Scratchy* episode the "worst episode ever," sparking a much-used catchphrase.

[August 31, 1997 — At age 36, Princess Diana dies in a car crash in Paris.]

April 26, 1998 — The 200th episode, "Trash of the Titans," airs.

[May 14, 1998 — *Seinfeld* ends after nine seasons on NBC.]

May 28, 1998 — Phil Hartman dies; Troy McClure, Lionel Hutz, and many other characters are silenced.

[January 31, 1999 — *Family Guy* premieres on Fox. It is met with mixed reviews, including praise for being irreverent but funny, and criticism for mimicking storylines and humor too much like *The Simpsons*. Fans and critics continue to make similar observations.]

[July 1999 — Denise and Karma meet at Florida State University. That winter, Karma teaches Florida State University's first course on *The Simpsons*; Denise teaches the university's second *Simpsons* course the following winter.]

December 31, 1999 — *Time* declares *The Simpsons* the best television show of the 20th century.

January 14, 2000 — The Simpsons are awarded a star on the Hollywood Walk of Fame.

February 13, 2000 — Maude Flanders dies in the episode "Alone Again, Natura-Diddily."

[January 20, 2001 — President George W. Bush takes office.]

June 14, 2001 — "Doh"/"D'oh" added to *Oxford English Dictionary*. (It appears in scripts and subtitles as "annoyed grunt." *The Simpsons'* neologisms are discussed in Chapter 3.)

September 11, 2001 — Terrorists attack New York and Washington, D.C., with hijacked aircraft. "The City of New York vs. Homer Simpson" stops airing (permanently, in some markets), due to its depiction of the World Trade Center.

[February 12, 2002 — After threatening more than once, Fox cancels *Family Guy*.]

March 31, 2002 — "Blame It on Lisa," the episode in which the family goes to Brazil, airs. Brazil complains about its portrayal. (This is discussed further in Chapter 5).

June 26, 2002 — *South Park* airs the episode "*Simpsons* Already Did It."

February 2, 2003 — 300th episode, "Strong Arms of the Ma," appears.

November 23, 2003 — Prime Minister Tony Blair appears as himself in "The Regina Monologues."

[May 2005 — *Family Guy* returns to Fox.]

February 28, 2006 — The Associated Press reports on a study that confirms that Americans know more about *The Simpsons* than the First Amendment.

May 20, 2007 — 400th episode: "You Kent Always Say What You Want."

July 27, 2007 — *The Simpsons Movie* opens.

April 28, 2008 — *The Simpsons Ride* opens, replacing *Back to the Future* at Universal Studios Florida.

April 2008 — Venezuelan TV replaces *The Simpsons* with *Baywatch* after the former is criticized as inappropriate for children.

May 19, 2008 — *The Simpsons Ride* opens, replacing *Back to the Future* at Universal Studios Hollywood.

February 15, 2009 — *The Simpsons* is broadcast in HD and features a new opening sequence in "Take My Life, Please."

March 17, 2009 — "In the Name of the Grandfather" premieres in the UK before being broadcast in the U.S.

July 25, 2009 — Morgan Spurlock meets with fans at Comic-Con San Diego to audition for *The Simpsons' Twentieth Anniversary Special — In 3-D! On Ice!*

[September 13, 2009 — *King of the Hill* airs its final episode, with the status of second-longest-running American animated series (after *The Simpsons*).]

Awards/Accomplishments (So Far):

- 24 Emmy Awards
- 26 Annie Awards
- Peabody Award
- Named by *Time* as the best television show of the 20th century
- Record holder for "Most Guest Stars Featured in a Television Series"
- Longest-running sitcom in history
- Longest-running American prime-time show

Episode Guide

The episode guide that follows is designed specifically for teachers. Each episode (up to the time of this writing) is listed in chronological order. The notes provided include narrative structure and parody, as well as discussion points for the classroom such as social issues, censorship, and other noteworthy information. All information consists of the authors' own observations or were learned from the DVD commentaries (such as incidents of censorship).

This is not an exhaustive list of jokes and allusions. Included are only allusions that are extended or developed strongly enough to be teachable. For more extensive information (allusions, additional jokes, couch gags) see the *Our Favorite Family* books or snpp.com (The Simpsons Archive).

We have not included references that exist across almost all episodes.

For example, most episodes include some use of literary foils and have foci on the family, relationships, community, forgiveness, and the like; we list such repeating themes only when they are the essential theme of the episode.

Season Number and Episode	Cumulative Episode Number	Title	Themes, Discussion Points, Teachable Elements Other Notes
1.1	1	Simpsons Roasting on an Open Fire	Holidays (Christmas); economics/class; family values; censorship (censors tried to change Lisa's costume)
1.2	2	Bart the Genius	Education; gifted education; family; cheating in school; parenting
1.3	3	Homer's Odyssey	Job loss; employment; safety; suicide; social protest
1.4	4	There's No Disgrace Like Home	Family therapy; family relationships/expectations
1.5	5	Bart the General	Bullies; war; censorship (Grampa writes a letter about language such as that used in the episode)
1.6	6	Moaning Lisa	Depression; family; education; music
1.7	7	The Call of the Simpsons	Economics/class; nature/wilderness; envy; camping
1.8	8	The Telltale Head	Narrative structure (the majority of the story is flashback, in medias res); peer pressure; guilt; parody (*The Tell-Tale Heart*)
1.9	9	Life on the Fast Lane	Marriage; adultery; temptation; overcompensation; bowling; birthdays
1.10	10	Homer's Night Out	Feminism; objectification of women; parenting

Season Number and Episode	Cumulative Episode Number	Title	Themes, Discussion Points, Teachable Elements Other Notes
1.11	11	The Crepes of Wrath	Fine art, France (stereo-types); linguistics (language acquisition); education abroad; exchange students; international espionage; Albania
1.12	12	Krusty Gets Busted	Crime (theft and framing); children's television; heroes
1.13	13	Some Enchanted Evening	Crime (theft); marital problems; censorship (censors tried to edit the line about Marge's nightie); babysitting; "most wanted" shows
2.1	14	Bart Gets an *F*	Education; prayer; religion; knowledge; teaching
2.2	15	Simpson and Delilah	Appearance prejudice; employment; hair growth/loss; public speaking; body image
2.3	16	Treehouse of Horror (Bad Dream House; Hungry Are the Damned; The Raven)	Holidays (Halloween); parody ("The Raven"); censorship (Marge appeals to parents to put their children to bed rather than writing angry letters); aliens; hauntings
2.4	17	Two Cars in Every Garage and Three Eyes on Every Fish	Politics; elections; nuclear safety/waste; political campaigns; mudslinging/ spinning; homemaking; (when the episode was rerun, the chalkboard gag made fun of V.P.'s inability to spell potato — perhaps he had seen how Bart spelled it in "Dead Putting Society")

Season Number and Episode	Cumulative Episode Number	Title	Themes, Discussion Points, Teachable Elements Other Notes
2.5	18	Dancin' Homer	Sports (baseball); narrative structure (flashback); employment; small town vs. big city
2.6	19	Dead Putting Society	Sports (mini golf); competition; Zen; sportsmanship; gender roles; betting
2.7	20	Bart vs. Thanksgiving	Holidays (Thanksgiving); economics/class; homelessness; family dynamics; poetry; sibling rivalry
2.8	21	Bart the Daredevil	Extreme sports; popularity; parental discipline
2.9	22	Itchy & Scratchy & Marge	Censorship; children's cartoons/television; classical art; social protest; self-referentiality
2.10	23	Bart Gets Hit by a Car	Heaven/Hell; injury attorneys; law/lawsuits
2.11	24	One Fish, Two Fish, Blowfish, Blue Fish	Marriage; death; life affirmation; bucket lists; poetry
2.12	25	The Way We Was	Narrative structure (flashbacks); storytelling; high school; feminism; romance/dating
2.13	26	Homer vs. Lisa and the 8th Commandment	Crime (theft); morality; cable television
2.14	27	Principal Charming	Dating; school
2.15	28	Oh Brother, Where Art Thou?	Automobile industry; adoption
2.16	29	Bart's Dog Gets an *F*	Pets; obedience; education
2.17	30	Old Money	Death; inheritance; charity; treatment of the elderly
2.18	31	Brush with Greatness	Painting; art; dieting; the Beatles
2.19	32	Lisa's Substitute	Education; role models; father-daughter

Season Number and Episode	Cumulative Episode Number	Title	Themes, Discussion Points, Teachable Elements Other Notes
			relationships; elections; campaigns; voting
2.20	33	The War of the Simpsons	Marital counseling/marital problems; fishing
2.21	34	Three Men and a Comic Book	Sharing; paranoia; comic books
2.22	35	Blood Feud	Charity; morality; blood donation
3.1	36	Stark Raving Dad	Employment; conformity; sanity; birthdays, George H. W. Bush (in repeat, this episode was revised to respond to his slander of *The Simpsons*); Michael Jackson
3.2	37	Mr. Lisa Goes to Washington	*Reader's Digest*; politics; patriotism; scandal; George H. W. Bush; nerds (feelings of isolation); essay writing
3.3	38	When Flanders Failed	Business; jealousy; morality
3.4	39	Bart the Murderer	School; the Mafia; crime; law/trial, TV movies
3.5	40	Homer Defined	Nuclear safety; heroes; censorship (reruns changed one use of "ass" to "butt" after Fox received complaints)
3.6	41	Like Father, Like Clown	Father-son relationships; Judaism; intertextuality/ parody (*The Jazz Singer*, *The Godfather II*); children's television; narrative structure (flashback)
3.7	42	Treehouse of Horror II (Monkey's Paw; The Bart Zone; If I Only Had a Brain)	Holidays (Halloween); censorship (Marge warns parents again); parody (*The Monkey's Paw*, *The Twilight Zone*, *Frankenstein*)

Season Number and Episode	Cumulative Episode Number	Title	Themes, Discussion Points, Teachable Elements Other Notes
3.8	43	Lisa's Pony	Father-daughter relationships; *The Yearling*; intertextuality (*The Godfather*); employment; economics
3.9	44	Saturdays of Thunder	Father-son relationships; sports (soapbox racing); competition; heroes; Bill Cosby
3.10	45	Flaming Moe's	Friendship; business; revenge
3.11	46	Burns Verkaufen der Kraftwerk	Business; job loss; respect/fear; fantasy sequence; Germans (stereotypes)
3.12	47	I Married Marge	Economics/class; employment; pregnancy; narrative structure (flashback); shotgun marriage
3.13	48	Radio Bart	Birthdays; practical jokes; community; charity, celebrities; intertextuality (*Ace in the Hole*, USA for Africa)
3.14	49	Lisa the Greek	Sports (football); father-daughter relationships; gambling; continuity (repeats of this episode have changed the names of teams to reflect the teams in that year's Super Bowl; this is in contrast to "Sunday, Cruddy Sunday"); Malibu Stacy; gender
3.15	50	Homer Alone	Stress; spas; emotional breakdowns; homemaking; parenting; mother-infant attachment; intertextuality (Hanna-Barbera)

Season Number and Episode	Cumulative Episode Number	Title	Themes, Discussion Points, Teachable Elements Other Notes
3.16	51	Bart the Lover	Love letters; dating; divorce; impersonation; yo-yos; personal ads; profanity; educational films
3.17	52	Homer at the Bat	Sports (baseball); cheating; coincidences; the Heimlich maneuver; gambling (first to beat *The Cosby Show* in ratings)
3.18	53	Separate Vocations	Education; standardized testing; career prep paths; homemaking; rebellion; law enforcement; crime (theft); sibling relationships
3.19	54	Dog of Death	Lottery; pets; animal care/surgery; economics/thrift; brainwashing (Ludovico technique); psychology; educational funding
3.20	55	Colonel Homer	Adultery; temptation; music; marital problems; investment/management (Groening writing credit)
3.21	56	Black Widower	Crime (murder); marriage; prison romance
3.22	57	The Otto Show	Spinal Tap; music; charity; driving; riots
3.23	58	Bart's Friend Falls in Love	Friendship; first love; obesity; subliminal tapes; public vs. Catholic education
3.24	59	Brother, Can You Spare Two Dimes?	Workers' compensation, sterility; communication; inventing; history
4.1	60	Kamp Krusty	Summer camp; rebellion; child labor; parody (*The Lord of the Flies*); Tijuana (stereotypes); discipline

Season Number and Episode	Cumulative Episode Number	Title	Themes, Discussion Points, Teachable Elements Other Notes
4.2	61	A Streetcar Named Marge	Community theater; parody (*A Streetcar Named Desire*; *The Great Escape*); Ayn Rand's philosophy (Objectivism); acting; literary adaptations; controversy (for the song "New Orleans"— the blackboard gag for the next episode, "Homer the Heretic," contained an apology); day care
4.3	62	Homer the Heretic	Religion; heresy; church; dreams/visions
4.4	63	Lisa the Beauty Queen	Smoking; ads aimed at children; beauty pageants; father-daughter relationships; body image; self-esteem, gender
4.5	64	Treehouse of Horror III (Clown Without Pity; King Homer; Dial "Z" For Zombies)	Holidays (Halloween); censorship (Homer warns the audience about the episode); parody (*Child's Play, King Kong*); zombies
4.6	65	Itchy & Scratchy: The Movie	Parenting (discipline); animation history; self-referentiality (guest stars using fake names, Korean studios)
4.7	66	Marge Gets a Job	Sexual harassment; employment; home repair; crying wolf; censorship (a joke about Tourette's syndrome was taken out after complaints; the DVD, confusingly, has the Tourette's imitation without Krabappel's reference to it)

Season Number and Episode	Cumulative Episode Number	Title	Themes, Discussion Points, Teachable Elements Other Notes
4.8	67	New Kid on the Block	First love; lawsuits; neighbors; babysitting
4.9	68	Mr. Plow	Friendship; competition; business; commercials/advertisements; censorship (the censors did not want to allow a joke where Homer says "they were gay" for fear of a libel suit)
4.10	69	Lisa's First Word	Storytelling; narrative structure (flashback); pregnancy; Olympics; fast food; sibling rivalry
4.11	70	Homer's Triple Bypass	Health; insurance; surgery; law enforcement; parody (*COPS*); economics; medical care
4.12	71	Marge vs. the Monorail	Con men; transit; parody (*The Music Man*); community management/spending; EPA; safety
4.13	72	Selma's Choice	Death; funerals; amusement parks; biological clock; health; food poisoning; inheritance
4.14	73	Brother from the Same Planet	Parenting; father-son relationships; Big Brother program; addiction; 900 phone lines; *Ren and Stimpy*; parody (*Saturday Night Live*); revenge
4.15	74	I Love Lisa	Holidays (Valentine's Day, President's Day); American history; love and rejection; television retrospective specials; controversy (a Vietnam Vet objected to the show's reference to Vietnam)

Season Number and Episode	Cumulative Episode Number	Title	Themes, Discussion Points, Teachable Elements Other Notes
4.16	75	Duffless	Alcoholism; drunk driving; sibling relationships; science fairs; advertising; AA
4.17	76	Last Exit to Springfield	Health insurance; unions; strikes; dentistry; economics
4.18	77	So It's Come to This: A Simpsons Clip Show	Holidays (April Fool's Day); health care; insurance; coma; censorship (censors did not want the episode to link beer to cancer for fear of losing advertising dollars)
4.19	78	The Front	Cartoon writing and production; *Itchy & Scratchy*; high school reunions; adult education; narrative structure (episode has stand-alone short featuring Ned Flanders); censorship (censors objected to the dream sequence and a cut clip featuring animal cruelty); cartoon violence; self-referentiality
4.20	79	Whacking Day	Holidays (Whacking Day/ St. Patrick's Day); animal cruelty; education; expulsion; home-schooling; politics; logical fallacies (appeal to tradition); community
4.21	80	Marge in Chains	Crime (shoplifting); riots; community; trial; prison; illness (communicable diseases; SARS); alcoholism/AA
4.22	81	Krusty Gets Kancelled	Advertising (marketing); children's television;

Season Number and Episode	Cumulative Episode Number	Title	Themes, Discussion Points, Teachable Elements Other Notes
			comebacks; catchphrases; depression; dieting; censorship (Krusty asks the Red Hot Chili Peppers to change their lyrics as the Doors were once asked to do); communism/Eastern European animation
5.1	82	Homer's Barbershop Quartet	Music; flashbacks; the Beatles; agents; conceptual art; censorship (the censors did not like the Malibu Stacy breast joke)
5.2	83	Cape Feare	Crime (murder); parody (*Cape Fear, HMS Pinafore*); stalking; witness protection
5.3	84	Homer Goes to College	Education; college; admissions; authority; nerds; cheating; nuclear power; pranks; expectations/stereotypes
5.4	85	Rosebud	Birthdays; class/wealth; power; stand-up comedy/roasting; history; mobs; depression; parody (*Citizen Kane*)
5.5	86	Treehouse of Horror IV (The Devil and Homer Simpson; Terror at 5½ Feet; Bart Simpson's Dracula)	Holidays (Halloween); Satan; parody (*Gremlins; Bram Stoker's Dracula; The Lost Boys; The Twilight Zone*'s "Nightmare at 20,000 Feet"; *The Devil and Daniel Webster*); trial; vampires; censorship (Marge warns us about content); ironic punishment (*Inferno*); history
5.6	87	Marge on the Lam	Parody (*Thelma and Louise*);

Season Number and Episode	Cumulative Episode Number	Title	Themes, Discussion Points, Teachable Elements Other Notes
			crime (car theft); girls' night; babysitting; ballet; feminism; friendship
5.7	88	Bart's Inner Child	Self-help; identity; marital trouble; responsibility; infomercials; riot
5.8	89	Boy-Scoutz 'n' the Hood	Boy Scouts; father-son relationships; rafting
5.9	90	The Last Temptation of Homer	Adultery; marriage; temptation; insurance; HMOs; sexism; nerds; worker safety; conventions; guardian angels; fortune cookies
5.10	91	$pringfield (Or, How I Learned to Stop Worrying and Love Legalized Gambling)	Gambling; economics; addiction; paranoia; germ phobia; community
5.11	92	Homer the Vigilante	Crime (theft, assault); aging; treatment of the elderly; vigilantes
5.12	93	Bart Gets Famous	Self-referentiality; television; catchphrases; field trips; personal assistants; employment; show business; fame
5.13	94	Homer and Apu	Consumer protection; forgiveness; India (stereotypes); actor training; undercover reporting; employment; job loss
5.14	95	Lisa vs. Malibu Stacy	Barbie; feminism; treatment of the elderly; self-esteem; marketing; sexism; Malibu Stacy
5.15	96	Deep Space Homer	Television; popular culture; high vs. low culture; NASA; space exploration; space-themed films; respect; competition (a

Season Number and Episode	Cumulative Episode Number	Title	Themes, Discussion Points, Teachable Elements Other Notes
			copy of this episode resides at the space station)
5.16	97	Homer Loves Flanders	Friendship; football; censorship (censors wanted the LSC joke taken out); self-referentiality
5.17	98	Bart Gets an Elephant	Pets; radio contests; economics; treatment of animals; ivory
5.18	99	Burns' Heir	Parenting; adoption; brain-washing; inheritance; class; power; sexism; auditions; family
5.19	100	Sweet Seymour Skinner's Baadasssss Song	Education; show and tell; job satisfaction/identification; employment; job loss; discipline; plagiarism; military training; loneliness; friendship (chalkboard: I will not celebrate meaningless milestones)
5.20	101	The Boy Who Knew Too Much	Truancy; trials; crime; justice; bravery; class; jury duty; linguistics (accents); the French (stereotypes)
5.21	102	Lady Bouvier's Lover	Romance; birthdays; parody (*The Graduate*); dating; treatment of the elderly
5.22	103	Secrets of a Successful Marriage	Marital problems; adult education; secrets; indiscretion/gossip; marital counseling; teaching
6.1	104	Bart of Darkness	Parody (*Rear Window*); swimming pools; isolation; paranoia; popularity, gender

Season Number and Episode	Cumulative Episode Number	Title	Themes, Discussion Points, Teachable Elements Other Notes
6.2	105	Lisa's Rival	Competition; parody (*The Fugitive*, *The Tell-Tale Heart*); dioramas; greed; crime (theft); linguistics (anagrams)
6.3	106	Another Simpsons Clip Show	Romance; love; adultery; temptation; montages; prank calls
6.4	107	Itchy & Scratchy Land	Theme parks; vacation; parody (*Westworld*); robotics (1st rule); violence (cartoon and actual); self-referentiality; Disney; Jurassic Park; censorship (censors had threatened to cut all *Itchy & Scratchy* episodes after new censorship laws were enacted)
6.5	108	Sideshow Bob Roberts	Politics; campaigns; Republicans; crime (fraud); debate; Democrats; intertextuality (many references to actual political events and many films)
6.6	109	Treehouse of Horror V (The Shinning; Time and Punishment; Nightmare Cafeteria)	Holidays (Halloween); parody (*The Shining*, *A Sound of Thunder*); time travel; cannibalism; insanity; dystopia; censorship (Marge issues the warning; Mirkin injected more violence due to complaints from Congress)
6.7	110	Bart's Girlfriend	Crime (theft); morality; parenting; young love; church; Sunday school; "bad boys"
6.8	111	Lisa on Ice	Sibling rivalry; youth sports (hockey); physical

Season Number and Episode	Cumulative Episode Number	Title	Themes, Discussion Points, Teachable Elements Other Notes
			education; competition; sportsmanship; grades; crime (rioting); gambling
6.9	112	Homer Badman	Babysitting; feminism; sexual harassment; professional conventions; media; social protest; made for TV movie-bios; crime (theft); parody (*Hard Copy*); public access TV
6.10	113	Grampa vs. Sexual Inadequacy	Sexuality; sex; home remedies; father-son relationships; conspiracy theories; parenting; Occam's razor
6.11	114	Fear of Flying	Parody (*Cheers*); fear of flying; phobias; pranks; psychology; therapy; gender roles; community abjection
6.12	115	Homer the Great	Self-esteem; secret societies; hazing; Freemasonry; exclusion; acceptance; philanthropy; charity
6.13	116	And Maggie Makes Three	Pregnancy; storytelling; narrative structure (flashbacks); job satisfaction; debt; economics/budgeting; sports (bowling)
6.14	117	Bart's Comet	Astronomy; comet; apocalypse; science; bomb shelters; community; sacrifice; parody (*Twilight Zone*); punishment; pranks
6.15	118	Homie the Clown	Education; trade school; clowns; debt; gambling; crime (mafia); Italian-Americans (stereotypes, mafia); greed;

Season Number and Episode	Cumulative Episode Number	Title	Themes, Discussion Points, Teachable Elements Other Notes
			impersonation; advertisements
6.16	119	Bart vs. Australia	Australia (stereotypes); crime (fraud); international relations/politics; Coriolis effect (note that Lisa is wrong about the science here); ecosystem health (cane toads); offense (the Australian Parliament condemned the episode); tourism; parenting; pranks
6.17	120	Homer vs. Patty and Selma	Debt; speculating/investment; in-laws; ballet; gender roles
6.18	121	A Star Is Burns	Films; film production; film festivals; *The Critic;* advertising/controversy (Groening pulled his name from this episode, as he felt it was just an ad for *The Critic*); tourism; alcoholism; self-referentiality
6.19	122	Lisa's Wedding	Fortune-telling; future; college; romance; wedding; family loyalty; Renaissance fairs; American/English stereotypes; parody (*Love Story*)
6.20	123	Two Dozen and One Greyhounds	Crime (theft; animal cruelty); pets; parody (*101 Dalmatians*); censorship (censors had problems with the dog sex scene)
6.21	124	The PTA Disbands	Education; educational funding; employment; job satisfaction; substitute

Season Number and Episode	Cumulative Episode Number	Title	Themes, Discussion Points, Teachable Elements Other Notes
			teachers; unions; strikes; physics; field trips; tutoring
6.22	125	'Round Springfield	Death and life affirmation; lawsuits; appendicitis; surgery; sibling relationships
6.23	126	The Springfield Connection	Law enforcement; corruption; gender roles; crime (counterfeiting, gambling, theft)
6.24	127	Lemon of Troy	Town pride; crime (graffiti, theft); parody (Trojan Horse/War); legends; rivalry; parenting; community; treatment of the elderly
6.25	128	Who Shot Mr. Burns, Part 1	Crime; guns; school funding; narrative structure (mystery, cliff-hanger); monopolies; greed; self-referentiality (Mr. Burns mentions memories of each member of the Simpson family — except Homer — when he sees a picture)
7.1	129	Who Shot Mr. Burns, Part 2	Law enforcement; detective work; narrative structure (mystery, cliff-hanger)
7.2	130	Radioactive Man	Film production; parody (*Batman*); acting
7.3	131	Home Sweet Homediddly-Dum-Doodily	Parenting; foster parents; child protective services; baptism; religious choices; custody
7.4	132	Bart Sells His Soul	Religion; faith; philosophy; pranks; church; chain restaurants; dreams; narrative structure (fantasy, daydreams)
7.5	133	Lisa the Vegetarian	Vegetarianism; petting zoos;

Season Number and Episode	Cumulative Episode Number	Title	Themes, Discussion Points, Teachable Elements Other Notes
			animal cruelty; corporate propaganda; father-daughter relationships; education; "other" status/ abjection; competition
7.6	134	Treehouse of Horror VI (Attack of the 50-Foot Eyesores; Nightmare on Evergreen Terrace; Homer[3] [Homer cubed])	Holidays (Halloween); computer animation; 3D; parody (*A Nightmare on Elm Street*; *Little Girl Lost*); advertising; self-referentiality; physics; math
7.7	135	King-Size Homer	Workers' compensation; disabilities; obesity/ treatment of the obese; medical quackery; nuclear power; nuclear accidents; marriage; sexual attraction; narrative structure (montage)
7.8	136	Mother Simpson	Parenting; absent parents; 1960s; radical groups; parody (60s films' moments of clarity and music, *Dragnet*, *Laugh-In*); crime; narrative structure (flashback); storytelling; linguistics (grammar: seen/saw)
7.9	137	Sideshow Bob's Last Gleaming	Self-referentiality (Fox, Murdoch is in prison); justice system; the military; *Dr. Strangelove*; air shows; nuclear threat; advertising
7.10	138	The Simpsons 138th Episode Spectacular	Parody (sitcoms, clip shows, *The Flintstones*, Madonna); homo-sexuality; outtakes; viewer letters; audience; self-referentiality

Season Number and Episode	Cumulative Episode Number	Title	Themes, Discussion Points, Teachable Elements Other Notes
7.11	139	Marge Be Not Proud	Holidays (Christmas); video games; crime (shoplifting); parenting; parody (advertising, video games); narrative structure (fantasy sequence)
7.12	140	Team Homer	Sports (bowling, bowling leagues); *Mad* magazine; friendship; competition
7.13	141	Two Bad Neighbors	Politics; President George H. W. Bush; President Ford; spanking/discipline; parenting; competition; parody (*Dennis the Menace*)
7.14	142	Scenes from the Class Struggle in Springfield	Class; economics; status; sports (golf, horseback riding); acceptance; country clubs; designer clothing; outlet malls
7.15	143	Bart the Fink	Money; offshore accounts; banking; impersonation; crime (tax fraud/insurance fraud); childhood heroes
7.16	144	Lisa the Iconoclast	History; historical revision; icons; father-daughter relationships; cultural mythology; linguistics (neology: cromulent; embiggens); mystery; town pride; Gilbert Stuart's unfinished painting of George Washington; self-referentiality (inside joke about Harvard)
7.17	145	Homer the Smithers	Job satisfaction; self-reliance; job loss; stereotypes (the elderly, homosexuality)

Season Number and Episode	Cumulative Episode Number	Title	Themes, Discussion Points, Teachable Elements Other Notes
7.18	146	The Day the Violence Died	Self-referentiality; *Itchy & Scratchy*; theft/plagiarism; bankruptcy; trials; law; cartoon production and history; parody (*Schoolhouse Rock*); resisting an ending
7.19	147	A Fish Called Selma	Marriage; Hollywood; sexual perversion; sexuality; insincerity; acting; parody (*Planet of the Apes*; *The Muppets*); fame; marriage of convenience
7.20	148	Bart on the Road	Vacation; spring break; crime; impersonation; road trip; friendship; adventure; father-daughter relationships; Take Your Children to Work Day; travel
7.21	149	22 Short Films About Springfield	Parody (*Pulp Fiction*; *Thirty Two Short Films About Glenn Gould*); crime (robbery); medicine; lying; guns/ gun shops; narrative structure (vignettes)
7.22	150	Raging Abe Simpson and His Grumbling Grandson in "The Curse of the Flying Hellfish"	World War II; veterans; storytelling; narrative structure (flashbacks); tontines; crime (theft, assassination); grandfather-grandson relationships; heroes
7.23	151	Much Apu about Nothing	America; politics; government; illegal immigration; scapegoating; red herring fallacy; deportation; taxes; American history; citizenship; crime (fraud);

Season Number and Episode	Cumulative Episode Number	Title	Themes, Discussion Points, Teachable Elements Other Notes
			stereotypes (Indian, American, Italian-American); democracy; voter propositions; xeno-phobia; linguistics (grammar, accents)
7.24	152	Homerpalooza	Music festivals; carnival freaks; carpooling; rock music; generation gap; Generation X; popularity; the idea of coolness
7.25	153	Summer of 4 Ft. 2	Holidays (Independence Day); popularity; jealousy/sibling rivalry; summer vacation; friendship; parody (*American Graffiti*); nerds; acceptance
8.1	154	Treehouse of Horror VII (The Thing and I; The Genesis Tub; Citizen Kang)	Holidays (Halloween); conjoined twins; science fair projects; Genesis; creation; God; religion; history; civilization; politics; elections; two-party systems; aliens; abduction; Bob Dole; President Clinton; parody (*The Twilight Zone* "The Little People")
8.2	155	You Only Move Twice	Intertextuality and parody (*James Bond* movies); job satisfaction; moving; remedial education; allergies; managerial styles; marriage/family harmony; aspirations
8.3	156	The Homer They Fall	Sports (boxing); bullying; parody (Mike Tyson; Don King)
8.4	157	Burns, Baby Burns	Illegitimate children; kid-napping; parental love; class; *Caddyshack*

Season Number and Episode	Cumulative Episode Number	Title	Themes, Discussion Points, Teachable Elements Other Notes
8.5	158	Bart after Dark	Burlesque; oil spills; environment, environmentalists; punishment; parenting; community morals; parody (*The Best Little Whorehouse in Texas*)
8.6	159	A Milhouse Divided	Divorce; dinner parties; marriage; family
8.7	160	Lisa's Date with Density	Dating; bullies; crushes; crime (fraud); telemarketing; parody (*Rebel without a Cause*)
8.8	161	Hurricane Neddy	Anger; psychotic breakdown; hurricane; parenting; prayer; faith; psychotherapy; spanking; linguistics (neologism: "spankological")
8.9	162	*El Viaje Misterioso de Nuestro Jomer*	Parody (spaghetti westerns, *The Magical Mystery Tour*); marriage; relationships; hallucinations; Carlos Castaneda (spirit guides, spiritual journeys)
8.10	163	The Springfield Files	Parody/crossovers (*Plan Nine from Outer Space*, *The X-Files*); marriage; alcoholism; mob rule; storytelling (framing); self-referentiality (Homer on T-shirts, Fox's *Alien Autopsy*)
8.11	164	The Twisted World of Marge Simpson	Franchises; investing; organized crime; competition; feminism
8.12	165	Mountain of Madness	National Park System; John Muir; management strategies (team-building exercises); competition; cheating

Season Number and Episode	Cumulative Episode Number	Title	Themes, Discussion Points, Teachable Elements Other Notes
8.13	166	Simpsoncalifragil-isticexpiali(annoyed grunt)cious	Parody (musicals, *Mary Poppins, Mrs. Doubtfire*); stereotypes (American, British); parenting; stress; nannies; dysfunction
8.14	167	The Itchy & Scratchy & Poochie Show	Linguistics (semantics, jargon); self-referentiality (this episode was in response to Fox executives' actual suggestion to add another character to the show, including one possibly voiced by Jenny McCarthy; the writers for *Itchy & Scratchy* are drawn in the likeness of Simpsons writers; the animator who draws Poochie is David Silverman); cartoons; cartoon violence; geeks/geek culture
8.15	168	Homer's Phobia	Homosexuality; homophobia; stereotypes (homosexuals, homophobes); kitsch/camp; mise-en-scène; parenting; hunting; censorship (Fox censors originally wanted all references to homosexuality removed from the episode, but executive turnover occurred. Later, the episode was cleared and ultimately won an Emmy and a GLAAD award)
8.16	169	The Brother from Another Series	Parody (Johnny Cash, television, crossovers); prison/rehabilitation/recidivism; sibling rivalry; crime (fraud)

Season Number and Episode	Cumulative Episode Number	Title	Themes, Discussion Points, Teachable Elements Other Notes
8.17	170	My Sister, My Sitter	Family/sibling relationships; babysitting; parody (*The Baby-sitters Club*); pranks
8.18	171	Homer vs. the Eighteenth Amendment	Holidays (St. Patrick's Day); prohibition; laws/law enforcement; alcohol; drunkenness; crime (bootlegging); parody (*The Untouchables*)
8.19	172	Grade School Confidential	Relationships; school romance; bribery; social protest
8.20	173	The Canine Mutiny	Crime (credit card fraud, marijuana possession); drugs (amphetamines, marijuana); corruption; pets; service animals
8.21	174	The Old Man and the Lisa	Recycling; environmentalism; stock market loss/ bankruptcy; treatment of the elderly; parody (*That Girl*)
8.22	175	In Marge We Trust	Advertising; stereotypes (Japanese); church; job satisfaction; role of clergy; faith; narrative structure (flashback); volunteering; crime
8.23	176	Homer's Enemy	Literary foils; self-referentiality (Homer shows Frank pictures, each of which refer to previous episodes); job satisfaction; envy; hatred; American dream; death; funerals; reality vs. television fantasy
8.24	177	The Simpsons Spin-Off Showcase	Parody (*My Mother the Car*, *The Brady Bunch Variety Hour*, sitcoms, variety shows, television conventions, spin-offs,

Season Number and Episode	Cumulative Episode Number	Title	Themes, Discussion Points, Teachable Elements Other Notes
			crime/mystery dramas, magical sitcoms, laugh tracks); New Orleans (stereotypes); self-referentiality; narrative structure (framing)
8.25	178	The Secret War of Lisa Simpson	Education; school system; pranks; sibling relationships; military school; bullies; alienation/outsiders; private vs. public education; feminism; women in the military (inspired by the Citadel)
9.1	179	The City of New York vs. Homer Simpson	Stereotypes (New Yorkers, Asians, films about New York); bus travel; censorship (when Homer urinates, the zipper and urine sounds were removed; the episode was pulled from syndication after 9/11/2001); alcoholism; advertising (bus ads; "Duffman" is a parody of 1960s "Budman")
9.2	180	The Principal and the Pauper	Community; the status quo; fear of change; Vietnam; self-referentiality (sitcom conventions, narrative self-containment); narrative techniques (deus ex machina); impersonation; aspirations
9.3	181	Lisa's Sax	Gifted children; education; music; starting school; heat waves; storytelling; parental sacrifice; narrative structure (flashback, framing);

Season Number and Episode	Cumulative Episode Number	Title	Themes, Discussion Points, Teachable Elements Other Notes
			parody (*All in the Family*); behavioral problems; psychology; private school tuition; self-referentiality
9.4	182	Treehouse of Horror VIII (The HΩmega Man; Fly vs. Fly; Easy-Bake Coven)	Censorship (the Fox censors requested the opening to be changed from a dagger to a sword); parody (*The Omega Man*; *The Crucible*; *The Fly*); nuclear holocaust; matter transport; Salem witch trials; witches; mob rule
9.5	183	The Cartridge Family	NRA; guns; gun laws/the Brady Bill; marriage/separation; sports (soccer); satire (soccer, soccer fans, soccer riots, gun nuts)
9.6	184	Bart Star	Sports (football); youth sports; parenting; living through children; childhood obesity; competition; coaching
9.7	185	The Two Mrs. Nahasapeemapetilons	Arranged marriages; India (stereotypes); Hinduism; parenting; lying; charity (bachelor auction); weddings
9.8	186	Lisa the Skeptic	Archaeology; faith; religion vs. science controversy; malls/consumer culture; "A Very Old Man with Enormous Wings" by Gabriel García Márquez; mob rule; advertising; publicity stunts
9.9	187	Realty Bites	Police auction, ethics; honesty; competition; realty/real estate; parody (*Glengarry Glen Ross*)
9.10	188	Miracle on Evergreen Terrace	Holidays (Christmas); lying; human interest stories;

Season Number and Episode	Cumulative Episode Number	Title	Themes, Discussion Points, Teachable Elements Other Notes
			charity; game shows; mob rule
9.11	189	All Singing, All Dancing	Clip shows; musicals; parody (*The Music Man*, "New York, New York," *Paint Your Wagon*); Censorship (Snake points the gun at Maggie and the censors wanted it changed, but it was not changed and ended up with a G rating)
9.12	190	Bart Carny	Parenting/discipline; carnivals; carnival rides/safety; grifting; police corruption/bribes; linguistics (neology: "Euroific")
9.13	191	The Joy of Sect	Religion; cults; cult tactics; brainwashing
9.14	192	Das Bus	Parody (*Lord of the Flies*); ethnic stereotypes: Libya, Polish jokes; Internet boom; model UNs; narrative structure (narrator; deus ex machina)
9.15	193	The Last Temptation of Krust	Comedians/comedy festivals; politically incorrect vs. offensive humor (Krusty's outdated routine); selling out; parody (Lenny Bruce; George Carlin); stand-up comedy; SUVs; advertising
9.16	194	Dumbbell Indemnity	Romance/dating; montage; crime (insurance fraud); friendship; guilt
9.17	195	Lisa the Simpson	Self-esteem; growing up; fear; genetics; cryogenics; brain teasers; freak shows; intelligence; success

Season Number and Episode	Cumulative Episode Number	Title	Themes, Discussion Points, Teachable Elements Other Notes
9.18	196	This Little Wiggy	Bullies; playdates; capital punishment; prison; peer pressure; linguistics (morphemes)
9.19	197	Simpson Tide	The Naval Reserve; fads; "Don't Ask, Don't Tell"; parody (parody of *Crimson Tide*, basic training in comedies such as *Private Benjamin*); war games
9.20	198	The Trouble with Trillions	Taxes/tax fraud; Cuba; larceny; FBI (spying)
9.21	199	Girly Edition	Parody of television (ratings, cartoons, kids' news shows, human interest stories); sibling rivalry; family relationships
9.22	200	Trash of the Titans	The environment; sanitation; elections; campaign promises; public office; parody (advertising, rock concerts); running for office; censorship (Censors wanted "wanker" removed from the episode at first)
9.23	201	King of the Hill	Publicity stunts; parenting; role models; nutrition bars; fitness; mountain climbing; cannibalism
9.24	202	Lost Our Lisa	Museums; Egyptian artifacts; public transportation; parenting; health care; crime (breaking and entering); mystery; father-daughter relationships
9.25	203	Natural Born Kissers	Marriage; sex; sexuality; exhibitionism; *Casablanca*; nudity/censorship (Current censorship rules won't permit the same nudity in new episodes,

Season Number and Episode	Cumulative Episode Number	Title	Themes, Discussion Points, Teachable Elements Other Notes
			although repeats of this episode are shown)
10.1	204	Lard of the Dance	Growing up; peer pressure; new students; dating; school dances; popularity; grease recycling; economics; profit; parody (*Grease*)
10.2	205	The Wizard of Evergreen Terrace	Mid-life crisis; inventing; self-esteem; heroes; Thomas Edison; envy
10.3	206	Bart the Mother	Parenting; mother-son relationships; peer pressure; invasive species; ecosystem; linguistics (passive language)
10.4	207	Treehouse of Horror IX (Hell Toupee; The Terror of Tiny Toon; Starship Poopers)	Capital punishment; parody (*Shocker*; *Pleasantville*; *Alien*; *Jerry Springer*); crime (murder); cartoon violence; self-referentiality; *Itchy & Scratchy*; extramarital impregnation; alien abduction
10.5	208	When You Dish upon a Star	Hollywood stereotypes, celebrity; court system; corruption; marriage; betrayal; self-referentiality (Basinger remarks that no one knows where Springfield is)
10.6	209	D'oh-in in the Wind	Parody (Ben & Jerry's ice cream, Fruitopia); marijuana; the Beatles; personal discovery; hippies; spirit of the 1960s
10.7	210	Lisa Gets an A^5	Academic dishonesty; video games; *The Wind in the Willows*; public school funding; narrative structure (false ending); pets; treatment of animals

Season Number and Episode	Cumulative Episode Number	Title	Themes, Discussion Points, Teachable Elements Other Notes
10.8	211	Homer Simpson in: Kidney Trouble	Urban legends (waking up without a kidney, fears of becoming an organ donor); health care; surgery anxiety; satire (the Old West); narrative structure (flashback); father-son relationships; tourist towns; cowardice; abjection
10.9	212	Mayored to the Mob	Parody (sci-fi conventions, geek culture, *The Bodyguard*); self-referentiality (Üter wears a T-shirt for Groening's other TV creation, *Futurama*); JFK assassination; corruption
10.10	213	Viva Ned Flanders	Bigamy; Las Vegas; gambling; responsibility; censorship (Barney's birthday was changed in reruns and the crowd running from a building demolition was removed in some syndicated versions after 9/11); lying
10.11	214	Wild Barts Can't Be Broken	Sports (baseball); fans; intoxication; curfews; secrets; vandalism; parody (*Village of the Damned*; *Bye Bye Birdie*); voter apathy; generation conflict
10.12	215	Sunday, Cruddy Sunday	Sports (football/Super Bowl); narrative structure (resisting an ending); self-referentiality; con jobs; crafting; advertising (Super Bowl commercials); censorship (the term "Catholic" was taken out of the Super Bowl ad

Season Number and Episode	Cumulative Episode Number	Title	Themes, Discussion Points, Teachable Elements Other Notes
			parody in reruns after complaints[6]); President Clinton
10.13	216	Homer to the Max	Television programming; self-referentiality; name changes; environmentalism; environmental protesting; President Clinton; popularity; power; parody (*Miami Vice*)
10.14	217	I'm with Cupid	Holidays (Valentine's Day); sabotage; peer pressure; workaholism; marital problems; romance
10.15	218	Marge Simpson in: "Screaming Yellow Honkers"	Road rage; masculinity; cars/SUVs; talent shows; zoos; self-referentiality (at gunpoint, Homer praises Fox); linguistics (semantics, pejoration)
10.16	219	Make Room for Lisa	Father-daughter relationships; drinking; museums; cell phones; voyeurism; debt; fines; psychosomatic illness; stress; sensory deprivation; holistic medicine; pranks
10.17	220	Maximum Homerdrive	Truck driving; eating contests; death; doorbells; scams; automation; secrets
10.18	221	Simpsons Bible Stories	Parody (The Bible; action movies; *The People's Court*); dreams; sin; forgiveness; holidays (Easter); Egypt
10.19	222	Mom and Pop Art	Popular art ("outsider" art); high vs. low art; jealousy; ambiguous sexuality; self-referentiality (Homer's face on T-shirts); crime (theft); anger; crafts

Season Number and Episode	Cumulative Episode Number	Title	Themes, Discussion Points, Teachable Elements Other Notes
10.20	223	The Old Man and the C Student	Ethnic stereotypes; patriotism; the Olympic Games; corruption; community service; treatment of the elderly; *Gone with the Wind*; *Titanic*
10.21	224	Monty Can't Buy Me Love	Consumerism; megastores (the "Fortune Megastore" in the episode is a spoof of Virgin and its CEO; "Arthur Fortune" is based on Richard Branson); wealth/happiness; charity; shock jocks; linguistics (passive language, Scottish dialect); ethnic jokes/ stereotypes; legends (Loch Ness monster); parody (*King Kong*); popularity
10.22	225	They Saved Lisa's Brain	Anti-intellectualism; mob rule; Mensa; corruption; government; utopia
10.23	226	Thirty Minutes over Tokyo	Technology; self-referentiality (Lisa warns Homer not to invest in Fox); seminar culture (money and budgeting); Japan and America (stereotypes); television shows (cartoons, game shows); crime; jail; controversies (Japan was insulted by the treatment of the emperor, although Homer is punished for said treatment in the episode)
11.1	227	Beyond Blunderdome	Parody (*Mr. Smith Goes to Washington*); Hollywood (celebrity, film violence, filmmaking); test screenings; jealousy

Season Number and Episode	Cumulative Episode Number	Title	Themes, Discussion Points, Teachable Elements Other Notes
11.2	228	Brother's Little Helper	ADD; children on prescription drugs; self-help books; authority; conspiracy theories
11.3	229	Guess Who's Coming to Criticize Dinner	Road rage; educational system; newspaper industry; peer pressure; ethnic stereotypes; self-referentiality (Homer introduces the commercial break, the ending shows multiple enemies from previous episodes); writing; ghost writing; criticism
11.4	230	Treehouse of Horror X (I Know What You Diddily-Iddly-Did; Desperately Seeking Xena; Life's a Glitch, Then You Die)	Holidays (Halloween, New Year's Eve); self-referentiality (Kang and Kodos wonder what aliens have to do with Halloween); parody (superheroes, superhero television shows; *I Know What You Did Last Summer*); geek culture; technology; Y2K; mob rule; apocalypse; were-wolves
11.5	231	E-I-E-I-(Annoyed Grunt)	Parody (music, B-52s, hip-hop; *Zorro*); stereotypes (southerners); President Carter; cigarettes/nicotine/cigarette companies; genetically modified foods; addiction; dueling; cowardice
11.6	232	Hello Gutter, Hello Fadder	Parenting; stereotypes (New Yorkers, police officers); sports (bowling); puns; bucket lists; parody (*Hollywood Squares*); fleeting fame; religious

Season Number and Episode	Cumulative Episode Number	Title	Themes, Discussion Points, Teachable Elements Other Notes
			faith; father-daughter relationships
11.7	233	Eight Misbehavin'	Marriage; parenthood; pregnancy; fertility drugs/ multiple births; idiomatic expressions; narrative structure (flash-forward technique); the media (predates *Jon and Kate Plus Eight,* and creates an interesting comparison)
11.8	234	Take My Wife, Sleaze	Kitsch (1950s); authority; motorcycles; subcultures (motorcycle gangs); violence; marriage; crime (kidnapping); class
11.9	235	Grift of the Magi	Holidays (Christmas); educational system/ funding; advertising; organized crime; toys
11.10	236	Little Big Mom	*Itchy & Scratchy;* ambiguous sexuality; sports (skiing); linguistics/semantics (snowboarding lingo); parenthood; homemaking; medicine (Western, Eastern, and Internet); Hansen's disease; leper colonies; Hawaii
11.11	237	Faith Off	College; fraternities; faith; faith healing; skepticism, science (heat makes metal expand); linguistics (grammar — double negatives, neologism); sports (football); gambling; alumni associations
11.12	238	The Mansion Family	Awards shows; celebrity; wealth/class; health care; laws/lawlessness; the military; treatment of animals

Season Number and Episode	Cumulative Episode Number	Title	Themes, Discussion Points, Teachable Elements Other Notes
11.13	239	Saddlesore Galactica	State fairs; patriotism; justice; politicians (President Clinton); treatment of animals/ horse racing; self-referentiality (Comic Book Guy remarks that the family had already had a horse [3.8], then he reappears when Lisa tells Marge she may have a gambling problem[7]; Moe's heart beats out of his chest à la old Warner Brothers cartoons)
11.14	240	Alone Again, Natura-Diddily	Death (of spouse); class (satire of the NASCAR crowd); self-referentiality (catchphrases; scan of the cemetery headstones shows previous deaths on the show; the crowd waiting for someone to die mirrored the audience, who had been told by an expansive ad campaign that a Simpsons character would perish); dating; religious faith; Christian rock; grief
11.15	241	Missionary: Impossible	Public television (fund drives); missionary work; religion/conversion; linguistics (British humor); sexism; gambling/casinos; self-referentiality (anti–Fox comments such as "crude, low-brow humor" are allowed because the show makes much money for the network)
11.16	242	Pygmoelian	Alcohol; plastic surgery;

Season Number and Episode	Cumulative Episode Number	Title	Themes, Discussion Points, Teachable Elements Other Notes
			body image; revenge; Hollywood; superficiality; parody (soap operas, sitcoms, narrative self-containment [the ending mocks the formulaic nature of sitcoms])
11.17	243	Bart to the Future	Narrative structure (flash-forward); Native American stereotypes/casinos; *Pinocchio*; linguistics (idiomatic expressions); politics/politicians
11.18	244	Days of Wine and D'ohses	Stereotypes (Italians); alcoholism/AA; relationships; co-dependency; parody (*The Days of Wine and Roses*); competition
11.19	245	Kill the Alligator and Run	Stereotypes (Southerners, Floridians, police officers); Florida; spring break; mental health; crime; chain gangs
11.20	246	Last Tap Dance in Springfield	Stereotypes (Latin Americans); sports (dance); parenting; parody (*Flubber*); pressure/expectations
11.21	247	It's a Mad, Mad, Mad, Mad Marge	Marriage; jealousy; parody (*The Hand That Rocks the Cradle*); mental health; crime (attempted murder)
11.22	248	Behind the Laughter	Parody (*Behind the Music*, Beatlemania); celebrity culture (fame, wealth); self-referentiality (television families, television shows, Fox, *Simpsons* merchandise, clips of fake episodes mixed in with actual episodes); linguistics (mixed and absurd metaphors in the

Season Number and Episode	Cumulative Episode Number	Title	Themes, Discussion Points, Teachable Elements Other Notes
			narration); awards shows[8]
12.1	249	Treehouse of Horror XI (G-G-G-Ghost D-D-Dad; Scary Tales Can Come True; Night of The Dolphin)	Holidays (Halloween); religion; heaven; parody (*Ghost Dad*, Grimm's fairy tales, *Day of the Dolphin*, *The Birds*); cartoon violence; ghosts; witches; parenting; poverty
12.2	250	A Tale of Two Springfields	Community ("Us vs. Them" mentality); rock music; class warfare; governance
12.3	251	Insane Clown Poppy	Gulf War; book festivals; parenthood; organized crime; storytelling (montage); parody (mafia movies); gambling; illegitimate children; USO shows
12.4	252	Lisa the Treehugger	Environmentalism; social protests; clearcutting; vegetarianism/veganism; crushes; self-referentiality (Lisa is on a T-shirt); capitalism
12.5	253	Homer vs. Dignity	Parody (*The Magic Christian*, Macy's Thanksgiving Day parade); dignity; ethics; pranks
12.6	254	The Computer Wore Menace Shoes	Computers; muckraking; watchdogs; gossip; corruption; journalism; parody (*The Prisoner*); ethics
12.7	255	The Great Money Caper	Grifting; magic acts; alcohol; parody (*Paper Moon*); father-son relationships; con artists
12.8	256	Skinner's Sense of Snow	Parody (Cirque du Soleil, Pennants, *Zero for Conduct*); snowstorms; narrative

Season Number and Episode	Cumulative Episode Number	Title	Themes, Discussion Points, Teachable Elements Other Notes
			structure (flashback); authority; holidays (Christmas); hallucinations
12.9	257	НОМЯ	Parenting; father-daughter relationships; parody (cartoons, animation; *Flowers for Algernon*); anti-intellectualism; self-referentiality (discussion of animation); medical testing
12.10	258	Pokey Mom	Art; prison system; chiropractic vs. Western medicine; volunteering; trust
12.11	259	Worst Episode Ever	Romance; May-December relationships; healthcare system; heart problems; comic books; crime (bootlegging); memes (Comic Book Guy's collection is a precursor to YouTube)
12.12	260	Tennis the Menace	Sports (tennis); popularity; treatment of the elderly; death preparation; competition; fears
12.13	261	Day of the Jackanapes	Parody (*The Manchurian Candidate*; *Who Wants to Be a Millionaire?*); revenge; hypnotism; crime (attempted murder); retirement
12.14	262	New Kids on the Blecch	Boy bands; subliminal messages; military recruiting; sibling rivalry; censorship (the episode was pulled from syndication for a few months after 9/11/2001 because a building is blown up. Note that the

Season Number and Episode	Cumulative Episode Number	Title	Themes, Discussion Points, Teachable Elements Other Notes
			film *Josie and the Pussycats* [with a similar storyline] was released after this episode aired)
12.15	263	Hungry, Hungry Homer	Parody (Legos, Legoland); protests (hunger strike); sports (baseball)[9]; freak shows
12.16	264	Bye, Bye, Nerdie	Linguistics (neologism); bullies; nerds; science fairs; babyproofing
12.17	265	Simpson Safari	Africa (stereotypes); safari; travel; animals; Jane Goodall; diamond mines; unions; strikes
12.18	266	Trilogy of Error	Storytelling (perspective); the Butterfly Effect; parody (*Run, Lola, Run*; *Go*); science fair; crime (theft; mafia); health; linguistics/grammar; narrative structure
12.19	267	I'm Goin' to Praiseland	Faith; charity; mourning/grief (dead spouse); satire (Heritage, USA); hallucinations; community
12.20	268	Children of a Lesser Clod	Sports; YMCA; ethnic stereotypes; health care; child care/day care centers; morphine; jealousy; parenting
12.21	269	Simpsons Tall Tales	Storytelling; narrative structure (frame plot); folktales; environmentalism; parody (*Huck Finn*; *Tom Sawyer*; *Johnny Appleseed*; *Paul Bunyan*); guns; extinction; hobos
13.1	270	Treehouse of Horror XII (Hex and the City; House of Whacks; Wiz Kids)	Holidays (Halloween); parody (*Harry Potter*; *Demon Seed*; *2001*); magic; gypsies; mythical creatures;

Season Number and Episode	Cumulative Episode Number	Title	Themes, Discussion Points, Teachable Elements Other Notes
			stereotypes (British charm); sibling rivalry; curses; automation
13.2	271	The Parent Rap	Justice system (creative sentencing); father-son relationships; parenting; crime
13.3	272	Homer the Moe	Suicide; postmodernism; trends; job satisfaction; satire (universities, education, television conventions [narrative self-containment]); hunting; hunting accidents
13.4	273	A Hunka Hunka Burns in Love	Fortune cookies; romance; May–December relationships; aphrodisiacs; narrative structure (montage); sitcom conventions (wacky misunderstandings); crime (kidnapping)
13.5	274	The Blunder Years	Advertising; pranks; parody (*Stand by Me*, murder mysteries, Brawny paper towels); narrative structure (flashbacks); post-traumatic stress; hypnotism
13.6	275	She of Little Faith	Christianity; Buddhism; spirituality; holidays (Christmas): religious tolerance; meditation; commercialism
13.7	276	Brawl in the Family	Politics; Republican Party; Strom Thurmond; pollution; the environment; Monopoly (the game); parody (dating shows); social work; neologism ("mouth whoopie");

Season Number and Episode	Cumulative Episode Number	Title	Themes, Discussion Points, Teachable Elements Other Notes
			bigamy; marriage; team-work; crime and punishment
13.8	277	Sweets and Sour Marge	Parody (*Guinness Book of World Records*); obesity; American diet (sugar); corporate responsibility; class action lawsuits (*Erin Brockovich*); censorship (Britain's Channel 4 cuts out a cocaine reference and Bart's line referring to Erin Brockovich as a "prostitute with a heart of gold")
13.9	278	Jaws Wired Shut	Class distinction; marriage; silence; parody (gay pride parade, attending the cinema, *The View*); narrative structure (voiceover)
13.10	279	Half-Decent Proposal	Parody (*Indecent Proposal*); health care; snoring; narrative structure (flashback); marriage; satire (oil industry, Texas)
13.11	280	The Bart Wants What It Wants	Canada (stereotypes, eh?); crushes; filmmaking; stand-up comedy; jealousy; break-ups
13.12	281	The Lastest Gun in the West	Hero worship; alcoholism; Westerns; crime (bank robbery); father-son relationships; aging stars
13.13	282	The Old Man and the Key	Branson, Missouri (stereo-types); competition; romance; parody (*Grease*, '50s films with drag-racing scenes)
13.14	283	Tales from the Public Domain (D'oh	Narrative structure (frame plot); parody (*Iliad*;

Season Number and Episode	Cumulative Episode Number	Title	Themes, Discussion Points, Teachable Elements Other Notes
		Brother, Where Art Thou?; Hot Child in the City; Do the Bard, Man)	*Odyssey*; Odysseus; Troy; Trojan Horse; Joan of Arc; *Hamlet*); competition; storytelling; censorship (Marge won't tell Lisa how the story of Joan of Arc ends); Shakespeare
13.15	284	Blame It on Lisa	Brazil (stereotypes); children's television shows; Stockholm syndrome; controversy (Brazilian leaders and the Rio de Janeiro Tourist Board were very upset by the episode; there was an apology, but the show has made many more negative references to Brazil since); charity; orphans; Carnival; crime (theft, kidnapping)
13.16	285	Weekend at Burnsie's	Parody (*Weekend at Bernie's*); medical marijuana; gardening; narrative structure (montage); voting
13.17	286	Gump Roast	Narrative structure (frame plot); parody (*Forrest Gump*); roasts; clip shows
13.18	287	I Am Furious Yellow	Comic strips; guest speakers; pranks; parody (*Incredible Hulk*); anger
13.19	288	The Sweetest Apu	Marriage; infidelity; forgiveness; intertextuality (*My Fair Lady*, *The Godfather*)
13.20	289	Little Girl in the Big Ten	Poetry; intertextuality (*Kafka*, *Robert Pinksy*, *The Boy in the Plastic Bubble*, *Jem and the Holograms*; *Bouncing Boy*); double life; college; meta-reference/self-

Season Number and Episode	Cumulative Episode Number	Title	Themes, Discussion Points, Teachable Elements Other Notes
			referentiality (in the episode, a college course about *Itchy & Scratchy* could be a reference to college courses about *The Simpsons*); anti-intellectualism; media analysis; sports (gymnastics)
13.21	290	The Frying Game	Reality television; endangered species; intertextuality (*Ghost-busters*); community service; death penalty
13.22	291	Papa's Got a Brand New Badge	Heat wave; riots; mob rule; parody (*High Noon, Dragnet, The Sopranos*); stereotypes (police officers, Italian-Americans); police departments, vigilantism; self-referentiality (Homer lists previous jobs he's held, every example of which refers to previous *Simpsons* episodes; the mobsters are shot by Maggie Simpson, who shot Mr. Burns in "Who Shot Mr. Burns? Pt. 1")
14.1	292	Treehouse of Horror XIII (Send in the Clones; The Fright to Creep and Scare Harms; The Island of Dr. Hibbert)	Cloning; parody (*Multiplicity, Apocalypse Now, The Island of Dr. Moreau*); gun control, Billy the Kid; time travel; violence
14.2	293	How I Spent My Strummer Vacation	Rock music; parody (summer camp); satire (rock music, rock-n-roll lifestyle); competition
14.3	294	Bart vs. Lisa vs. the Third Grade	Narrative structure (hallucination sequence); grade skipping; sibling

Season Number and Episode	Cumulative Episode Number	Title	Themes, Discussion Points, Teachable Elements Other Notes
			relationships; sitcom conventions (narrative self-containment — the status quo is restored at the end of the episode); education
14.4	295	Large Marge	Marriage; parody (musicals, television conventions [narrative self-containment — "classic Marge" returns at the end, preserving the status quo], *Batman*); political corruption; plastic surgery; breast implants; body image; modeling
14.5	296	Helter Shelter	Reality shows; sports (hockey); intertextuality ("The Entertainer," *King of the Hill*); meta-reference (at the end, Homer has had it with reality TV and wants to stick to scripted tele-vision); Victorianism
14.6	297	The Great Louse Detective	Mystery/detective stories; sadism; holidays (Mardi Gras); alcohol; revenge; narrative structure (flashback); satire (musicals)
14.7	298	Special Edna	Pranks; teaching; teacher of the year; parody (Disney World, EPCOT Center)
14.8	299	The Dad Who Knew Too Little	Birthdays; parenting; private detectives; father-daughter relationships
14.9	300	Strong Arms of the Ma	Celebrity; bodybuilding; steroids; femininity; crime (mugging); PTSD

Season Number and Episode	Cumulative Episode Number	Title	Themes, Discussion Points, Teachable Elements Other Notes
			(agoraphobia); parody (fight scene from *The Godfather*)
14.10	301	Pray Anything	Sports (WNBA, bowling); prayer; church; blasphemy; Bible stories; court system; religion
14.11	302	Barting Over	Emancipation; court system; self-referentiality (the lawyer has a Bart doll; Lisa says this skate-boarding stunt is the 300th crazy thing Homer's done[10]); sports (skateboarding)
14.12	303	I'm Spelling As Fast As I Can	Advertising; spelling bees; anti-intellectualism; fast food (Ribwich is a parody of McDonalds' McRib); ethics; parody of visual cue (the sequence when Homer becomes addicted to the Ribwich is a reference to the drug use sequences in the film *Requiem for a Dream*); parental neglect
14.13	304	A Star Is Born-Again	Parody (*Notting Hill*); self-referentiality (Fox); celebrity; Hollywood; community; premarital sex
14.14	305	Mr. Spritz Goes to Washington	Self-referentiality (Homer eats the *Joe Millionaire* promo, Fox News is mocked); airspace; *The Three Stooges*; the government; the Republican Party; running for office
14.15	306	C.E. D'oh	Holidays (Valentine's Day); parody (*Glengarry Glen Ross*; corporate inefficiency,

Season Number and Episode	Cumulative Episode Number	Title	Themes, Discussion Points, Teachable Elements Other Notes
			white collar crime); self-referentiality (Homer laments that Bart won't be 10 forever); parenthood; scapegoating; adult education; sexuality
14.16	307	'Scuse Me While I Miss the Sky	Astronomy; light pollution; crime (vandalism); mob rule; narrative structure (frame plot)
14.17	308	Three Gays of the Condo	Marriage; fidelity; stereo-types (homosexuality); parody (Weird Al Yankovic; trends such as the medieval-themed restaurant); narrative structure (flashback, flash-forward)
14.18	309	Dude, Where's My Ranch?	Radio play (one-hit wonders); intertextuality (Britney Spears, William Shatner, *The Lord of the Rings*); treatment of animals; Native Americans; the American West; linguistics (accents); songwriting; crushes; dude ranches
14.19	310	Old Yeller Belly	Intertextuality (advertising, Spuds McKenzie); alcoholism; treatment of animals/pets
14.20	311	Brake My Wife, Please	Aquariums; treatment of animals; marriage/marital stress; community; driving; walking; dependency
14.21	312	Bart of War	Intertextuality (*South Park*); The Beatles/Beatlemania; linguistics (discussion of the words "hijinks" and changes in spellings); Native Americans; youth

Season Number and Episode	Cumulative Episode Number	Title	Themes, Discussion Points, Teachable Elements Other Notes
			groups (one is a pseudo–Native American group called "The Pre-teen Braves," the other is "Calvary Kids); crime (riots); satire (America's violent past and present); competition
14.22	313	Moe Baby Blues	Loneliness; suicide; children's toys; storytelling; inter-textuality (*The Godfather*)
15.1	314	Treehouse of Horror XIV (Reaper Madness; Frinkinstein; Stop the World, I Want to Goof Off)	Holidays (Halloween); death; time manipulation; Nobel Prize; father-son relationships; parody (*The Twilight Zone*, "A Kind of a Stopwatch"; *On a Pale Horse*; *Frankenstein*)
15.2	315	My Mother the Carjacker	Mother-son relationships; puzzles; crime; escape; parody (*A Beautiful Mind*)
15.3	316	The President Wore Pearls	Parody (*Evita*); school fund-raisers; public school funding cuts; mobs/riots; elections; power; politics; strikes; labor unions; musicals
15.4	317	The Regina Monologues	Britain (stereotypes); travel; *Macbeth*; vacations; prison escape; self-referentiality (Bart opens a museum in his treehouse that houses a "Bart: the Early Years" exhibit); narrative technique (montage)
15.5	318	The Fat and the Furriest	Bears; holidays (Mother's Day); fear; confrontation; treatment of animals
15.6	319	Today, I Am a Klown	Bar Mitzvahs; treatment of animals; Judaism; local talk shows; television production; self-referen-

Season Number and Episode	Cumulative Episode Number	Title	Themes, Discussion Points, Teachable Elements Other Notes
			tiality (Lisa refers to the *Our Favorite Family* guide, discussion of the Fox network standards); fame
15.7	320	'Tis the Fifteenth Season	Holidays (Christmas); gifts; selfishness; parody (various Christmas specials, especially the "true meaning of Christmas" theme); jealousy
15.8	321	Marge vs. Singles, Seniors, Childless Couples and Teens, and Gays	Children's television; mobs/riots; parenting; voter initiatives; acronyms; lobbying; children; Pig Latin; music festivals (Lollapalooza, Woodstock)
15.9	322	I, (annoyed grunt)-Bot	Robots; robot wars (*Battlebots*); father-son relationships; pets; death
15.10	323	Diatribe of a Mad Housewife	Writing; romance novels; ambulances; whaling; publishing; biographical criticism
15.11	324	Margical History Tour	History; Henry VIII; Lewis, Clark, Sacagawea; Mozart; parody (*Amadeus*); libraries; marriage; fertility; succession; jealousy; sibling rivalry
15.12	325	Milhouse Doesn't Live Here Anymore	Friendship; brother-sister relationships; moving; anniversaries; panhandling; Native American artifacts; self-referentiality (Flanders appears at the TV museum, Isabel Sanford explains sitcom ending conventions at end of episode)
15.13	326	Smart and Smarter	Linguistics (language acqui-

Season Number and Episode	Cumulative Episode Number	Title	Themes, Discussion Points, Teachable Elements Other Notes
			sition); education; competition; running away from home; jealousy; identity construction; parody (*What Ever Happened to Baby Jane?*); narrative structure (montage); natural history museums; intelligence; sibling rivalry
15.14	327	The Ziff Who Came to Dinner	Parody (*Powers of Ten*); scary movies; fear; Securities Exchange; scapegoating; court trials; prison
15.15	328	Co-Dependent's Day	Parody (*Star Wars* series); alcoholism; co-dependency; drunk driving; framing for a crime; rehab
15.16	329	The Wandering Juvie	Juvenile delinquency; grifting; escape; troubled children; parody (*The Defiant Ones*)
15.17	330	My Big Fat Geek Wedding	Weddings; marriage; cold feet; sci-fi conventions; relationships
15.18	331	Catch 'Em If You Can	Parenting; romance; *Love Story*; Niagara Falls; Miami; crime (credit card fraud); intertextuality/ parody (*Miami Vice*, *Catch Me If You Can*); air travel
15.19	332	Simple Simpson	Parody (superhero films); revenge; crime (assault); blackmail; heroes; vigilantism
15.20	333	The Way We Weren't	First love; first kisses; summer camp; romance; narrative structure (flashbacks); storytelling
15.21	334	Bart-Mangled Banner	Inoculations; patriotism;

Season Number and Episode	Cumulative Episode Number	Title	Themes, Discussion Points, Teachable Elements Other Notes
			political satire; media sensationalism; free speech; political debate/rhetoric ("Un-Americanism"); logical fallacies; prison escape (Alcatraz); stereotypes (France); immigration; civil liberties; talent shows
15.22	335	Fraudcast News	First Amendment; free speech; free press; poetry; National Parks; media monopolies; propaganda; independent newspapers; self-referentiality (references to Murdoch's media control, *Itchy & Scratchy* cartoon is made in Korea); intertextuality (*Pump Up the Volume*)
16.1	336	Treehouse of Horror XV (The Ned Zone; Four Beheadings with a Funeral; In the Belly of the Boss)	Heaven; stereotypes (English food); parody (*Innerspace*, *Fantastic Voyage*, Jack the Ripper, British detective stories); death; premonitions; opium; hallucinations
16.2	337	All's Fair in Oven War	Remodeling; cook-offs; integrity; cheating; role models; envy; parody (*Playboy*); sex education; competition; censorship (Marge says "BFD," and in some markets in repeats, the "F" is awkwardly dubbed out.)
16.3	338	Sleeping with the Enemy	Body image; anorexia; self-referentiality (Homer draws himself as Matt Groening would); parties; inducements for good grades; parenting;

Season Number and Episode	Cumulative Episode Number	Title	Themes, Discussion Points, Teachable Elements Other Notes
			bingeing; bullying; narrative structure (resisting an ending [Lisa refuses to provide Homer closure in this episode — the lack of said closure spills into the credits])
16.4	339	She Used to Be My Girl	Red herring fallacies; news coverage/journalism; jealousy; success; feminism; self-referentiality (the show criticizes Fox News's alleged bias)
16.5	340	Fat Man and Little Boy	Tooth fairy; artistic expression; job loss; small business; father-daughter relationships; crime (theft); toys; growing up
16.6	341	Midnight Rx	Insurance coverage; prescription plans; Canada (stereotypes); Canadian drugs; crime (drug smuggling, fraud); health care; racial profiling
16.7	342	Mommie Beerest	Health inspectors; mortgages; emotional infidelity; bar ownership
16.8	343	Homer and Ned's Hail Mary Pass	Sports; viral (Internet) entertainment; intertextuality/parody (*The Passion of the Christ*); religion; Super Bowl halftime shows; sportsmanship
16.9	344	Pranksta Rap	Rap music; sneaking out; lying; kidnapping; rap battle; parody (*The Passion of the Christ, Veggie Tales, 8 Mile*)

Season Number and Episode	Cumulative Episode Number	Title	Themes, Discussion Points, Teachable Elements Other Notes
16.10	345	There's Something About Marrying	Gay marriage; tourism; coming out; religion; capitalism; self-referentiality (Fox programming is mocked); intolerance; homophobia; narrative techniques (narrative self-containment); gender; sexuality; sexual orientation
16.11	346	On a Clear Day I Can't See My Sister	Global warming; glaciers retreating; field trips; sibling relationships; Walmart; working conditions; job satisfaction; restraining orders
16.12	347	Goo Goo Gai Pan	Adoption; single parenthood; China (stereotypes); menopause; globalization; Tiananmen Square; narrative structure/self-referentiality (episode credits feature a segment with a drawing lesson given by David Silverman)
16.13	348	Mobile Homer	Life insurance; budgeting; marriage (separation); mobile homes
16.14	349	The Seven-Beer Snitch	Architecture; prison; city funding; town pride; economics; pets; Frank Gehry; symphony; law; snitching
16.15	350	Future-Drama	Affording college; astrology; prediction; sibling relationships; marital separation
16.16	351	Don't Fear the Roofer	Home repair; black holes; hallucinations; mental illness

Season Number and Episode	Cumulative Episode Number	Title	Themes, Discussion Points, Teachable Elements Other Notes
16.17	352	The Heartbroke Kid	School funding; obesity; advertising; health; food; illness (heart attack); addiction; junk food; fat camp; youth hostels
16.19	354	Thank God It's Doomsday	Parody (*Left Behind*); rapture; numerology; predictions; religion; heaven; deus ex machina; the Last Supper; apocalypse; dreams/ visions
16.20	355	Home Away from Homer	Precious Moments figurines; Internet pornography; community; abjection; conformity
16.21	356	The Father, the Son, & the Holy Guest Star	Religion (Catholicism vs. Protestantism); community; belonging; conversion
17.1	357	Bonfire of the Manatees	Marital problems; mafia; lying; gambling; debt; animal cruelty; philan-thropy; manatees; endangered animals; rural Americans (stereo-types); pornography
17.2	358	The Girl Who Slept Too Little	Insomnia; fear; parody (*Where the Wild Things Are*); social protest; psychiatry; stamps
17.3	359	Milhouse of Sand and Fog	Reconciliation; attention; illness (chicken pox); lying; fidelity; trust; medicine/science (pox parties); vaccination
17.4	360	Treehouse of Horror XVI (Bartificial Intelligence; Survival of the Fattest; I've Grown a Costume on Your Face)	Self-referentiality (the opening scene with the aliens complaining about baseball mirrors audience members' anger about baseball forcing the

Season Number and Episode	Cumulative Episode Number	Title	Themes, Discussion Points, Teachable Elements Other Notes
			episode to air after Halloween); holidays (Halloween); witches; parody (*A.I.*, exorcism, *The Most Dangerous Game*); hunting; violence vs. sex on TV; public service announcements
17.5	361	Marge's Son Poisoning	Biking; mother-son relationships; tea; masculinity; karaoke; sports (arm wrestling; weight-lifting); gender roles
17.6	362	See Homer Run	Parody (2003 California recall election); politics; holidays (Father's Day); gift-giving; father-daughter relationships; acting out; psychological problems; bonding; safety awareness; peer pressure
17.7	363	The Last of the Red Hat Mamas	Crime (theft); friendship; holidays (Easter); peer pressure; morality; Italian (language); tutoring; parody (Red Hat Society); linguistics (second-language acquisition)
17.8	364	The Italian Bob	Travel; Italy (stereotypes); revenge; secrets; opera (*Pagliacci*); anti–Americanism; crime; plagiarism (self-reference); metafiction; parody (*Les Misérables*)
17.9	365	Simpsons Christmas Stories (The First D'oh El; I Saw Grampa Cussing Santa Claus; The Nutcracker ... Sweet)	Holidays (Christmas); the Nativity; Santa Claus; World War I; Christmas gift-giving; suicide attempts; parody (The Bible, *The Nutcracker*); self-referentiality (the

Season Number and Episode	Cumulative Episode Number	Title	Themes, Discussion Points, Teachable Elements Other Notes
			family starts singing after an acknowledgment of public domain)
17.10	366	Homer's Paternity Coot	Mystery; paternity testing; narrative structure (flashback sequence); sitcom conventions (narrative self-containment); class/wealth
17.11	367	We're on the Road to D'ohwhere	Punishment; crime (destruction of property); father-son relationships; no-fly list; behavior modification; prescription drug trafficking/abuse; intellectual theories (ontogeny recapitulates phylogeny)
17.12	368	My Fair Laddy	Parody (*My Fair Lady*); class; manners; gym class; advertising; musicals
17.13	369	The Seemingly Never-Ending Story	Narrative structure (framing, resisting an ending); archaeology; crime; greed; storytelling
17.14	370	Bart Has Two Mommies	Motherhood/parenting; animals in zoos and show business; babysitting
17.15	371	Homer Simpson, This Is Your Wife	Reality television; marital support; envy
17.16	372	Million Dollar Abie	Sports (football); treatment of the elderly; assisted suicide
17.17	373	Kiss Kiss, Bang Bangalore	Outsourcing; workers' rights; India (stereotypes); capitalism, unions; MacGyver; crime (kidnapping); escape; parody (*MacGyver; Misery; Apocalypse Now*)
17.18	374	The Wettest Stories Ever Told	Storytelling; the *Mayflower*; parody (*The Poseidon*

Season Number and Episode	Cumulative Episode Number	Title	Themes, Discussion Points, Teachable Elements Other Notes
			Adventure); history; Captain Bligh
17.19	375	Girls Just Want to Have Sums	Education (math, gender-segregated education); essentialist feminism, sexism; impersonation; gender roles
17.20	376	Regarding Margie	Love; marriage; amnesia; parody (*Regarding Henry*)
17.21	377	The Monkey Suit	Evolution vs. creationism; education; religion; history (Scopes "Monkey Trial"); *The Origin of Species*
17.22	378	Marge and Homer Turn a Couple Play	Marital problems/advice; sports; celebrity marriages
18.1	379	The Mook, the Chef, the Wife and Her Homer	Parody (*The Godfather*); crime; mafia; cooking; aspirations; corporal punishment; carpooling
18.2	380	Jazzy and the Pussycats	Sibling relationships; jazz; jealousy; psychiatry; anger management; music; death; overdose; animal rescue
18.3	381	Please Homer, Don't Hammer 'Em	Gender roles; carpentry; sexism; fraud (front); food allergies; parody (*Remington Steele*)
18.4	382	Treehouse of Horror XVII ("Married to the Blob"; "You Gotta Know When to Golem"; "The Day the Earth Looked Stupid")	*Golem of Prague*; monsters; holidays (Halloween); nuclear mutation; weight gain; golem/Frankenstein; Jewish humor; parody (*War of the Worlds, Tales from the Crypt, Meteorite, Alien Invasion*, military occupation)
18.5	383	G.I. (Annoyed Grunt)	Army recruiting; war games (field training exercises); parody (*Looney Tunes, Full*

Season Number and Episode	Cumulative Episode Number	Title	Themes, Discussion Points, Teachable Elements Other Notes
			Metal Jacket); Abu Ghraib prisoner abuse
18.6	384	Moe'N'a Lisa	Poetry; plagiarism; popularity; authorship; Senior Olympics; friendship; memory; Bread Loaf Writers' Conference
18.7	385	Ice Cream of Margie (with the Light Blue Hair)	Job loss; ice cream trucks; artistic expression; sculpture; depression; *The Feminine Mystique*; feminism; success
18.8	386	The Haw-Hawed Couple	Bullies; best friends; jealousy; birthday parties; children's books
18.9	387	Kill Gil, Volumes I & II	Holidays (Christmas, Valentine's Day, St. Patrick's Day); toys; Malibu Stacy; assertiveness
18.10	388	The Wife Aquatic	Memory; nostalgia; commercial fishing; overfishing; parody (*The Perfect Storm*)
18.11	389	Revenge Is a Dish Best Served Three Times (The Count of Monte Fatso; Revenge of the Geeks; Bartman Begins)	Revenge; storytelling; parody (*Batman*; *The Count of Monte Cristo*); France (stereotypes)
18.12	390	Little Big Girl	Romance; marriage; driver's license; Native American heritage appropriation; fire
18.13	391	Springfield Up	*Seven Up!*; documentaries; self-esteem; economics/class; impersonation
18.14	392	Yokel Chords	Education; class; child entertainers; exploitation; parody (*The Sound of Music*; Edward Gorey–style art); tutoring; child psychology; psychotherapy; urban legends; education

Season Number and Episode	Cumulative Episode Number	Title	Themes, Discussion Points, Teachable Elements Other Notes
			funding; depression; cultural literacy
18.15	393	Rome-old and Juli-eh	Economics/bankruptcy; employment; marriage; aging; senility
18.16	394	Homerazzi	Celebrities; paparazzi; tabloids; privacy
18.17	395	Marge Gamer	Parody (video games [MMORPS, or massively multi-player online role playing games, fantasy]); sports (soccer); computer literacy; mother-son relationships; cheating; sportsmanship; coaching
18.18	396	Boys of Bummer	Sports (Little League baseball); self-esteem; depression; sales; sex; community
18.19	397	Crook and Ladder	Crime (theft); firefighting; parenting advice; sleeping pills; insomnia; charity/volunteerism; ethics
18.20	398	Stop or My Dog Will Shoot	Pets; police; Tremaux's algorithm; show and tell; chemistry; presidential candidacies (Giuliani had recorded a guest voice, but the original airing could not include his scene because he was a candidate at that time); crime-fighting
18.21	399	24 Minutes	Parody (*24*); surveillance; crime-fighting; moles; truancy
18.22	400	You Kent Always Say What You Want	Censorship/FCC fines; free speech; Fox News; Republicans; politics; news media; *Tracey Ullman* shorts; self-referentiality

Season Number and Episode	Cumulative Episode Number	Title	Themes, Discussion Points, Teachable Elements Other Notes
19.1	401	He Loves to Fly and He D'ohs[11]	Chicago (Second City); life coaches; flying (private planes); class distinction; envy; lying; job satisfaction
19.2	402	Homer of Seville	Opera (*La Bohème*); fame; fans (the head of Homer's fan club, Julia, is obsessed with Homer, perhaps in a similar way that Yolanda Saldívar, who was the president of Selena's fan club, was obsessed with Selena. Saldívar murdered Selena in 1995)
19.3	403	Midnight Towboy	Towing cars; parenting; dependency; crime (kidnapping); greed; territorialism
19.4	404	I Don't Wanna Know Why the Caged Bird Sings	Crime (robbery, stalking); promises; parental involvement in child's achievements
19.5	405	Treehouse of Horror XVIII (E.T. Go Home, Mr. and Mrs. Simpson, Heck House)	Holidays (Halloween); parody (*E.T., Mr. and Mrs. Smith*); Hell; the Seven Deadly Sins
19.6	406	Little Orphan Millie	Marriage/remarriage; grief; popularity
19.7	407	Husbands and Knives	Comic books; business competition; crime (destruction of property); weight loss; gyms; small business; success; cosmetic surgery; body image
19.8	408	Funeral for a Fiend	Crime (attempted murder); revenge; TiVo; advertising; guilt
19.9	409	Eternal Moonshine of the Simpson Mind	Memory; forgetting; parody (*Eternal Sunshine of the*

Season Number and Episode	Cumulative Episode Number	Title	Themes, Discussion Points, Teachable Elements Other Notes
			Spotless Mind, Internet memes [Picture a day for a Year]); suicide; birthdays
19.10	410	E Pluribus Wiggum	Politics; elections; controversy (called Juan Peron a dictator); parody; Bayeux Tapestry; fire; presidential primaries; undecided voters
19.11	411	That 90's Show	Parody (Nirvana, Weird Al Yankovic); *The Treachery of Images*; college; grunge music; MTV; stereotypes (intellectuals, political correctness); relationships; narrative structure (flashbacks)
19.12	412	Love, Springfieldian Style	Holidays (Valentine's Day); storytelling; parody (*Bonnie and Clyde*, *Lady and the Tramp*; *Sid and Nancy*, the Sex Pistols/ punk rock, Tunnel of Love ride); danger/ violence kink; crime; pets; addiction; censorship (episode the first to be broadcast in the UK after prime time due to adult content)
19.13	413	The Debarted	Parody (*The Departed*); moles/ snitches; crime; automobiles; pranks; narrative structure (fourth wall)
19.14	414	Dial 'N' for Nerder	Pranks; murder; parody (TV mystery series, *Columbo*, *Cheaters*); diet cheating; reality TV; diets
19.15	415	Smoke on the Daughter	Sports (ballet); parenting; living through children;

Season Number and Episode	Cumulative Episode Number	Title	Themes, Discussion Points, Teachable Elements Other Notes
			smoking, smoking with eating disorders; beef jerky; parody (*Harry Potter* book release); pests/raccoons
19.16	416	Papa Don't Leech	Taxes; tax evasion; city funding; father-daughter relationships; abandonment; plagiarism
19.17	417	Apocalypse Cow	4-H; animal rights; marriage; rural stereotypes; slaughterhouses; feedlots; advertising; children's cartoons; pets
19.18	418	Any Given Sundance	Sundance Film Festival; filmmaking; confessional art; family dysfunction
19.19	419	Mona Leaves-a	Mother-son relationships; forgiveness; death; environmental activism; parody (*James Bond* movies); grief
19.20	420	All About Lisa	Parody (*All About Eve*); fame; sidekicks; narrative structure (flashbacks; narrator); coin collecting; children's television
20.1	421	Sex, Pies, and Idiot Scrapes	Holidays (St. Patrick's Day); Ireland; job satisfaction; bounty hunting; narrative structure (montage); baking; friendship
20.2	422	Lost Verizon	Pranks; cell phones; Machu Picchu
20.3	423	Double, Double Boy in Trouble	Parody (*The Prince and the Pauper*); class/wealth; inheritance
20.4	424	Treehouse of Horror XIX (Untitled Robot Parody, How to Get Ahead in Dead-	Holidays (Halloween; Thanksgiving); parody (*It's the Great Pumpkin, Charlie Brown*; *Peanuts*;

Season Number and Episode	Cumulative Episode Number	Title	Themes, Discussion Points, Teachable Elements Other Notes
		vertising, It's the Grand Pumpkin, Milhouse)	*Transformers*; *Mad Men*); advertising; heaven
20.5	425	Dangerous Curves	Parody (*Two for the Road*); narrative structure (flashbacks); holidays (Independence Day); relationships; premarital sex; adultery
20.6	426	Homer and Lisa Exchange Cross Words	Meta/genre crossover (the Sunday *New York Times'* crossword included a message to fans); parody (*Wordplay*); crosswords; father-daughter relationships
20.7	427	Mypods and Broomsticks	Satire (Apple, Inc.); religion; Muslims; racial profiling; prejudice
20.8	428	The Burns and The Bees	Bees; (Africanized bees, mysterious bee disappearance, colony collapse); holidays (Christmas); wealth/class
20.9	429	Lisa the Drama Queen	Fantasy; utopias; mental illness; parody (*Heavenly Creatures*); running away from home
20.10	430	Take My Life, Please	High school; midlife crisis; alternate realities; election fraud
20.11	431	How the Test Was Won	Education, education funding; No Child Left Behind; health insurance; testing, test anxiety
20.12	432	No Loan Again, Naturally	Economics; mortgage crisis; friendship; landlords; renters; holidays (Mardi Gras); local media; loans
20.13	433	Gone Maggie Gone	Parody (*The Da Vinci Code*);

Season Number and Episode	Cumulative Episode Number	Title	Themes, Discussion Points, Teachable Elements Other Notes
			camera obscura; stress; puzzles
20.14	434	In the Name of the Grandfather	Ireland (stereotypes); smoking ban; relaxation; pubs/bars; treatment of the elderly; Irish literature; self-referentiality (there's a note about guest voices)
20.15	435	Wedding for Disaster	Parody (*Bridezillas*); religion; weddings; mysteries
20.16	436	Eeny Teeny Maya Moe	Parenthood; romance; little people; height bias; Internet dating
20.17	437	The Good, The Sad and the Drugly	Pranks; discipline; deception; friendship; antidepressants, children on prescription drugs
20.18	438	Father Knows Worst	Parenting (hovering parents); competition; cliques
20.19	439	Waverly Hills 9021 D'oh!	Satire (Hannah Montana–esque teen stars); public education; sibling relationships; class
20.20	440	Four Great Women and a Manicure	Parody (*The Fountainhead, Macbeth, Snow White,* Disney); feminism; Queen Elizabeth I; history; Ayn Rand's philosophy (Objectivism); artistic expression
20.21	441	Coming to Homerica	Satire (border crossing, attitudes towards immigration); economy; agriculture; stereotypes; linguistics (dialects)
21.1	442	Homer the Whopper	Comic books; superheroes; parody (Hollywood, actors, filmmaking, montages)

Chapter 1

They Have the Internet on Computers Now — A Collection of *Simpsons* Resources

The Internet wrote it. I just handed it in. — Bart Simpson

Don't you worry about Wikipedia. We'll change it when we get home. We'll change a lot of things. — Homer Simpson

After more than twenty years of programming, there are now many secondary sources[1] to use when teaching or researching *The Simpsons*. This chapter provides a guide to *some* of these resources. This list is not exhaustive but highlights many useful books, articles, and websites. We won't examine news articles, although there is a plethora (a daily news Google search will yield an average of five new pieces). It should be noted that many issues surrounding audience response and the production of the show can be found in news articles, as opposed to scholarly work. That is, news articles often have updated information about the show's production problems and progress, as well as audience reactions and scandals.

The early years of *The Simpsons* yielded little critical work, although the show was controversial and popular. As the years went on, many pieces surfaced in defense of the show, arguing not only that the show was *not* damaging to American culture but that it was "more than just a cartoon." There are still works whose main point is the same, even after all the years that the show has been fair fodder for scholarship. These works may seem relevant and necessary, as there are still people who dismiss the show due to its genre and popularity. The texts often discuss the satiric, postmodern, and/or literary methods of *The Simpsons*; unfortunately, they tend to feel repetitive and unnecessary to seasoned *Simpsons* scholars. It is also doubtful that the philistine holdouts will be won over by one more article expounding the merits of the series.

77

The following are organized by category and then roughly by year. We continue to add reviews of sources to our website as more are written and discovered.

Books (Single Author and Anthologies)

The Simpsons: *A Complete Guide to Our Favorite Family*, created by Matt Groening, edited by Ray Richmond (1997). This is an authorized episode-by-episode guide to seasons 1–8, including basic production information, quotes, basic plot, minor character profiles, and stuff viewers may have missed (usually an explanation of quick visual jokes, like what's written on the newspapers characters read). The index is useful for when you can remember something about an episode, but you can't quite place *which* episode you want. This guide also features main character overviews, a synopsis of the *Tracey Ullman Show* shorts, a guide to voice talents, and lists of such fun things as billboards around town and an *Itchy & Scratchy* filmography. Karma often uses this as a required text, as it allows students to access information about the first eight seasons quickly and introduces them to characters they may not know well.

The Simpsons Forever!, created by Matt Groening, edited by Scott M. Gimple (1999). This is a continuation of the *Complete Guide*, with episodes from seasons 9 and 10 chronicled. In addition to the features of the first book, Troy McClure (Phil Hartman) is honored in his own spread and *Simpsons* songs are highlighted.

The Simpsons *and Philosophy: The D'oh of Homer*, edited by William Irwin, Mark T. Conard, and Aeon J. Skoble (2001). Unlike another book on this list, *The Psychology of* The Simpsons, the editors of this collection make it clear that while they may enjoy the show, they do not consider it serious literature. Additionally, "Matt Groening studied philosophy in college, but none of the contributors to this book believes there is deep underlying philosophy to Groening's cartoon. This is *not* 'the philosophy of *The Simpsons*' or '*The Simpsons* as philosophy'; it's *The Simpsons and Philosophy*" (2). Thus, the contributors' motive is to use the show as the medium to make you read about philosophy. Many articles barely mention the show, and a few have serious errors, as if the writers have only seen a few episodes and thus make erroneous generalizations about the show and its characters. Following is our take on each chapter.

- Raja Halwani, "Homer and Aristotle." This essay explores Homer's character through Aristotle's four basic character types — virtuous, continent, incontinent, and vicious. Halwani finds that Homer is morally problematic, but gives reasons why the audience likes him anyway.
- Aeon J. Skoble, "Lisa and American Anti-Intellectualism." Skoble's thoughtful piece discusses how the show represents our ambivalent relationship to intellectualism. Skoble wants to use Lisa as his example of intellectualism and thus as the example of the victim of anti-intellectualism, but he simplifies her for being both an intellectual and having the drives of a little girl, when surely she can be a person with contradictory drives.
- Eric Bronson, "Why Maggie Matters: Sounds of Silence, East and West." Bronson attempts to use Maggie to discuss the relationship between silence and enlightenment in Eastern philosophy and between language and thought in Western philosophy. However, this essay suffers because it seems to have been written after Maggie had said her first word. There is also a detour into discussing Marge and Homer as bad parents.
- Gerald J. Erion and Joseph A. Zeccardi, "Marge's Moral Motivation." This piece uses Marge to illustrate Aristotle's view of morality and virtue, concluding that Marge is "a Christian-flavored Aristotelian" (57).
- Mark T. Conard, "Thus Spake Bart: On Nietzsche and the Virtues of Being Bad." This essay's tone is markedly different from the rest of the collection, as Conard asserts that Nietzsche is "as bad as they come, honey." While the purpose of the essay is supposedly to determine if Bart is the Nietzschean ideal, Bart is mentioned only at the very end and the author does not engage with counterexamples of Bart's behavior.
- William Irwin and J. R. Lombardo, "*The Simpsons* and Allusion: 'Worst Essay Ever.'" This useful essay successfully defines allusion and its use in *The Simpsons*, including self-referential allusions. The authors distinguish actual allusions from accidental associations, that is, those that are unintended or anachronistic.
- Deborah Knight, "Popular Parody: *The Simpsons* Meets the Crime Film." Using "Bart the Murderer," Knight relates the show to Linda Hutcheon's theory of parody, noting that

Hutcheon's definitions and examples are all limited to high, rather than popular, art. Knight concludes that this episode is not parody, as it is not critical of the genre of crime film, and thus concludes that it is closer to homage.

- Carl Matheson, "*The Simpsons*, Hyper-Irony, and the Meaning of Life." Matheson discusses irony, parody, allusion, and quotationalism. These and other articles on parody serve to reinforce how slippery "parody" is as a term. Unlike Jonathan Gray, Matheson holds that the show does not parody the sitcom as genre. Matheson explains that the show undercuts moral agendas and then undercuts its own undercutting, which he calls "hyper-irony" (118). Matheson believes that comedy is invariably linked to cruelty, and perhaps this is why he believes that the show has no "underlying moral commitment" (122).

- Dale E. Snow and James J. Snow, "Simpsonian Sexual Politics." The show's stereotypical treatment of gender is shown in three ways: the characters are mostly male; the episodes mainly focus on Bart and Homer; and the characterizations of Lisa and Marge are somewhat sexist. While many of the critiques are valid, other claims are debatable, including a claim that "sexism" is inherent in the voice work.

- James Lawler, "The Moral World of the Simpson Family: A Kantian Perspective." This analysis concludes it is the entire Simpson family that ultimately resolves and surmounts the contradictions of duty and desire (148).

- Paul A. Cantor, "*The Simpsons*: Atomistic Politics and the Nuclear Family." The author seems to be defending a conservative view of the family, apparently believing that the show (and Hollywood) is not defensive of the family; however, he says that the family unit is problematic in contemporary American democracy.

- Jason Holt, "Springfield Hypocrisy." Holt uses Chief Wiggum to argue that the traditional definition of hypocrisy is flawed and that it is possible to be true to oneself while being false to others.

- Daniel Barwick, "Enjoying the So-called 'Iced Cream': Mr. Burns, Satan, and Happiness." Barwick uses Mr. Burns to discuss happiness and to conclude that happiness is about who you are, not what happens to you.

- David Vessey, "Hey-diddily-ho, Neighboreeños: Ned Flanders and Neighborly Love." Vessey explores a moral dilemma raised in "Home-Sweet Homediddily-Dum Doodily," wherein Ned, having temporary custody of the Simpson children, tries to baptize them. Most of the discussion focuses on Kant, though there is some mention of Ned and why he attempts to baptize the children only when he has control over them (that is, why he doesn't do so when they are simply his neighbors).
- Jennifer L. McMahon, "The Function of Fiction: The Heuristic Value of Homer." Rather than talking about what the show teaches, this essay simply argues that fiction (and thus the show) is capable of teaching. This defense of fiction is unlikely be needed by those with a background in the humanities.
- James M. Wallace, "A (Karl, Not Groucho) Marxist in Springfield." While the author finds that the show may be considered de-centered art (240), Wallace ultimately concludes, "*The Simpsons*—despite its barbs at commercialism and corporations—not only reflects, but conserves and propagates a traditional bourgeois ideology" (249).
- David L. G. Arnold, "'And the Rest Writes Itself': Roland Barthes Watches *The Simpsons*." This is an effective overview of Barthes and a discussion of how the show disrupts binaries.
- Kelly Dean Jolley, "What Bart Calls Thinking." There are a few paragraphs on Bart at the end, but this work is basically a discussion of Heidegger.

The Gospel According to The Simpsons, by Mark I. Pinsky (2001). The very first page of the book, the "advance praise," tells the reader what to expect, as various religious commentators reassure us that Pinsky is about to convince us that *The Simpsons* is not anti-religious. Pinsky's assessment of the show is not as eloquent as Gerry Bowler's 1996 article "God and *The Simpsons*," however. In fact, although Pinsky is able to address a few more issues (such as adultery), the book does not advance beyond the point Bowler originally made. Pinsky's book, though accessible to those with faith, is also problematic due to frequent errors in action/line attribution and the treatment of fantasy moments as canonical.

Everyday Apocalypse: The Sacred Revealed in Radiohead, The Simpsons *and Other Pop Culture Icons*, by David Dark (2002). Professor Dark explains in the introduction of his book his use of the word "apocalypse."

What he calls apocalyptic (he uses it as a noun[2]) means "that which is revelatory, that which engenders epiphany." In his defense of popular culture, Dark holds that "any song or story that deals with conflict by way of strained euphemistic spin, a cliché, or a triumphal cupcake ending strikes us as the best in family entertainment. This is the opposite of apocalyptic" (10). In other words, apocalyptic is that which shakes the reader from complacency and causes him/her to see the world anew. Dark is situated firmly within a Christian context. He believes that the popular culture he discusses is not an attack on Christian values, but an opportunity for Christians to reexamine themselves. Dark, in fact, seems at odds with modern Christians who obsess about the apocalypse, as he calls for Christians to have a positive change on the world today, rather than settling for the status quo until the rapture.

Flannery O'Connor's fiction is cited for its use of distortion to achieve what Dark calls apocalypse: "I am interested in making up a good case for distortion, as I am coming to believe it is the only way to make people see" (O'Connor quoted in Dark 13). *The Simpsons* as satire naturally fills Dark's vision of apocalyptic. Thus, he argues that the show is society's mirror and that some viewers will reflexively shrink from the reflection, becoming offended on behalf of themselves or others. We are warned that "viewing *The Simpsons* can be an intensely liberating experience, but it requires a disconcerting task that the viewer might not have the wit to perform" (48).

In addition to *The Simpsons*, Dark examines O'Connor, Radiohead, *The Matrix*, *The Truman Show*, Beck, and films by the Coen brothers. Although Dark's writing is eminently readable (one imagines how dynamic his class lectures must be), he tends to make claims with broad generalizations, often trusting the readers to be able to provide their own examples, to understand his quick references, and to follow his literary connections; there is very little analysis of specifics.

The Simpsons Beyond Forever!, created by Matt Groening, edited by Jesse L. McCann (2002). Seasons 11 and 12 are listed here, with highlights of production art and the usual information and extras.

Leaving Springfield: The Simpsons *and the Possibility of Oppositional Culture*, edited by John Alberti (2004). This excellent collection is academic in nature and addresses a series of relevant concepts to deeper thinking about *The Simpsons*. The introduction gives a thorough history of the show and contextualizes the show within television history. Alberti believes that television perpetuates an individualistic approach to life (American television, anyway): "The approach taken by most sitcoms usually represents the given [social] issue as a matter of individual lifestyle or personality" (xiv). *The Simpsons*, in contrast, "consistently works at connecting the personal to the political, in the classic sense, by taking advantage of the creative freedoms offered by animation to place the behavior of individual characters in social and historical context" (xv).

This anthology seeks to answer questions about how the show can be oppositional and mainstream, how it can reconcile a critique of consumer culture while perpetuating it through advertising and merchandise, and how it combines high and low culture. Refreshingly, Alberti declares that the collection is not meant to situate the show as worthy of attention and as more valuable than other shows, "for this argument reproduces the standard hierarchical construction of contemporary culture" (xix).

- David L. G. Arnold, "'Use a Pen, Sideshow Bob': *The Simpsons* and the Threat of High Culture." This is an intriguing article about intellectualism, high culture, and *The Simpsons*, through an analysis of Sideshow Bob. Arnold takes us through theories of culture and elitism before broaching interesting claims, such as, "We can read Bart as an avatar of the kind of culture available in and defined by Springfield, and Sideshow Bob's persistent attempts to kill him represent an attack on, and defense against, the gradual evacuation of high-cultural taste and values" (13). This provides a solid close reading of relevant episodes and connects Bob to larger ideological frames.
- Kurt M. Koenigsberger, "Commodity Culture and Its Discontents: Mr. Bennett, Bart Simpson, and the Rhetoric of Modernism." In many ways, this article is an attempt to revive scholarship on writer Arnold Bennett by linking his work to *The Simpsons*. The thesis: "The potential for oppositionality both in the pre-high modernist fiction of Bennett and in the postmodernist *Simpsons* is partially constrained by an inclusivity designed to solve the problem of the 'great divide' between high and low texts, on the one hand, and to represent a whole way of life, on the other" (32). The readings of commodity culture in *The Simpsons* contrasted with the commodified production world of the Fox product are astute.
- Megan Mullen, "*The Simpsons* and Hanna-Barbera's Animation

Legacy." This essay grounds *The Simpsons* in the history of television family sitcoms in general and of Hanna-Barbera's work
specifically, to show *The Simpsons'* progenitors.

- Kevin J. H. Dettmar, "Countercultural Literacy: Learning Irony
  with *The Simpsons.*" Dettmar's excellent essay explores how "*The
  Simpsons* is the most consistently, intelligently ironic show on
  television. Running against the implicit logic of the sitcom, it
  relentlessly works to explore and exploit the gap between the
  American Dream and contemporary American reality" (88). He
  gives special attention to the highly ironic episode "The Cartridge Family" and how the irony at play reinforces many sides
  in the political argument over gun control.
- Valerie Weilunn Chow, "Homer Erectus: Homer Simpson As
  Everyman ... and Every Woman." Chow begins with an interesting discussion of the "ironic hyperconsciousness" (107) of *The
  Simpsons* and how both the characters and the viewer (the latter
  as intended consumers for the products advertised by commercials in the break) are "both the consumer and the consumed"
  (108). She then traces the role of television on the show and
  Homer's role as the to-be-deconstructed picture of white, heterosexual, normative patriarch.
- Robert Sloane, "Who Wants Candy? Disenchantment in *The
  Simpsons.*" Sloane believes that *The Simpsons* was part of a shift
  into independent film and programming (although he acknowledges its rather mainstream production and appeal). It is, in fact,
  this tension between being mainstream and critiquing the mainstream that Sloane explores as he mines several episodes in depth,
  most significantly "The Itchy & Scratchy & Poochie Show,"
  "Homer's Enemy," and "*The Simpsons* Spin-Off Showcase," all of
  which are required viewing for those interested in postmodern
  self-reference, play, and audience interaction/positionality.
- Vincent Brook, "Myth or Consequences: Ideological Fault Lines
  in *The Simpsons.*" Drawing on his ethnographic study (basically,
  his experience teaching the show), Brook discusses how the
  show satirizes American culture. The article is noteworthy in
  that it acknowledges the role "of active producers as well as
  readers" (173). Brook discusses the open-endedness of the show,
  referring to the way "happy" endings are undercut.

- William J. Savage, Jr., "'So Television's Responsible!': Oppositionality and the Interpretive Logic of Satire and Censorship in *The Simpsons* and *South Park.*" Savage's smart essay uses two episodes, "Itchy & Scratchy & Marge" and "Death," from *The Simpsons* and *South Park*, respectively, to discuss how the shows satirize cartoon censorship.
- Matthew Henry, "Looking for Amanda Hugginkiss: Gay Life on *The Simpsons.*" While gay life on *The Simpsons* has become more varied and more visible since Henry wrote this article, this is a useful exploration of one of the least discussed aspects of the *Simpsons* world. Henry's engaging take on Mr. Smithers exposes the difficulty of the subject — while *The Simpsons* is liberal in its sexual politics, certain aspects of its depiction of gay characters can be troubling.
- Mick Broderick, "Releasing the Hounds: *The Simpsons* As Anti-Nuclear Satire." This is an intriguing essay on the undercurrent of the threat of nuclear disaster on the show.
- Duncan Stuart Beard, "Local Satire with a Global Reach: Ethnic Stereotyping and Cross-Cultural Conflicts in *The Simpsons.*" This article poses questions about national identity in a globalized world, as *The Simpsons* represents and misrepresents identities in episodes that are broadcast all over the world. Specifically, Beard looks at "Bart vs. Australia" and depictions of Apu.
- Douglas Rushkoff, "Bart Simpson: Prince of Irreverence." This brief essay by the author of *Media Virus! Hidden Agendas in Popular Culture* touches on the meme transmissions made possible by the format of the show and the popularity of characters like Bart. Rushkoff posits that the plot serves only to satisfy older viewers, while "Bart's generation" of viewers finds pleasure in "pattern recognition ... those moments when we recognize which other forms of media are being parodied" (296).

Planet Simpson: How a Cartoon Masterpiece Defined a Generation, by Chris Turner (2004). Turner states his central thesis in his title, but amplifies it in the text: "If there was a single cultural signpost announcing the emergence of a generation/era/movement/whatever; a monument to a widespread yearning for progress, truth, honesty, integrity, joy; a final goddamn rejoinder to every vacuous corporate press release and cloying commercial script and prevaricating political sound bite — it was *The Simpsons*" (6). Obviously a great fan of music, Turner makes the point with musical references and terminology throughout, which is fitting, as he believes *The Simpsons* filled the void that music left when, he believes, it ceased to have the power to define the '90s generation. Turner traces many cultural movements, including cyberspace, cult of personalities, and cultural activism, through character analysis and episode dissection. His intro, which details the early history of *The Simpsons* is eminently useful for setting the stage for *Simpsons* analysis. Wonderfully readable, Turner tempers his encyclopedic knowledge with enough references to make a true fan smile.

The Simpsons One Step Beyond Forever!, created by Matt Groening, edited by Jesse L. McCann (2005). This contains the necessary information and extraneous materials for seasons 13 and 14.

The Psychology of The Simpsons*: D'oh!*, edited by Alan Brown, Ph.D., with Chris Logan (2006). Extremely readable, this book is a valuable introduction to a plethora of psychological concepts. Chapters include brief conclusions that summarize main points. There is a good balance of teaching concepts and discussions of the show.

- Misty K. Hook, Ph.D., "The Family Simpson: Like Looking in a Mirror?" The article is a brief analysis of Simpson family demographics, family hierarchy, family roles, family rules, communication and emotional patterns, parenting, conflict resolution, social interaction, and overall familial health.
- Wind Goodfriend, Ph.D., "For Better, or Worse?: The Love of Homer and Marge." This piece serves as an introduction to interdependence theory, which can look at the health of a relationship based on satisfaction, dependence, and investment level. This analysis concludes that Homer and Marge *are* happy together.
- Molly Snodgrass, M.A., and Irene Vlachos-Weber, "Which One of Us Is Truly Crazy?: Pop Psychology and the Discourse of Sanity and Normativity in *The Simpsons*." The authors argue that the show, for the many times it engages with psychology, is ambivalent towards it, as it reifies the idea that we can all benefit from self-awareness but is skeptical of aspects of psychiatric treatment and discourse.
- Nelson Cowan, Michael J. Kane, Andrew R. A. Conway, and

Alexander J. Ipsa-Cowan, "Stupid Brain!: Homer's Working Memory Odyssey." Taking the form of Homer's diary after Homer removes the crayon from his brain (from episode 257, "НОМЯ"), this continues to follow his thoughts after it is re-inserted, though Lisa must write the entries. This work is a creative, but sometimes tedious, way to introduce terminology and concepts surrounding the idea, quantification, and study of intelligence. One of the authors is a high school student, and the essay writing was supported by a grant (thus serving as examples for us all).

- Paul Bloom and David Pizarro, "Homer's Soul." This article discusses how we can use the show to think about how we think about consciousness, noting that we distinguish between brain, body, and soul.
- Denis M. McCarthy, "Alcohol — The Cause of, and Solution to, All Life's Problems." McCarthy considers what it means to have an alcohol problem and discusses risk factors for developing alcoholism. While the former focuses on Homer, his children are the focus for the latter.
- Mike Bryne, "The Cafeteria Deep Fryer Is Not a Toy." This is a smart essay about engineering psychology, with insights into the show and real-life examples.
- Sally D. Stabb, Ph.D., "Righteousness and Relationships: Feminine Fury in *The Simpsons*, or How Marge and Lisa Taught Me to Embrace My Anger." A discussion of socialization as relating to femininity and masculinity that presents and deconstructs myths about anger. This piece demonstrates a qualitative content analysis.
- Robert M. Arkin and Philip J. Mazzocco, "Self-Esteem in Springfield: Self and Identity in the Land of D'oh." This provides a solid discussion of how self-esteem forms identity.
- W. Robert Batsell, Jr., "Can Bart or Homer Learn?" An exploration of three distinct types of learning and a consideration of which members of the Simpson family can use them, this essay also discusses negative reinforcement and how characters use it for manipulation.
- Linda Heath, Ph.D., and Kathryn Brown, "Sex and Gender in Springfield: Male, Female, and D'oh." This clever piece is able

to discuss characters on the show, community, and representation, while it introduces key concepts that you'd learn in any sociology or women's studies course and leaves the audience with intriguing questions about the masculine/feminine spectrum and members of *The Simpsons* community.

- Karin H. Bruckner, M.A., LPC, "Hope Springs Parental: *The Simpsons* and Hopefulness." This is a discussion of the idea of hope.
- Frank C. Keil, Kristi L. Lockhart, Derek C. Keil, Dylan R. Keil, and Martin F. Keil, "Looking for Mr. Smarty Pants: Intelligence and Expertise in *The Simpsons*." The authors make a good distinction between the two concepts. The piece includes short discussions of how the show views scientists and academics.
- David A. Kenny and Deirdre T. Kenny, "The Personalities of *The Simpsons: Simpsons'* Big Five." Discusses and classifies the Simpson family members according to the big traits: extroversion, agreeableness, conscientiousness, neuroticism, and openness. Displays various forms of graphs and types of representation of data.
- Chris Logan, "Lyle Lanley, You're My Hero!: The Social Psychology of Group Membership and Influence." This is one of our favorite articles from the book, as it's useful in teaching Rogerian argument and rhetoric. Overall, this is about how characters on the show influence each other, but it can be used to discuss rhetoric, politics, persuasion, and advertising techniques.
- David A. Rettinger and James Rettinger, "Springfield — How Not to Buy a Monorail: Decision Making (Mostly Bad) in *The Simpsons*." This seems to serve as a counterpoint to the previous essay, as it discusses resisting Lyle Lanley's influence. This is an exploration of heuristics, algorithmic decision making, and utility/value decisions.
- Harris Cooper, "(A) None of the Above: Psychology Testing on *The Simpsons*." This is a wonderful tongue-in-cheek piece about how to write and take psychological/intelligence tests, as demonstrated by the show. Formatted as a guide, this piece can be used to demonstrate parody and satire in addition to beginning a discussion of psychological testing.

Watching with The Simpsons: *Television, Parody, and Intertextuality*, by Jonathan Gray (2006). To understand Gray's text, one must first understand his terminology. As the title promises, this is primarily a discussion of parody and intertextuality (with *The Simpsons* as a conduit for exploring both). Gray understands parody as distinct from "uncritical pastiche" (5) and uses the term only when parody of genre is used to satirize. He explains, "Parody is often confused with satire or with pastiche, but neither of these forms shares parody's interest in a genre's form and conventions. Parody can be satiric, but pure satire bypasses concerns of form and aims straight at the content, whereas pastiche alludes to form and/or content, but with no critical comment on either" (47). Intertextuality is "the fundamental and inescapable interdependence of all textual meaning upon the structures of meaning proposed by other texts" (3–4). Gray provides a sweeping history of reader-response criticism, but assures us that this isn't a reception study (12); however, Part III of this text is a mixture of the two, as Gray reports findings from a small empirical study of subjects' responses to the show.

Gray's explication of *The Simpsons* as parody focuses on both the show's potential disruption of the sitcom genre and the sitcom's depiction of the suburban family (44), though he seems more interested in the former. The book also covers how *The Simpsons* parodies ads and news media. Although Gray holds that the show, as a piece of popular entertainment that relies on ad revenue, cannot be entirely radical, he concludes: "The optimism lies in its belief that revolution with a substantial audience is possible on prime time, mainstream television, whereas the pessimism lies in the complete inability to see what substantial gains are made nevertheless" (164); and that "Of the king's court, *The Simpsons* as fool lives in the realm of King Murdoch" (168). This clever analysis of form would be useful in discussions/classes on American studies, media, and cultural studies.

The World According to The Simpsons, by Steven K. Keslowitz (2006). Keslowitz's first book, *The Simpsons and Society*, was updated and expanded to create *The World According to the Simpsons*. Both books have the same central thesis — "*The Simpsons* is more than just a cartoon" (11). That, and its reluctance to close without throwing in just one more *Simpsons* quote (and then another), may be less than useful for some readers. Keslowitz highlights many important issues, such as education, exceptionalism, politics, and globalization. While Keslowitz gives some of the episodes astute close readings, he deals with the larger issues in broad strokes (which may only be suitable for younger or beginning scholars). The book occasionally makes assertions that might open debate — that *The Simpsons* is always evenhanded, that Bart has been toned down over the seasons, that Marge is no longer a feminist, for example. Overall, what distinguishes Keslowitz is the clarity of his prose and the fact that he wrote both books before receiving his bachelor's degree. He can be held up as an example to our students — to use their passions both in learning and in teaching others.

The Bluffer's Guide to The Simpsons, by Paul Couch (2007). This is exactly what it sounds like — it's a very short breakdown of the show, from the obvious to the arcane, for those who have never seen it. It has a British slant, resulting in a view of the show as satirizing American subjects from the outside. It's cute, but we really recommend watching the show rather than memorizing names and factoids from a book. As instructors, we value experiential knowledge over rote memorization.

What's Science Ever Done for Us? What The Simpsons *Can Teach Us about Physics, Robots, Life, and the Universe*, by Paul Halpern (2007). This book opens with a colloquial description of Springfield and its inhabitants, and notes that "[a]ny town listing Gould, Hawking, Herschbach, and Pynchon as residents (or at least visitors) would seem to have great potential for a healthy attitude toward science" (6). Halpern admits that the town does not always uphold a love of science, but claims that the show does:

> *The Simpsons* offers a perfect venue for informal science education. It's one of the few comedy programs with no laugh track — and plenty of brains.
> In the absence of an authority telling you when to laugh or learn, you are forced to sift through cutting sarcasm, conflicting opinions, and occasionally even sly misrepresentations to figure out the truth [8].

Halpern envisions his book as "a field guide to the science behind the series" (9). To that end, he discusses "Lisa the Simpson" in light of genetics; "E-I-E-I-(Annoyed Grunt)" for grafting; "Two Cars in Every Garage and Three Eyes on Every Fish" for pollution, industrial waste, genetic mutation, and three-eyed fish fakes in history. "The Springfield Files" allows for an overview of genetics, radiation, and the EPA; "In the Belly of the Boss" (from "Treehouse of Horror XV") for an explanation of why we can't shrink organisms beyond a certain point; and "The Genesis Tub" (from "Treehouse of Horror VII") for evolutionary processes. "Lisa the Skeptic" provides fodder for a synopsis of evolution versus intelligent design; "The Wizard of Evergreen Terrace" for inventions/machines; "The PTA Disbands" for perpetual-motion machines; "B.I.: Bartificial Intelligence" (from "Treehouse of Horror XVI") for emotional links between robots and humans; "I, (Annoyed Grunt)-bot" for Asimov's laws of robotics; and "Itchy and Scratchy Land" for chaos theory. Halpern uses "Fly vs. Fly" (from "Treehouse of Horror VIII") to explicate quantum transportation; "Stop the World, I Want to Goof Off" (from "Treehouse of Horror XIV") for temporal experience and disturbance; "Time and Punishment" (from "Treehouse of Horror V") for time travel; and "Lisa's Wedding," "Bart to the Future," and "Future-Drama" for future prognostication. "'Scuse Me While I Miss the Sky" serves to discuss astronomy; "Don't Fear the Roofer" serves up black holes and electromagnetic waves; "Bart vs. Australia" debunks the Coriolis effect and inertia; and "'Tis the Fifteenth Season," astrolabes. Finally, "Bart's Comet" generates discourse on comets and asteroids; "Deep Space Homer" on space travel; "Life's a Glitch, Then You Die" (from "Treehouse of Horror X") on global catastrophe; Kang and Kodos on extraterrestrial life; "They Saved Lisa's Brain" on general relativity and the shape of the universe; and "Homer³" on dimensions. The book ends with a handy list of scientific questions related to *The Simpsons Movie*. Many of the chapters are insightful (especially the tangents), but most are abrupt, because the ties to episodes are tenuous at best. Some college-level students have reported that the science presented is too elementary, so this book might better be used for high school or young college students.

Thank You for Arguing: What Aristotle, Lincoln, and Homer Simpson Can Teach Us about the Art of Persuasion, by Jay Heinrichs (2007). This is a highly readable text on how the lessons of classical rhetoric may be applied to modern argument. Heinrichs references examples from the classics, from popular contemporary media, and from his own experience. There are a few quotes from and references to *The Simpsons*, but the book is not at all related to the show. Even chapter titles, such as "Control the Argument: Homer Simpson's Canons of Logic" are misleading. Heinrich seems to be taking his own advice on how to get an audience interested in your subject — divert them with what they're interested in, but then take them to what you want to talk about.

Simpsonology: There's a Little Bit of Springfield in All of Us, by Tim Delaney (2008). Delaney's enthusiasm for his subject is contagious. His purpose here is "to entertain and inform the reader on the social significance and relevancy of the TV show *The Simpsons*" (13). With such a broad purpose, it's no surprise that the subjects here are covered in very broad strokes. Delaney tackles the family, high versus low culture, friendship and community, relationships and romance, gender roles, race and nationality, religion, environmental politics, general politics, sports, education, physical and mental health, pranks (sometimes associated with holidays), Halloween, and the show's success. Although readable, the book is addressed to a very general audience. Due to its emphasis on summary over analysis and its sometimes jarring transitions, this book might best be used for high school or for non-academic purposes.

Homer Simpson Goes to Washington: American Politics through Popular Culture, edited by Joseph J. Foy (2008). There are few articles that deal with *The Simpsons* here, so we'll only discuss those that do. This is an intriguing collection, however, dealing with such diverse topics as *The West Wing*, news parodies, and *24*. Foy's collection is premised on the idea that "entertainment media can help bring politics to life for those people who have always felt it a distant machine that has nothing to do with them" (3).

- Greg Ahrenhoerster, "Aye on Springfield: Reasons to Vote 'Yes' on Popular Culture." Ahrenhoerster's article is one of those that defends teaching subjects like *The Simpsons* (for those who need convincing — and Foy's collection assumes that people do; it also assumes there's a distinct difference between high and low culture). Ahrenhoerster gives specific examples of how he used *Simpsons* episodes in his class, successfully arguing that it is "wise to allow students to practice their critical thinking skills and political analysis on subject matter they already know" because "they will be better able to apply sound judgment to the political issues they will continue to be confronted with as they go through life" (13).
- Jo Michael Bitzer, "Political Culture and Public Opinion: The American Dream on Springfield's Evergreen Terrace." Bitzer gives brief examples from the world of *The Simpsons* to illustrate basic political concepts, such as political culture, public opinion, and the American dream. His discussion of the show as artifact can be useful if assigning our cultural artifact essay, detailed in Chapter 2 of this text.

The Springfield Reformation: The Simpsons, *Christianity, and American Culture*, by Jamey Heit (2008). This is a well-written, thoughtful analysis of both *The Simpsons* and the role of contemporary Christianity in America. Not surprisingly, the text is written from a Christian point of view, specifically a Protestant (and perhaps a Calvinist) one. The author thus assumes both that the audience is Christian and that they have a good working knowledge of Christian history and modern practices. There are fewer assumptions about the audience's working knowledge of *The Simpsons*. Rather than being an apologist for the show or an apologist for Christianity (as are some authors who decry *The Simpsons*; they maintain that the show's ideology is at odds with religious righteousness[3]), the author mostly holds that *The Simpsons* both depicts a vibrant Christian life and that it rightly satirizes the foibles of modern Christianity and its practitioners. The thesis:

> The goal in identifying how Christian beliefs and practices unfold in a town that reflects contemporary American culture is to examine in depth how *The Simpsons* understands a fundamental social institution that affects Springfield. The results formulate a critique of Christianity that recalls Martin Luther's need to confront the church's increasingly secularized character. Likewise, *The Simpsons* portrays how Christianity has lost, or actively given away, its integrity as a socially relevant institution in contemporary American culture [2].

Heit's analysis calls to mind Flannery O'Connor's writings about Christianity; he seems to see *The Simpsons* filling the same role O'Connor's stories did. His analysis contains a surprising critique of Ned Flanders, fitting with O'Connor's ideas about Christian satirists needing to focus their energy on the failings of the faithful. Of special note are his chapters on economics/capitalism and on religion and science. While some readers may feel alienated by the author's assumptions, they will find that Heit is not a fundamentalist but, rather, a devoted moderate.

Academic Articles[4]

"Clinical Assessment of TV Cartoon Family: Homework to Encourage Systemic Thinking in Counseling Students," by Richard D. Mathis and Zoe Tanner (*Family Therapy* 1991). A test of the Clinical Rating Scale (CRS). While the sample (n = 12) was small and *The Simpsons* not essential for this study, results showed that graduate-level students were able to apply skills developed with a make-believe family to real clients. Further, students reported that using *The Simpsons* as a medium for understanding counseling made reading and homework more interesting.

"The Theory of Infantile Citizenship," by Lauren Berlant (*Popular Culture* 1993). Berlant's powerful article about the construction of American citizen as (failed) subject makes its point through a close reading of "Mr. Lisa Goes to Washington." Berlant finds that "Lisa's assertion that the system works counts as even a parodic resolution to her epistemic murk because consciousness that a system exists at all has become what counts as the ideal pedagogical outcome of contemporary politics: thus, in the chain that links the fetus, the wounded, the dead, and the 'children' as the true American 'people,' the linkage is made through the elevation of a zero-sum mnemonic, a consciousness of the nation with no imagination of agency — apart perhaps from voting, here coded as a form of consumption" (407).

"Homer Simpson's Eyes and the Culture of Late Nostalgia," by Jerry Herron (*Representations* 1993). Herron interrogates the idea of nostalgia for the present, as constructed by agents of late capitalism. This theory-laden article is not for beginners, but makes for an intriguing read of Bart and *Simpsons* products.

"Family Communication on Prime-Time Television," by Mary Strom Larson (*Journal of Broadcasting & Electronic Media* 1993). Larson's striking study of family communication compared the Huxtables of *The Cosby Show* with the Simpsons, when they faced off in prime time. Larson's findings are that the Simpsons scored higher in supporting and directing communication, while the majority of the Huxtables' conversations centered on informative communication. Besides rebutting the popular idea that the Simpson family provides a poor model for family relationships, the piece serves as an illustration in quantitative/qualitative information gathering and analysis.

"Simpsons as Subculture: Multiple Technologies, Group Identity and Authorship," by Kurt Borchard (*The Image of Technology in Literature, the Media, and Society*, edited by Will Wright and Steve Kaplan, 1994). Borchard takes postings from alt.tv.simpsons to analyze how group and individual identity is formed through both television viewing and audience interaction via media such as newsgroups.

"The Triumph of Popular Culture: Situation Comedy, Postmodernism and *The Simpsons*," by Matthew Henry (*Studies in Popular Culture* 1994). A review of the show's rise to pop icon status, this is a comprehen-

sive look at situation comedy history and how *The Simpsons* revolution-
ized it. The article specifically addresses *The Simpsons* as a form of postmodern art — paradoxical art that, while being critical of popular culture,
is also a part of it.

"God and *The Simpsons*: The Religious Life of an Animated Sitcom,"
by Gerry Bowler (The Simpsons Archive[5] 1996). This excellent article was
among the first to address positive religious messages in *The Simpsons*.
Bowler recounts what might be called his conversion to the show, as he
went from forbidding his children to watch it to touting the show as one
of the most religious on television. He details characters' church attendance, biblical reading, saying grace, and prayer (which is always answered
by an attentive god), as well as analyzing the critique of some religious
practices and proclivities. He ends by exploring why the religious community does not appreciate the show.

"King-Size Homer: Ideology & Representation," by Barry Hodge
(The Simpsons Archive 1996). Hodge uses Vladimir Propp's schematic of
narrative functions to illustrate that *The Simpsons* adheres to folktale structures. He then goes on to describe ideological values in the show, finding
the overall ideology to be open enough to appeal to a wide demographic.
For teachers using Propp-esque analysis, this would be a good example.

"*The Simpsons*: From an Obscure Hell to Life in the Fast Lane:
'Whoo-hoo!,'" by W. Keith Work (The Simpsons Archive 1996). An
extremely short article tracing the early evolution of *The Simpsons*.

"In Praise of Television: The Greatest TV Show Ever," by Paul A.
Cantor (*The American Enterprise* 1997). This was one of the first defenses
of *The Simpsons* written by a Shakespeare scholar. Cantor holds that "if
praise for *The Simpsons* makes you sneer in condescension, it's dollars to
Homer's doughnuts you've never watched an entire episode" (34). He bol-
sters his case with a focus on "the creation of the cartoon-within-the-
cartoon" (34). His argument is helpful, both for students who don't
remember a world without *The Simpsons* and for those who need to be
persuaded of the show's literary merits.

"*The Simpsons* and Quality Television," by Dan Korte (The Simpsons Archive 1997). Korte uses Robert J. Thompson's criteria for quality
television to evaluate *The Simpsons*.

"Homer Simpson: Classic Clown," by Ellen Amy Cohen (The Simpsons Archive 1998). In a clever analysis of how Homer fits the "Classic
Clown" archetype, Cohen compares Homer to Shakespeare's Falstaff.

"*The Simpsons* Meet Mark Twain: Analyzing Popular Media Texts in the Classroom," by Renée Hobbs (*The English Journal* 1998). Hobbs links *The Simpsons* to Mark Twain, noting Twain's rise from "low" culture to "high" culture art and the similarities shared with *The Simpsons*. This connection reportedly makes students excited about learning "high culture" texts.

"D'oh! An Analysis of the Medical Care Provided to the Family of Homer J. Simpson," by Robert Patterson, M.D., and Charles Weijer, M.D., Ph.D. (*Canadian Medical Association Journal* 1998; online in The Simpsons Archive). This tongue-in-cheek piece contrasts the medical practices of Dr. Nick and Dr. Hibbert. The authors purport to be in favor of Dr. Nick, while actually critiquing what they see as a new model of medicine in which the patient becomes a consumer whose whims must be granted. We routinely pair this article with relevant episodes to spur discussion among pre-med students, or use it on its own to discuss analysis and satire.

"'I Will Not Expose the Ignorance of the Faculty': *The Simpsons* As a Critique of Consumer Culture" by Sam Tingleff (The Simpsons Archive 1998). Tingleff argues that despite the show's criticism of American culture through the hypocrisy of the Simpsons family, it is still able to thrive within the confines of prime-time network television because of the Fox network's identity in the '80s, conformity of the narrative, and animated format. The show is able to criticize various aspects of American life (politics, values, sexuality, knowledge, injustice to women, dismissal of reason, capitalism, etc.) through the presentation of the characters as ideas (not personalities). *The Simpsons* subtly urges the viewers to think critically about their culture and what injustice they are doing to themselves.

"'Karmic Realignment': Transnationalism and Trauma in *The Simpsons*," by Eva Cherniavsky (*Cultural Critique* 1999). This article presumes that we've left behind a "disdain for popular culture" (139) and moves forward to assert of the show, "If *The Simpsons* as image-commodity are [*sic*] paradigmatic of Agger's thing-texts, things through which circulate an increasingly circumscribed repertoire of cultural meanings, then I would argue that it is the aspiration of *The Simpsons* to make of its very conscription a critical resource" (140). Using the episode "Homer and Apu," Cherniavsky interrogates transnationalism and neocolonial capitalist domination.

"Mmm ... Television: A Study of the Audience of *The Simpsons*," by

Jon Horowitz (The Simpsons Archive 1999). This piece discusses how the show is written for adults with a high level of what might be called teleliteracy. Horowitz specifically analyzes moments when the characters are watching television.

"Writing for *The Simpsons*," by Alexander Kippen (*Creative Screenwriting* 1999). Kippen provides a short interview with Mike Scully, *Simpsons* executive producer. The author highlights the importance of writing for animated productions since it is the characters who become stars and not the actors who play them.

"Theory and Practice: Revisiting Critical Pedagogy in Studio Art Education," by Susan E. McKenna (*Art Journal* 1999). McKenna addresses the problem of integrating theory into art school curriculum, noting that many see theory and art as mutually exclusive. This piece breaks down the binary, noting that formalist concerns taught in school are "theory." She also notes that the difficulty many students have with reading theory points to a larger problem of students not being taught critical reading skills, rather than a problem with theory itself. This piece is light on *The Simpsons*, however, as it only briefly mentions using "Itchy & Scratchy & Marge" in class.

"*The Simpsons*, American Satire," by Brett Mullin (The Simpsons Archive 1999). This is a short article that touches on a few aspects of society satirized by the show.

"*The Simpsons*—Just Funny or More?," by Gerd Steiger (The Simpsons Archive 1999). "Or More," obviously. The fact that this piece is a bit dated and doesn't really provide a new analysis of the show makes it fit for neophytes, but not hardcore fans.

"You Can't Argue with the Little Things," by Michael Frost (The Simpsons Archive 2000). This intriguing reading of "You Only Move Twice" argues that Cypress Creek (where the Simpson family moves in the episode) is dystopic due to its undermining of identity and because of the relativity of utopia. That is, since each person longs for a different utopia, Cypress Creek cannot fulfill everyone's needs.

"*The Simpsons*: Religious Dialogues in Prime Time," by James L. Hall (The Simpsons Archive 2000). Using "Homer the Heretic" as its primary example, this piece discusses how *The Simpsons* relates to Camus, Kierkegaard, de Certeau, and Pascal's "wager." Hall concludes, "*The Simpsons* does not say that theism is undesirable; it merely puts forward the idea that blind obedience to dogma and lack of awareness towards the self are undesirable qualities in modern western society."

"Postmodern Philosophy Meets Pop Cartoon: Michel Foucault and Matt Groening," by Margaret Betz Hull (*The Journal of Popular Culture* 2000). Hull argues that Foucauldian ideas of "the normalizing power aimed at individuals in contemporary society" are found in *The Simpsons* and in Matt Groening's *School Is Hell* (57). While Hull finds that Foucault and Groening share a mistrust of power, she believes that Groening offers "a Nietzschean lightness and humor in the face of Foucault's dismal description of the oppressive force of disciplinary power" (61).

"Make Room for Daddy: An Analysis of the Differentiating Parenting Techniques of Homer Simpson to His Three Children," by Elise Lipoff (The Simpsons Archive 2000). Lipoff's analysis finds that Homer is an inconsistent though effective father. His parenting techniques are differentiated in that "Homer has the most substantial relationship with Bart, the most trying with Lisa, and the most loving with Maggie," causing/being caused by his different tactics with them.

"The Cartoon Society: Using *The Simpsons* to Teach and Learn Sociology," by Stephen J. Scanlan and Seth L. Feinberg (*Teaching Sociology* 2000). As an account of positive *Simpsons* use in upper-level sociology classes at Ohio State University, this article includes a list of useful episodes and topics, and a warning about the potential misinterpretation of satire.[6]

"Religion in *The Simpsons*," by Jeff Shalda (The Simpsons Archive 2000). This is a brief and readable discussion of religion and of a few religious controversies generated by the show.

"This Is College?," by Tanya Schevitz (http://www.simpsonsfolder. com/scrapbook/articles/college.html). This article, originally from the *San Francisco Chronicle*, is quite old (2000), but it stands the test of time as it addresses how schools and students often feel the need to justify offering and taking courses in popular culture.

"*The Simpsons*: An Imperfect Ideal Family," by Eliezer Van Allen (The Simpsons Archive 2000). Van Allen asserts that, rather than the ideal family portrayed in several 80s and 90s sitcoms, *The Simpsons* focuses on a plausible representation of a nuclear family. A close analysis of Homer, Marge, Bart, Lisa, and Maggie serves to determine why *The Simpsons* is a favorite among all types of families in America.

"The Simpsons and Their World — A Mirror of American Life?," by Bastian Vogl (The Simpsons Archive 2000). The thesis seems to be that the critique of American culture (and even a larger global culture) is not accidental, which we find fairly obvious.

"'We're All Pigs': Representations of Masculinity in *The Simpsons*," by Karma Waltonen (The Simpsons Archive 2000). This essay explores the tension between the liberal inclinations of the show and the conservative nature of the sitcom format. Even if, for example, Homer learns to expand his definition of masculinity in one episode, he "unlearns" his lesson by the start of the next episode, as the format demands that the situations and attitudes of the characters must remain static.

"Homer the Heretic and Charlie Church," by Lisle Dalton, Eric Michael Mazur, and Monica Siems (*God in the Details: American Religion in Popular Culture*, edited by Eric Michael Mazur and Kate McCarthy, 2001). A comprehensive analysis of *The Simpsons* and its use of religion, this is essentially an outline of how *The Simpsons* debunks traditional rigid religious practices yet highlights the importance of morality, and the way it shows how religion is seen and has been integrated into contemporary America.

"Simpsons Have Soul," by John Dart (http://www.religion-online. org/showarticle.asp?title=2113). In this 2001 article, Dart claims that there is at least one reference to religion in 70 percent of all episodes. He observes that religion can be interpreted through individual standards, as shown in an example when God agrees with Homer that Lovejoy's sermons are tedious, but closes by acknowledging that, while some religious leaders have issues with the show, most understand that *The Simpsons* is not an anti-religious show because there is goodness at the end of each episode and they are a family who love each other. Unfortunately, this article is like many others that focus on debating how to watch the show instead of recognizing religious parody and satire in the show; nor does it discuss how Christianity functions in Springfield.

"Discourse Stu Likes Discourse Theory: An Analysis of Meaning in *The Simpsons* As It Relates to Democracy," by Michael Frost (The Simpsons Archive 2001). As it's heavy on theory and jargon, Frost's piece is meant for educated readers, but his discussion of the indeterminacy of meaning is intriguing, especially as he argues that this indeterminacy leads to antimaterialist postlinguistics being more useful to political theory than materialist theories used to understand democracy. This indeterminacy ultimately makes meaning "a realm of political action." "A Streetcar Named Marge" and "Much Apu about Nothing" are the primary texts in play.

"Tones of Morality through Layers of Sarcasm: *The Simpsons* and Its Underlying Themes," by Gabe Durham (The Simpsons Archive 2001).

Durham illustrates how *The Simpsons* promotes several moral standards through sarcastic means. Values such as family unity and religion as essential parts of life are expressed to a great extent within the show. The show also suggests the problems to be attended to within American government and society by poking fun at its politics.

"*The Simpsons*: A Reflection of Society and a Message on Family," by Eric Garrison (The Simpsons Archive 2001). An analysis of whether *The Simpsons* is an effective medium for expressing values on family membership. Discussed are problems (limitations) with using *The Simpsons* as a medium, main principles behind the show, and benefactors of the show (writers versus audience).

"The Evolution of the Seven Deadly Sins: From God to the Simpsons," by Lisa Frank (*The Journal of Popular Culture* 2001). Frank's very readable article, which starts with a list of her morning's sins, details how the seven deadly sins have evolved into celebrated aspects of American culture, using examples from *The Simpsons* to illustrate the ideas.

"Sephardic Tradition and *The Simpsons* Connection," by Richard Kalman and Josh Belkin (The Simpsons Archive 2001). The piece argues that what is known as the Sephardic tradition of Jews is well portrayed by *The Simpsons*. Many of the writers for *The Simpsons* are Jews who follow the Sephardic tradition and thus try to impart knowledge of that tradition — like "Food should not be taken to repletion" or "One should not sleep in the day."

"Animation and Teaching: Enhancing Subjects from the Curriculum by Using *The Simpsons* in High School English Teaching," by Andreas Kristiansen (The Simpsons Archive 2001). Kristiansen writes from a Norwegian perspective, giving a few close readings of the animation of the show. The article discusses how the show might be taught (with practical, specific examples) and goes over the problems inherent in doing so.

"*The Simpsons*: Sitcom Satire at Its Finest," by Kirstyn Miller (The Simpsons Archive 2001). Miller explores the show as an example of deviance from the typical TV sitcoms because it portrays the lives of a typical working-class family, rather than a dream family living a near-perfect life. Instead of focusing on an American dream like other sitcoms, *The Simpsons* thrives off the fact that its characters are imperfect and thus realistic. The imperfect qualities of the Simpsons family are what allows the show to express deep messages through satire and parody, easily achieving a high level of brilliance.

"Cartoon Realism: Genre Mixing and the Cultural Life of *The Simpsons*," by Jason Mittell (*The Velvet Light Trap* 2001). Mittell addresses "how genre impacts *The Simpsons* regarding issues of cultural hierarchies, assumptions about target audiences, codes of realism, and the implications of genre parody" (15). He mentions postmodernism long enough to declare it irrelevant to public discourse and then moves into an analysis of how the press and critics discuss genre in the show.

"The Social 'Simpson': Psychology Found Within," by Chris Moyer (The Simpsons Archive 2001). This is a list of episodic events that occur within *The Simpsons* that apply to specific social psychology theories.

"The Simpsons: Portrait of a Heroic Family," by Dan Rousseve (The Simpsons Archive 2001). Rousseve begins with a history of the show and a contextualization within the history of television, before moving on to an analysis of how the family practices various communication strategies and conflict resolution.

"Individualism versus Paternalism: An Analysis of Homer J. Simpson," by Dan Rousseve (The Simpsons Archive 2001). Rousseve borrows some material from the opening of the other piece (or vice versa, we're not sure) to begin his Social Values Model analysis of Homer. He finds "*The Simpsons* uses a dialectical transformation from individualism to paternalism to tell its audience that people must be committed to one another because of the large scale neglect and apathy towards one another in modern society."

"*The Simpsons* as a Religious Satire," by Scott Satkin (The Simpsons Archive 2001). Though made funny by both the lack and surplus of religious intent (Homer and Ned, respectively), the show demonstrates its foundations by acknowledging the importance of religion in people's lives.

"*The Simpsons*: Morality from the 'Immoral,'" by Frank G. Sterle, Jr. (The Simpsons Archive 2001). Sterle argues that the show is in fact moral, using a variety of examples, such as the show's stance on homophobia, gun nuts, and nationalism. Sterle's bias comes through, as he does not stop to define morality and as he only believes the show "takes an ideologically partisan position" in regards to vegetarianism. As Sterle notes, he's "a fairly avid meat eater." This piece might be an interesting one to use in teaching assumptions, qualifiers, defining parameters, and audience awareness.

"Worst Paper Ever: *The Simpsons*, Morality, and Religion," by Josh Cashion (The Simpsons Archive 2002). Cashion analyzes five key episodes of *The Simpsons* ("Homer the Heretic," "Bart Sells His Soul," "In Marge

We Trust," "Homer vs. Lisa and the 8th Commandment," and "Hurricane Neddy") to establish whether the show can properly communicate theology and philosophy. The author explores in detail such concepts as the role of religion in everyday life, existence of souls, reason against sin, and keeping the faith.

"'The Whole World's Gone Gay!': Smithers' Sexuality, Homer's Phobia, and Gay Life on *The Simpsons*," by Matthew Henry (*Popular Culture Review* 2002). Henry's piece is a discussion of gays and their history on TV, drawing attention to episodes in which *The Simpsons* questions preconceived notions of homosexuality and heterosexuality.

"Advertising of America's Beer Companies and the Duff Corporation," by Jeffrey Katzin (The Simpsons Archive 2002). An analysis of how *The Simpsons* satirizes American culture. A prime example of such parody is the parallel drawn between the make-believe Duff Corporation and various real American beer companies. More often than not, the beer-selling corporations (make-believe or not) target the middle-aged and young through characteristic history, humor, music, promise of good taste, and emergence of quality personality.

"Religious Rhetoric and the Comic Frame in *The Simpsons*," by Todd V. Lewis (*Journal of Media and Religion* 2002). Lewis begins his analysis by citing a series of critics who believe the show ultimately respects religion. He agrees, using a Burkean analysis of comic frames and burlesque.

"Bart's Parts and Other Stories About Using Cabri in the Classroom," by Peter Ransom (*Micromath* 2002). This is a brief piece about having students "draw" Bart and other *Simpsons* images using Cabri software.

"Argumentative Writing and *The Simpsons*," by Ed Teall (*Kairos: A Journal for Teachers of Writing and Webbed Environments* 2002). A college professor uses the name of the Simpsons' hometown, Springfield, to develop writing and reasoning skills (without stirring political passions) by asking, "Which state is Springfield in?"

"*The Simpsons/Los Simpson*: Analysis of an Audiovisual Translation," by Lourdes L. Lorenzo (*Translator: Studies in Intercultural Communication* 2003). Lorenzo, who translates the show, gives a detailed look at translation based on Agost's model. Using four episodes and English-to-Spanish translations, the author identifies possible issues seen between the translated and original scripts. She found difficulties with puns, tone, cultural references, and idiomatic phrases. The author offers some possible options for improvement. This piece is significantly more detailed than Juan José Martinez-Sierra's translation article (cited below).

"'I'm Bart Simpson, Who the Hell Are You?': A Study in Postmodern Identity (Re)Construction," by Brian L. Ott (*Journal of Popular Culture* 2003). Ott uses Bart, Homer, and Lisa to examine how identity is constructed, and concludes that identity can be established only in relation to alterity. Overall, Ott is interested in how identity is constructed via media influence. Although his reading of the Simpson family isn't surprising, Ott extends his analysis to the consumer of *Simpsons* products, relating, for example, a consumer who buys a Bart Simpson doll but doesn't play with it as rebelling against the societal expectations of toy purchases. This clever reading of how we construct identities does not seem to envision a purchaser who sees a collectible rather than a toy, however.

"Mediasprawl: Springfield U.S.A.," by Douglas Rushkoff (*Iowa Journal of Cultural Studies* 2003). Rushkoff explains that "like a Trojan horse, *The Simpsons* sneaks into our homes" through its satire of mass media and forces audiences to see themselves (as receivers and responders) objectively. The article includes interviews with the show's writers.

"An Internationally Shared Health Frame of Reference Created by a Television Program: *The Simpsons*, a Content Analysis of Health Messages," by C. Byrd-Bredbenner (*Health Education* 2004). This study looks at health-related messages in *The Simpsons*, finding that nearly 40 percent are in contrast to professional recommendations, but that other messages are positive.

"Using *The Simpsons* to Teach Social Psychology," by Judy Eaton and Alyse K. Uskul (*Teaching of Psychology* 2004). These teachers from York University give us a valuable article, which discusses their subject from a practical standpoint. Like other teachers, Eaton and Uskul have found it useful to show clips from *The Simpsons* to get the students' attention, to "lighten up" the course, and to encourage discussion. They have found that using the show to illustrate sociological phenomena allows for better comprehension. The teachers conducted an informal study via questionnaire and found that the vast majority of students believe *The Simpsons* is useful to their coursework. Other teachers can find practical advice and specific examples to use with their own students here.

"The Ten Commandments vs. *The Simpsons*," by Jim Guida (The Simpsons Archive 2004). This article briefly examines how the *Simpsons* characters hold to (or fail to hold to) the ten commandments, finding that "they generally fall short."

"Individual and Neo-Tribal Consumption: Tales from the Simpsons of Springfield," by Steve Cooper, Damien McLoughlin, and Andrew Keating (*Journal of Consumer Behaviour* 2005). Through a semiotic analysis of *The Simpsons*, the authors make their case that consumption in the postmodern age creates a sense of individual identity and a sense of tribal belonging. The point is well made, although the reliance on theory makes this unsuitable for certain readers.

"Translating Audiovisual Humour: A Case Study," by Juan José Martinez-Sierra (*Perspectives: Studies in Translatology* 2005). A study of humor translatability, it focuses on dubbing, using four episodes as case studies. Results show minimal humor loss (even some increase). Cultural references often were the largest contributors to humor loss.

"The Influence of Friends and Family vs. *The Simpsons*: Scottish Adolescents' Media Choices," by John W. Robertson, Neil Blain, and Paula Cowan (*Learning, Media & Technology* 2005). Not surprisingly, this study tells us that 13–14 year olds prefer *The Simpsons* over TV soaps, and that parents and friends are highly influential to media choices.

"'Are We There Yet?': Searching for Springfield and *The Simpsons'* Rhetoric of Omnitopia," by Andrew Wood and Anne Marie Todd (*Critical Studies in Media Communication* 2005). The authors coin the term "omnitopia" to describe the urban everyplace that is Springfield. This analysis of Springfield itself is a valuable contribution to Simpsonology. Specifically, the authors address "the fictional town as a reflection of modernity marked by six practices: dislocation, conflation, fragmentation, mutability, mobility, and commodification" (209).

"*The Simpsons*: Public Choice in the Tradition of Swift and Orwell," by John Considine (*Journal of Economic Education* 2006). Considine ties *The Simpsons* to the satirical works of Jonathan Swift and George Orwell, making the case that extreme representation can serve as a useful tool for teaching students about public choice.

"Mister Sparkle Meets the *Yakuza*: Depictions of Japan in *The Simpsons*," by Hugo Dobson (*The Journal of Popular Culture* 2006). Dobson lists the show's references to Japan, Japanese culture, and Japanese people (to date). This is essentially a defense of such depictions, holding that *The Simpsons* is not racist, but rather that this is sophisticated humor.

"Reading the Ungraspable Double-Codedness of *The Simpsons*," by Simone Knox (*Journal of Popular Film and Television* 2006). Knox reads *The Simpsons* through the frame of Frederic Jameson, using his ideas to explore the show's double-codedness. Heavy on theory and light on concrete examples, the piece holds that the show's tension, as a postmodern artifact, is a product of it being both commercial and a critical cartoon parody that even parodies itself.

"Animated Fathers: Representations of Masculinity in *The Simpsons* and *King of the Hill*," by Suzanne Williams-Rautiola (*Animated "Worlds,"* edited by Suzanne Buchan, David Surman, and Paul Ward, 2006). Williams-Rautiola attempts to show that both *The Simpsons* and *King of the Hill* are "writerly" shows. Two models of masculinity are contrasted: traditional, hegemonic (Hank Hill) and postmodern, buffoonish (Homer Simpson). While both are typical representations of fatherly figures, according to Williams-Rautiola, it is through these dehumanized, animated worlds that we can accept a critique and explore behaviors that otherwise would be politically incorrect, controversial, and too bizarre to air in a live-action sitcom.

"Legally Speaking: D'oh! What *The Simpsons* Teaches Us About the Law," by John G. Browning (*The Southwest Texas Record* 2007). Although the title may lead some to think the article actually discusses what we can learn about the law, this brief newspaper piece is basically just a list of moments when the Simpsons and the law intersect.

"Using *The Simpsons* to Teach Humanities with Gen X and Gen Y Adult Students," by Maxwell A. Fink and Deborah C. Foote (*New Directions for Adult and Continuing Education* 2007). Undergraduate instructor Maxwell Fink and Professor Deborah Foote discuss their experience with *Simpsons*-heavy curricula. They note that literary works should be understood in the context of popular culture, that theatrics is often needed to exaggerate critiques (i.e., the importance of fiction), and that *The Simpsons* has the ability to inject and refine new age cynicism.

"Imagining American: *The Simpsons* Go Global," by Jonathan Gray (*Popular Communication* 2007). Gray interrogates new ideas of cultural imperialism through a small empirical study of *Simpsons* viewers, including subjects who are not fans of the show as well as those who are. Ultimately, he finds that the representation of America on the show is multiple, reflecting "numerous competing Americas" (131), and that shows are "engaged in an active debate over the semiotics of Americana, and this debate is being exported" (145).

"'Don't Ask Me, I'm Just a Girl': Feminism, Female Identity, and *The Simpsons*," by Matthew Henry (*The Journal of Popular Culture* 2007).

Henry tackles a subject that hasn't garnered enough critical attention — feminism and *The Simpsons*. He uses an analysis of Marge, Selma, and Lisa to discuss the traditional and simultaneously subversive treatment of women on the show.

"Through the Screen, into the School: Education, Subversion, Ourselves in *The Simpsons*," by Carla Meskill (*Discourse: Studies in the Cultural Politics of Education* 2007). Meskill begins her article with the common assumption that Springfield represents dysfunction, but argues, "[On] the contrary, Springfield USA can alternatively be read as being representative of all that is functionally democratic about life in the USA, particularly in US public schools" (38). While many articles discuss how *The Simpsons* celebrates the family or religious thought more than is supposed, Meskill defends the show's depictions of schools, finding them generally supportive.

"'Old People Are Useless': Representations of Aging on *The Simpsons*," by Darren Blakeborough (*Canadian Journal on Aging* 2008). Blakeborough gives an explanation of why the show's extreme stereotypical representations serve a postmodern aesthetic that critiques stereotypes, rather than reinforcing them. Age is the author's topic of choice; this same approach can be taken with various other cases of *Simpsons* "ignorance." This is an approachable resource for teaching postmodernism.

"D'oh! Using *The Simpsons* to Improve Student Response to Literature," by Ginger M. Eikmeier (*English Journal* 2008). Eikmeier activates prior knowledge before moving into literary discussion — that is, she uses students' affection for and knowledge of *The Simpsons* to enliven literary analysis. This short piece details a few of the pairings and suggests others.

"'What the Hell Is That?': The Representation of Professional Service Markets in *The Simpsons*," by Nick Ellis (*Organization* 2008). The professional service markets here are the legal and medical professions. Basically a close reading of Lionel Hutz and Dr. Nick Riviera, the article reassures us that dichotomies exist both in the professions and in the real world. Thus, we have the pasty-faced lawyer and Dr. Hibbert to balance the representation of professionals on the show. Ultimately, this is a discussion of the show as a satire of these professions and their practices.

"Media Representations of Attention Deficit Disorder: Portrayals of Cultural Skepticism in Popular Media," by Elizabeth England Kennedy (*The Journal of Popular Culture* 2008). This intriguing study on ADD

(ADHD) in the media focuses mainly on *Pecker*, *King of the Hill*, and *South Park*, but does briefly reference the "Brother's Little Helper" episode of *The Simpsons*.

"Trope and Irony in *The Simpsons'* Overture," by Martin Kutnowski (*Popular Music and Society* 2008). Nowhere else will one find a more detailed analysis of the opening musical sequence of *Simpsons* episodes. Kutnowski is writing to an audience with an understanding of musical terms, making his piece accessible to music students and teachers. While his description of the actual auditory text is remarkable, the way he relates the auditory to the visual is most helpful. That is, he reveals the characters we see on their daily commute via the types of sounds we hear as we see them.

"Gender, Politicians, and Public Health: Using *The Simpsons* to Teach Politics," by Pete Woodcock (*European Political Science* 2008). This article argues that the constructed society of *The Simpsons* can be used to illustrate lessons on gender, the nature of politicians, and censorship in regard to public health. Woodcock is writing from a European point of view, but his practical, detailed lessons and engaging writing style make this an invaluable article.

Internet Resources

Academic

The Simpsons Archive (http://www.snpp.com). Begun in 1994, The Simpsons Archive is the most complete Internet site for information about *The Simpsons*. Members of alt.tv.simpsons, academics and fans, U.S. and international, voluntarily maintain the site. The main page includes links to recent news regarding the show (under the heading *The Springfield Times*). Other selections from the main page include FAQs, guides, lists, complete episode information including future episodes and the network schedule, access to a list of interviews and academic papers, newsgroups, and a list of approved outside links. The episode information is incredibly detailed, encompassing writer, director, and guest voice information, along with transcripts, reviews, Easter eggs, allusions, and reviews, although the earlier episodes' entries are more complete than the later ones. The site also includes fan scripts. The Simpsons Archive is by far the most complete and reliable Simpsons-related site.

Heideas (http://heideas.blogspot.com). Since 2005, Heidi Harley has blogged linguistic jokes from *The Simpsons*. She gives each episode a close viewing and includes most (if not all) instances of wordplay. While it is a robust list, it may be confusing for linguistics beginners; not much explanation for each passage is provided and some of the linguistic terms and their definitions are a bit spurious.

Read Write Think (http://www.readwritethink.org/lessons/lesson_ view.asp?id=811). This website is a source for free lesson plans from the National Council of Teachers of English. Specifically, this link provides a lengthy and detailed lesson plan to analyze satire in *The Simpsons* (defining satire as exaggeration, incongruity, reversal, and parody). This lesson plan is recommended for grades 9–12 and covers three class days, divided by opening sequence, character analysis, and analysis of the episode "Two Cars in Every Garage and Three Eyes on Every Fish."

The Scientific Method According to the Simpsons (http://mrslattery. com/downloads/intro/ACTIVITY%20-%20Scientific%20Method%20 According%20to%20the%20Simpsons.pdf) This is a collection of word problems that work with "if/then" statements, independent and dependent variables, and control and experimental groups. (An additional handout for controls and variables in *The Simpsons* can be found on an unrelated site at http://www.biologycorner.com/worksheets/controls.html.

Simpsonsmath.com (http://www.simpsonsmath.com). Founders Sarah J. Greenwald (Appalachian State University) and Andrew Nestler (Santa Monica College) created and maintain this site to assist other math teachers with "fun ways to introduce important concepts to students, and to reduce math anxiety and motivate students in courses for non-majors." From problems and equations to quick jokes, the math presented on the show is compiled here in chronological order, searchable by season. There is also a helpful collection of classroom activity sheets, divided by type (geometry, arithmetic, calculus, etc.). A transcript of a talk the two gave in 2001 on using the show is available at http://www.mathsci.appstate.edu/ ~sjg/talks/simpsons. Their article on combining *The Simpsons* with math is also available on The Simpsons Archive.

Non-Academic Sites

Alt.tv.simpsons (http://groups.google.com/group/alt.tv.simpsons/ topics?lnk=srg). Created in 1990, this was one of the first *Simpsons* newsgroups, and has allowed fans to discuss all things *Simpsons* for years. The group is still active, though not as active as it was in the early to mid 1990s.

Last Exit to Springfield (http://www.lardlad.com). This site is noteworthy for its generous supply of wallpapers and images. This site's episode descriptions are much more thorough than those on another fan site with episode descriptions, *Simpson Crazy* (cited below).

Simpsons Channel (http://www.simpsonschannel.com). This site is dedicated to providing external news about *The Simpsons*, mainly regarding ways *The Simpsons* intersects with other elements of pop culture — for example, there are recent interviews and other video clips, *Futurama* news, and Comic-Con stories. The episode summaries provide text and a highlight picture as well as user comments.

Simpson Crazy (http://www.simpsoncrazy.com). Much of the episode guide and transcript information is blank (The Simpsons Archive is a much better resource for episode information), but this site is useful for the frequently updated news, such as upcoming guest voices. The site also provides substantial media (wallpapers, images, and magazine covers) and a collection of the music from the four main *Simpsons* albums to date, including lyrics.

The Simpsons Gallery (http://duffzone.org). This site really is a gallery for the show, with many images from each episode and an enormous amount of posters, desktops, and wallpapers. Unfortunately, this site is updated infrequently. Images cannot be used without permission.

The Simpsons Official Website (http://www.thesimpsons.com). Operated by Fox, the official website for *The Simpsons* offers the schedule of upcoming episodes, official news and contests, and streaming of recent episodes and extras, such as studio footage of guest voice talent.

The Simpsons Quotes (http://www.thesimpsonsquotes.com). This website offers favorite *Simpsons* quotes catalogued by character, popularity, and theme. This site could be useful for activities to analyze and interpret quotes divorced from the context of their episode. For example, consider this gem of Burns's: "What good is money if it can't inspire terror in your fellow man?" His perspective is one that considers currency as a means of making people cower before him.

Wacklepedia (http://www.wacklepedia.com/t/th/the_simpsons.html). Wacklepedia is an online encyclopedia. The entry for *The Simpsons* is noteworthy because it offers a list of guest stars in alphabetical order.

Simpsons Wiki (http://simpsons.wikia.com/wiki/The_Simpsons). As in any wiki, anyone with an account can update the information found here; unfortunately, many of the episode entries are sparse, but the "Notable Episodes" link provides some deep insight into particular episodes. "The Locations" link offers intricate details of well-known Springfield locations such as the Kwik-E-Mart and Springfield Elementary.

Wikipedia (http://en.wikipedia.org/wiki/Main_Page). The search in Wikipedia is easy to use and has a near-perfect success rate when searching for an episode name, often with more complete information than the *Simpsons Wiki.* As with any wiki, the information is fallible, but many episodes are chronicled not only in terms of plot but in terms of intertextual and cultural references. We have found that much of the information comes directly from the DVD commentaries, and is cited as such.

Research Tip

To locate information about individual contributors to *The Simpsons,* we recommend the Internet Movie Database (http://www.imdb.com) and searching by name. For example, if we wanted to quickly locate which episodes were directed by David Silverman, we would enter his name in the IMDb search field. All of Silverman's television and film projects appear, catalogued by his function (as director, producer, crew, art department, animation department, actor, writer, self, etc.).

Chapter 2

The Composition Class: Me Fail English? That's Unpossible!

Editor: This is a joke, right? I mean this is the stupidest thing I've ever read!

Homer: What's wrong with it?

Editor: You keep using words like "pasghetti" and "momatoes." You make numerous threatening references to the UN and at the end you repeat the words "Screw Flanders" over and over again.

Homer: Oh, it's so hard to get to 500 words.

About This Chapter

The first part of this chapter offers important definitions central to introductory composition courses similar to what is found in most composition texts, but with teachable examples from *The Simpsons*. Next, we describe composition paper assignments that we have used repeatedly. Also in this chapter are related in-class activities and handouts useful for composition classes, many of which, such as source citing, can be altered for technical writing and literature courses.

An Anecdote

Composition can feel daunting for many students, especially when they are expected to tackle unapproachable subjects on top of writing well, which can be equally intimidating. In Denise's freshman year of college, she took a course called "Writing about Irish Literature." She was nervous but pushed herself into it, deciding it was time to sink or swim. She sank. She was so preoccupied with her difficulties with the language and trying to make the right arguments about the literature that she forgot about the craft of writing. Poor paper grades derailed her self-confidence, not just about her analytical skills, but for the first time since junior high, about her writing skills as well.

She ended up withdrawing from the course, receiving the first (and most painful) of the three *W*s on her undergraduate transcript. She took an equivalent course during the summer, but with a more general writing theme and a teacher whose teaching style more closely matched her learning style, and gained back the self-confidence lost by tackling more than she could handle. This experience stayed with her and reminded her how it's not just the subject matter but a teacher's approach that can make all the difference in a student's learning.

Critical Thinking

Our experiences as students guide us as we design our writing courses. Before a student can be expected to think and write critically about Shakespeare or Chaucer or Foucault, the student must have a basic foundation of critical thinking skills. And with the trend in high schools leaning towards teaching for the standardized test rather than towards advancing critical thinking skills,[1] college composition instructors and students alike have a tough job ahead of them.

Teaching critical thinking and analysis through a familiar medium is not "dumbing down" the curriculum, as we have heard from instructors from the old school; but rather, it serves as an exercise in honing analytical skills, preparing students to apply these skills to the humanities, and writing through the lens of these new insights. Suddenly, Shakespeare isn't as intimidating as he used to be.[2]

The Simpsons is an ideal jumping-off point. Students are already familiar with sitcoms and cartoons, but few have taken the time to uncover exactly why the show works on different levels. *The Simpsons* makes literary concepts easier to grasp (such as figurative language, satire, theory, conflict, etc.) and offers myriad cultural and societal issues to analyze. Class discussions on tradition, religion, family values, race, consumerism, education, corporal punishment, and countless other topics offer students chances to formulate and defend their stances on these issues in a much more comfortable classroom environment than the average intro sociology or poli sci course. Most importantly, students learn to make arguments, which is the basis of freshman (and all subsequent) composition courses.

We instruct students to think of any piece of art as an argument. Every film, commercial, TV show, and song is an argument. Through breaking down the argument into components (analysis), the audience understands how the argument works and therefore becomes equipped to determine the validity of the argument (critical thinking). Critical thinking skills turn students of all majors into well-rounded, educated adults, capable of exercising common sense.

The Simpsons can be used in any type of composition course, including writing for personal discovery with the use of a viewer's journal (a description of which appears at the end of this chapter) and analytical writing.

Before moving into argumentative essays, it is wise to review argument terms and forms. Since these can be dry and often overwhelming for students, we recommend spreading out instruction of the concepts while having the students work on a narrative or similar warm-up essay. In a course relying heavily on *The Simpsons*, students might relate their history with the show and how it has affected them. In other courses, students should be encouraged to focus on specific topics rather than simply directed to tell a story. For example, our students in the past have been required to research and write about the history of their family's emigration, a specific food or meal, or their personal history of lying.[3] Working through narrative assignments can allow time to discuss more formal essays, which will require argumentative theses and the use of rhetorical tools, while enabling the students to focus on structure, clarity, and tone.

Working through Aristotle's appeals and the Toulmin argument system can be difficult, especially if the concepts are only treated as abstractions. Students should continually be encouraged to identify these concepts in the writings of others and to apply these concepts in their own work. In an advanced rhetoric course, it is imperative that students be able to distinguish and name logical fallacies and able to identify the claims, backing, warrants, and other parts of an argument. Most young writers, however, need to be able to see that faulty logic is at work in another's text and to avoid faulty logic in their own. They need to be able to formulate a solid argument, to back it up, and to write it clearly.

At the most basic level of the essay lies the thesis statement. Students must be reminded that a strong thesis is created by copious amounts of brainstorming and pre-writing. (A handout on creating a strong thesis statement is included later in the chapter.)

Thesis/Claim

The central argument of a piece of art is seldom blatantly stated; instead, the reader, viewer, or listener gleans it from the plot, style, and other elements working together. (A notable exception might be simplistic and didactic works like *Spider-Man*; it could be argued that Uncle Ben's phrase "With great power comes great responsibility" is the thesis.)

However, in a student essay, the central argument should appear as an identifiable thesis statement, which can be found anywhere in the essay as long as it is rhetorically effective. In the traditional five-paragraph essay most students remember from high school, the thesis is generally found in the introduction, often as the last sentence of the introduction. We generally encourage students to avoid the three-point thesis they may have relied upon in high school, as it does not often foster critical thinking. Deciding that an essay will have five paragraphs, no more, no less, before the topic is even chosen, will inevitably limit thinking.

The five-paragraph, three-point thesis essay is sometimes taught exclusively because it is an acceptable format for the SAT essay section. Many students who are taught that this is the *only* form are unprepared both for college entrance writing exams and for the variety of writing tasks they will encounter in college.

Types of Argument

It is often useful to have students categorize arguments, beginning with the arguments of others and then moving on to their own, as different types of arguments call for different writing strategies and organizational structures.

First, students may be asked to consider the purpose of an argument. The four basic purposes of argument are to inform, to entertain, to explore, and to persuade. Presumably, the pamphlet Marge is given by her doctor when she becomes pregnant the first time ("So You've Ruined Your Life") informs her about the difficulties she's about to encounter. Each one of Krusty's jokes is an argument that seeks to entertain. Springfield's copious town hall meetings open topics for the citizens to explore. When Bart and Lisa want to go to Itchy and Scratchy Land, they come up with several arguments to persuade their parents.

If an argument's purpose (like that of most composition arguments) is to persuade, then the essay form may be further subdivided into the following types: fact, definition, evaluation, causal, proposal. It should be noted that many arguments contain aspects of various types of argument, but a persuasive thesis should be easily classifiable into one of the above types. Determining whether the skeleton Lisa discovers is that of an angel is an argument of fact. An essay attempting to determine what denomination the Reverend Lovejoy represents would be one of definition. Evaluating Homer's argument tactics would require establishing criteria. Explaining that Homer caused Maude Flanders's death or that Marge's fear of flying was caused by her father's job would be causal analysis. Marge's attempt to convince Homer to raise emus when he was depressed is a proposal, though Bart's counter-proposal wins the day.

Reasons/Evidence

To back up the thesis, solid evidence must be presented. When making arguments about literature, textual evidence is key. Not only do the supporting paragraphs require evidence, but the arguments must be formulated and executed in an ethical manner. This means no heavy-handed emotional appeals and no logical fallacies. At the end of this chapter, we include some of our exercises for understanding logical fallacies and rhetorical analysis of sources.

Warrant/Assumption

The warrant serves as a connector between the claim, reasons, and data that support the claim. The warrant is the underlying, unspoken understanding of the values that the author shares with the reader. Especially when making an argument that the audience may have particularly strong feelings about, knowing the audience is the best way to provide a strong foundation. A speech given by a politician to a group of supporters, for example, will be very different from one delivered by that same politician invited to speak to a more diverse group, such as at a university commencement.[4] Most writing instructors hold that audience awareness is the key to a successful essay. That is, awareness of the audience will enable the writer to engage the audience, write in an appropriate voice, provide them with suitable evidence, and so on.

Students often have a difficult time identifying underlying warrants, unless they happen to disagree with the warrant. In other words, when students share assumptions with a writer, they often have problems detecting them. In these cases, the students need to be reminded that every argument has warrants. The author is always at least assuming the audience reads the language of the argument, that the audience understands the majority of the words, and so forth. There are basically two kinds of warrants — the author assuming that the audience already knows something (the definition of a scientific concept, for example) or the author assuming that the audience already believes something (that x is a "sin," for example).

For the author to achieve a strong warrant, he needs audience analysis skills. Activities for audience understanding are very useful, and several are included at the end of this chapter.

Qualifiers

A strong blanket statement as a thesis is easy to refute: "Professional athletes in the United States earn far too much money." A qualifier balances the statement to make it more reasonable. The thesis instead might be: "Some professional athletes earn an outrageous amount of money; thus, there should be caps on player salaries."[5] Ultimately, the essay behind that thesis statement will be stronger, and the extreme examples of pro athletes making an excessive amount of money back up the thesis. However, in the first thesis, the skeptical reader will have instant ammunition against the thesis, realizing that many pro athletes bank reasonable paychecks; the long snapper's contract seldom makes the news, and WNBA player contracts are laughable, comparatively speaking. Supply a list of qualifiers to the student, but warn against making the thesis too wishy-washy. Students should also be warned to qualify their knowledge — if they are basing their argument on a character or theme in *The Simpsons* but have seen only five episodes, they should say so. Otherwise, they invite being discredited by someone who has seen contradictory evidence in other episodes. Qualifiers in this sense are a type of proactive counter-argument. Above all, students should be encouraged to mean what they say and to say what they mean. For example, if they say that a certain piece

of evidence "proves" something, they shouldn't really mean "suggests."
Some frequently used qualifiers:

- sometimes
- very rarely
- under normal circumstances
- often
- in most cases
- frequently
- in certain situations
- until recently
- commonly

Aristotle's Three Appeals

A working knowledge of logos, ethos, and pathos is essential as students move from writer-centered assertions to reader-centered arguments. Successful arguments call for an awareness of audience. Without this, an argument runs the risk of being dismissed before it really begins. Even cretins like Moe can advise on appeals. For example, in "Marge Gamer," Moe tells Homer to appeal to Lisa's sense of reason (logos) and for Bart to appeal to Marge's feelings (pathos).

LOGOS

Logos is the way an argument appeals to the audience's sense of reason or logic. Although Jamey Heit reminds us that "[m]ost characters on *The Simpsons* lack reliable intellectual skills" (133), they are sometimes swayed by logic, such as when Lisa reminds various townspeople of the utility of snakes when she seeks to stop the Whacking Day celebration.

ETHOS

Ethos is the Greek word for "character." Ethos is the reliability of the author based on his or her (perceived or actual) authority on the subject. In class, ask the students which doctor they would trust more, Dr. Hibbert or Dr. Nick. Next, ask what qualities are exhibited by speakers/authors they trust, and then ask how they might establish their own credibility as authors — through reliable sources, the language they choose to employ, personal experience, education, and so on. Finally, ask whether students would trust Marge or Dr. Hibbert more to describe the pain of childbirth; this will enable them to think through the difference between academic expertise and experiential knowledge.

Note that most students will inevitably confuse ethos with ethics/

morals, especially since this is the "ethical appeal." Students should be reminded that arguments based on morality fall under pathos.

PATHOS

Pathos is the appeal to the audience's emotions. Lines of argument relying too heavily on emotion can be seen as manipulative, but just the right amount of pathos can be an effective, convincing tool in an argument. Students can often point to political tactics and commercials with excellent examples. Be sure to ask this question for discussion: Why do emotional appeals work, even when the audience is aware of the tactic?

Although logos should be the center of any argument, ethos and pathos must be present for an argument to work. For example, in "Simpson and Delilah," Homer makes a logical argument about saving money, but his audience dismisses him before he begins: "Some nerve, telling us how to run the plant. He doesn't even have hair!" (In addition to illustrating the importance of connecting with the audience, this example also illustrates a logical fallacy.)

Similarly, in *The Simpsons Movie*, Lisa realizes that counting on logic to get the town's citizens to stop polluting Springfield Lake is not working because she has not gotten them to care about the issue. Thus, she replaces the town meeting hall water with lake water.

Logical Fallacies

Understanding logical fallacies is the flip side of understanding logos, ethos, and pathos.[6] There are many different ways to classify logical fallacies and many different ways to describe them (for example, using the English or Latin names). One suggestion is to decide whether the fallacies are abuses of logos, ethos, or pathos.

For example, the red herring fallacy distracts the opponent from her argument. One of the most famous examples is from Nixon's "Checkers Speech," which is parodied in "Pranksta Rap," when Mayor Quimby is accused of hiding illegitimate children from the public: "I'm hiding nothing — except this puppy. Look into its eyes and tell me I'm lying." Kent Brockman's response? "Well, I'm placated."

Arguments abuse ethos when they appeal to improper or biased authority, such as when Homer believes that billboard ads have his best interest in mind in "Homie the Clown" or when townspeople conflate an actor playing Charles Darwin in a commercial with an actual person of science in "Two Cars in Every Garage and Three Eyes on Every Fish."

Arguers abuse pathos when relying on emotion rather than facts, often using ad hominem, appeals to tradition, and ad populum. An example of the last would be when Chuck Garabedian assures paying attendees that he can teach them how to save money: "Well, stick around, 'cause I'm gonna tell you the twelve savings secrets Wall Street *won't* tell you. Then, I'll show you the three ways to get back to the highway [sotto voce:] including one shortcut those Wall Street fat cats don't want you to know!" ("Thirty Minutes over Tokyo").

Students can be encouraged to see that even well-meaning and thoughtful arguers can sometimes fall prey to logical fallacies in debate. When Kent Brockman interviews Lisa Simpson after she discovers a mysterious skeleton, he challenges her assertion that the skeleton isn't that of an angel with the statement that it "looks like an angel." His circular logic is followed by her slippery slope, when she declares, "If you believe in angels, then why not unicorns, sea monsters, and leprechauns?" The argument then devolves into hypostatization, peer pressure, and the either/or fallacy:

> **Kent:** That's a bunch of baloney, Lisa. Everyone knows that leprechauns are extinct.
>
> **Lisa:** Look, you can either accept science and face reality, or you can believe in angels and live in a childish dream world. ("Lisa the Skeptic")

On Style

Although the show's characters do not often model expository writing, we can still find ways to use *The Simpsons* to illustrate the importance of style. Young writers, for example, may find that their writing resembles Homer's when he attempts to write restaurant reviews in "Guess Who's Coming to Criticize Dinner." Homer's diction is poor, his piece rambles off topic, and he attempts to make the word count by repeating "Screw Flanders" several times. We can thus illustrate that students need to reduce wordiness (wordiness meaning excessive or meaningless words), while developing their arguments through pertinent content or parallelism. We can also stress revision by showing what Lisa is able to do when she helps her father brainstorm. For example, when they need two more words to end the review, Lisa replaces "Screw Flanders" with "*Bon appétit.*"

Once writers gain confidence, however, they often fall prey to the inflated writing that they believe will impress audiences. Indiscriminate use of the thesaurus is usually involved (students' decisions to often choose the longest synonym rather than an appropriate one can be analyzed to illustrate the difference between denotation and connotation). *Simpsons* characters often use jargon or other diction choices that obscure meaning, and we can use these moments to remind students about the importance of clarity. For example, Mr. Burns's archaisms not only reveal his age, but also hinder understanding. Thus, his request is denied when he asks: "I'd like to send this letter to the Prussian consulate in Siam by aeromail. Am I too late for the 4:30 autogyro?" While using large words may impress audiences with small vocabularies, audience awareness precludes their use unless the only aim is to impress. When Mr. Burns insults Homer by saying "Your indolence is inefficacious!," he is not considering Homer's knowledge. When Homer does not understand whether he is being insulted or complimented, Mr. Burns must take the time to translate his own phrase.

We also remind students that pretentious diction in their essays often signals to the reader that the writer is faking mastery of a subject. For example, when an underage boy attempts to buy alcohol in "Much Apu about Nothing," his diction gives him away: "Furthermore to this beer, I would also like three of your finest, cheapest cigars. Here's my ID, which confirms my adultivity."

Clarity is also achieved by avoiding awkward syntax and extraneous nominalizations. Writing in the positive (avoiding *un-* and *not*) can further avoid double negatives and misunderstandings. Even Bart comments, when reading a safety text that instructs "Don't do what Donny Don't does," that "they could have made this clearer."

A discussion of euphemisms[7] can elicit great response. Many students hold that euphemisms that obscure meaning can be useful (from the point of view of the person who wants to obstruct meaning), though we tend to discourage them, as we prefer clarity. Several instances on *The Simpsons* seem to reinforce this preference. For example, when Marge is trying to tell Homer that his friend John is gay, she uses several euphemisms that go over Homer's head — that John is "festive," that "[h]e prefers the company of men." It is not until she uses the clear term — "homosexual" — that Homer understands ("Homer's Phobia").

In "Homer Defined," euphemisms become the more sinister "doublespeak"[8] when Mr. Burns tries to deflect attention away from a meltdown: "Oh, 'meltdown.' It's one of those annoying buzzwords. We prefer to call it 'an unrequested fission surplus.'"

Passive voice can also obscure clarity, so it's important that students be instructed in passive versus active voice. Often, students need to be told that each voice has value (science essays still tend to be written in passive voice, for example). They should also be warned about how passive voice can be used when people want to avoid responsibility for their actions. Thus, a politician might say "funds were misappropriated" or "thousands were slaughtered." Bart, in "Bart the Murderer," begins to use this tactic, but clarifies his language (though he doesn't change to active voice) when he begins to take responsibility for a wrong: "Mistakes were made. By me."

Even commonly misused language is critiqued in the show, such as when Dr. Nick doesn't understand that "flammable" and "inflammable" mean the same thing ("Trilogy of Error") or when Homer seems to think that Lisa is trying to tell him something about Moe's relationship with Marge:

> **Homer:** If what you are inferring...
> **Lisa:** I'm not inferring anything. You infer; I imply.
> **Homer:** Whew — that's a relief! ("Mommie Beerest")

Exercises and handouts on word choice and avoiding pretentious diction appear later in the chapter.

Introductions, Conclusions, and Titles

Many students, even after the research is done and the notes in the readers' journal are culled, have problems moving into the writing phase. The blank screen is daunting and procrastination is common. Karma has been known to convince herself that she can't possibly write when her bathroom is dirty. Denise requires quiet, and the barking of a dog is enough to render an afternoon worthless. Because of this, she knows that the best place to get work done is the Caribou Coffee near the medical college (full of students and rarely has children). Students should be encouraged to think through their writing hang-ups — they can confront their demons only by naming them first.

Beginning the writing process by attempting to write a title or an introduction can make everything more difficult, so students should be given permission to start in the middle. If they've done their pre-writing work, they know about an example they'll be giving in the essay or they'll have identified a term that they'll need to define. Even typing out simple parts of the paper like these will result in the student having something rather than nothing and will make the composition process go more smoothly.

At some point, of course, introductions and conclusions must be written. Students should be encouraged to see these as separate entities, not as the interchangeable paragraphs so often found in the three-point thesis paper. If a conclusion were supposed to be a reverse introduction, that's what we would call it. Introductions should set up the main idea and set the tone of the paper. There are several ways to do this — a student might open with a relevant anecdote, a surprising fact, or a common idea that she's about to deconstruct. We advise avoiding generalities, questions, and dictionary definitions. Super-generalities often don't need to be stated ("Many people watch television" or Denise's favorite: "High school is a difficult time for many students"). Often, overgeneralizations are incorrect. That is, when students decide to start their paper at the dawn of time, they say silly or irrelevant things. One of Karma's students, for example, once opened a paper by claiming that humans had practiced a certain behavior since the Jurassic period. Questions can be problematic if they put the reader off ("Have you ever wondered about X?") or if the paper doesn't really answer the question put forth. Dictionary definitions are often the beginnings of last resort. Cautioning against them can be a way to think through audience awareness. If the audience knows the word, we definitely don't need to define the word; if the audience does need a definition, the writer should be able to define the term in his own words.

Conclusions can be maddening — the writer has said everything she needs to, but there's another paragraph to write. Thankfully, conclusions (and introductions) have varying lengths, so if it only takes a sentence or two to give the audience a sense of conclusion, then the writer shouldn't belabor the point. The sense of closure is important, however. Often, the writer can use a strategy similar to an introduction — she might close with a story or quote, for example. The best conclusions either circle back to the introduction (a "hook and return" approach), finishing the opening anecdote, perhaps, or look forward to a larger world beyond the paper.

Scientific articles often end by elucidating what further research needs to be done, for instance.

Students should remember that the reader begins with a title, and while we endorse holistic grading, it's still important to make a good first impression. Essay titles should be as specific as possible. A student who titles his paper "Class" is being too vague; however, if he titles it "'Viva La Revolución!': Class Discrimination in 'A Tale of Two Springfields,'" he is off to a great start. Miss Hoover probably received many great papers on Jebediah Springfield, but we would most want to read Lisa's, just based on the title: "Jebediah Springfield: Superfraud" ("Lisa the Iconoclast").

Students should be encouraged to review the strategies of authors they're reading in the class so they may be able to imitate successful writing tactics.

Essay Assignments

Composition Essay #1: Argument Analysis

The first paper assignment in an argument-based composition course should be an argument analysis. Using either an episode watched collectively or by allowing students to view and choose on their own, the first step is for the students to identify an argument they feel is being made in the text. For the purposes of this explanation, we will be using examples from "Much Apu about Nothing," an episode in which the mayor of Springfield blames illegal immigrants for a frivolous new service that caused a tax hike completely unrelated to immigration. The student need not agree with the stance; using Toulmin's definition of argument structure, he just needs to be able to break down the argument into its component parts. The following four definitions may be altered for your specific class's needs and given as a handout:

1. Claim — The claim is the central argument ("argument," "claim," and "thesis" can be used almost interchangeably; the thesis is the argument but in succinct words). The student might conclude, after watching the episode, that the central argument is about how we should not use illegal immigrants as political scapegoats.

2. Reasons — Also called "evidence" by composition teachers, rea-

sons serve to back up the argument. They must be solid and logical. There are many instances in the episode that illustrate and back up the scapegoat claim, including the foreshadowing in the beginning of the episode, when a bear comes to Springfield and Kent Brockman speculates that he's looking "for employment."

3. Warrant — The warrant is the audience-centered connection between the claim and the reasons that support the claim; in essence, the warrant provides the author with the right to continue with the argument. If the reader disagrees with the warrant, there is no reasoning the arguer can do that will change the reader's mind. The warrants that might underlie an argument about this episode include the understanding that immigration is a complicated issue, that most people care deeply about their communities, or that the audience understands the basics of the controversy surrounding illegal immigration.

4. Qualifier — Qualifiers and qualifying phrases include "in many cases," "under these conditions," or "rarely." When an absolute blanket statement may be hard or impossible to prove, a qualifier functions to make a claim more honest and reasonable. The student would want to avoid saying the show "proves" that all immigrants are beneficial to the country or that "all" immigrants know more about American history than Americans do, based on Apu's knowledge versus Homer's.

In addition to the episode described above ("Much Apu about Nothing") we also recommend the following episodes in conjunction with Essay #1:

"Mr. Lisa Goes to Washington" 8F01: When Lisa wins an essay contest, the family travels to Washington, D.C. Once there, Lisa discovers the corruption therein. (This episode is also useful because Lisa must win her trip with a writing assignment, and she struggles to make her essay both appealing and engaging.)

"The Day the Violence Died" 3F16: This episode makes arguments about intellectual property and the damage caused by a litigious society. In addition, it features the "Amendment to Be" short (a spoof on *Schoolhouse Rock*) that argues that changing the Constitution through amendments opens the door to making "all sorts of crazy laws."

"Homer vs. the 18th Amendment" 4F15: In this episode, Homer is part of a beer-smuggling operation that supplies a speakeasy in Springfield because an old, previously unenforced prohibition law is discovered in the books. Arguments are made about individual responsibility for actions, the efficacy of prohibitive laws, and the power of taboo.

"Lisa the Iconoclast" 3F13: This episode makes arguments about society, tradition, patriotism, and even suggests that lying (or at least omitting the truth) might sometimes be justifiable.

"Whacking Day" 9F18: Lisa is troubled about the morality of the "Whacking Day" tradition: on a certain day of the year, the residents of Springfield hold a festival which includes the killing of snakes.[9] This is an interesting episode to place alongside "Lisa the Iconoclast" because, while both episodes show Lisa questioning the value of town tradition, in one episode she ultimately concludes that the tradition, though erroneous, has value and should remain, whereas in the other, she decides that the value in stopping the tradition outweighs the community fellowship created by the tradition.

"The Computer Wore Menace Shoes" CABF02: When the well of information for Homer's whistle-blowing website dries out, he turns to inventing rumors to keep it afloat. This episode examines just how loosely the First Amendment can be interpreted.

"Girls Just Wanna Have Sums" HABF12: In this episode, boys and girls are separated into different classes, and the girls are taught nothing useful about math. This episode suggests that gender disparity in the hard sciences (and gender disparity in some aspects of behavior) may have more to do with nurture than nature.[10]

"The Cartridge Family" 5F01: Marge, the kids, and even the NRA won't have Homer around when he becomes a gun nut.

"Coming to Homerica" LABF12: Springfield mirrors the United States' debate over immigration and the controversy over building a wall on the border.

"Weekend at Burnsies" DABF11: This episode shows sides of the medical marijuana issue and confronts the idea of legalization of marijuana.

"The Monkey Suit" HABF14: This episode tackles the evolution/creation debate.

Composition Essay #2: The Internal Research Paper

Once the student is able to identify and analyze existing arguments, she is ready to create and back up one of her own. The internal research paper works well to make the transition into writing research papers less stressful. Students become acquainted with the appropriate ways to conduct research and cite sources, but are not forced (for now) to go outside of themselves, *The Simpsons*, and the *Our Favorite Family* (OFF) guides.[11] It is up to the instructor to determine to what extent websites will be allowed as sources (see Chapter 1 for a list of reliable sites). After viewing and discussing several episodes, brainstorm as a class which themes appear frequently.[12] Examples might include:

- mob mentality
- fame/celebrity
- conservation
- patriotism

- parenting
- tradition
- sports
- the elderly

- others/outcasts
- substance abuse
- religion/faith
- corruption/crime

Starting with notes made in a viewer's journal, when the student has identified a theme, the next step is formulating an argument about that theme. It is useful to instruct the students to start with a research question.

We have seen students argue about the political affiliations of certain characters and the show's stance on different issues. One of the most interesting internal research papers we've seen was one in which a student very successfully argued that Homer is a better father than Ned Flanders.

Next, encourage the students to engage in counter-arguments — or, as we like to call them, "the old greet 'n' toss" (inspired by Bart in the episode "Bart After Dark"). The essay author should acknowledge that there are opinions that conflict with his thesis, but by addressing those opinions and invalidating them (or at least showing their limitations), he makes his essay stronger. Pretending opposing viewpoints don't exist weakens the argument by leaving noticeable holes in it.[13]

Suggested episodes for this assignment are listed below.

"Much Apu about Nothing" 3F20: As discussed above, this episode argues about immigration, but also brings into question issues of patriotism, ethnic stereotypes, entitlement, scapegoating, political corruption, and the role of law enforcement.

"Lisa the Vegetarian" 3F03: Tension mounts between Lisa and Homer when Lisa realizes that she can no longer bring herself to eat meat and she fervently opposes Homer serving meat at his barbeque. The "independent thought alarms" that upset Principal Skinner and the film shown in class, *Meat and You: Partners in Freedom*, suggest that this episode uses Lisa's vegetarianism as a vehicle to make points about individuality, what happens when the status quo is disrupted, and the role of the public school system.

"*El Viaje Misterioso du Nuestro Jomer*" 3F24: *The Simpsons* takes a stab at a familiar literary motif, inspired here by Carlos Castaneda: Homer goes on a mystical journey of self-discovery. Through his trip, he discovers that Marge is his soul mate. In this episode, marriage, community, and alcohol use are examined.

"Lisa on Ice" 2F05: When Lisa receives an "academic alert" for a failing grade in gym, her teacher strikes a deal with her that if she joins a team outside of school, she won't fail. When she discovers she has a talent for goaltending, she and Bart find themselves on competing peewee hockey teams. Kids' sports leagues, stage-parenting, bullies, school curricula, sexual double standards, and gambling are just a few of the discussion topics that can come out of this episode.

"Dead Putting Society" 7F08: Ned and Homer put Todd and Bart in a situation of competition. This episode analyzes issues of parenting, and facilitates conversations regarding gender stereotypes and a sports-obsessed, competitive society.

"Homer's Phobia" 4F11: As is obvious from the title, this episode deals with stereotyping, prejudice, and homophobia. When the family strikes a friendship with a gay man named John, Homer fears that the influence will make Bart gay too.

"She of Little Faith" DABF02: This episode shows Lisa's struggle as she grapples with religion and discovers Buddhism.

"You Kent Always Get What You Want" JABF15: This episode is self-referential, highlighting the contradictions of the Fox network. When a newscaster accidentally spouts a pain-induced expletive on air and gets in big trouble, Lisa wonders why the network is so strict about simple words and why its news reporting is so conservative, yet it consistently features so many raunchy shows. Issues of censorship, sponsorship, and the role of watchdog conservative groups come into play.

"Bart Sells His Soul" 3F02: This episode examines difference between religion and spirituality. In an argument with Milhouse about whether or not there is such a thing as a soul, Bart sells his soul (scrawled on a piece of paper) to Milhouse for five dollars. When weird things start happening, Bart becomes terrified that he has lost his soul and works hard to get it back.

"Home Sweet Homediddly-Dum-Doodily" 3F01: When a series of

unfortunate (and misunderstood) events cause the Simpson children to be placed in foster care at the Flanders home, Ned and Maude are disturbed to learn the children were never baptized. In addition to the topics of religion and family, this episode invites a discussion about the line between governmental protection and interference.

"Lisa the Drama Queen" KABF22: Lisa makes a friend with whom she feels a great connection, but whose fantasy world eventually becomes too much for Lisa to handle. This episode broaches the topics of how much imagination is healthy, when to cut people out of one's life, and when parents should get involved if worried about their children's friendships.

"Lisa vs. Malibu Stacy" 1F12: Lisa is excited to get her first talking Malibu Stacy doll, but is horrified by the doll's preprogrammed sexist phrases. She finds the original inventor of Malibu Stacy, and together they create a new, empowered doll called Lisa Lionheart. Sexism and consumer culture are the primary issues in this episode, and the subplot concerns the treatment of the elderly in society.[14]

This is by no means an exhaustive list; countless episodes can be presented in class (or assigned) to facilitate brainstorming of topics for Essay #2. To promote the habit of responsible citation practices, episodes must be quoted and cited properly (i.e., Episode 1F22: "Bart of Darkness"). We recommend limiting or banning the use of "Treehouse of Horror" episodes for this assignment because in such episodes, characters are frequently portrayed out of their usual behaviors.

Composition Essay #3: Four External Research Paper Assignments

Again, the student should begin with a viewer's journal and then a research question, but there are a couple of different approaches a teacher can take to implement a more traditional research paper in a *Simpsons* curriculum. Whichever type of research paper is chosen, teaching proper citation practices can be one of the most challenging elements. For that reason, we have included a citing activity later in the chapter.

SIMPSONS-INSPIRED ISSUE PAPER

The student may be instructed to research an issue *inspired* by the show. In this scenario, the research paper might have no reference to *The*

Simpsons at all. Similar issues may be used in this essay as in Essay #2, such as sexism in children's toys or approaches to immigration issues.

CULTURAL ARTIFACT PAPER

The research paper might be about a cultural artifact; seeing a piece of culture as an artifact helps students to view aspects of their culture anew. The paper should include a history of the artifact, an examination of the role this artifact plays in our society, and some thoughts on what this artifact says about us. Students should be encouraged to find something unique, not obvious like computers, the Internet, or cell phones; the more specific, the better. This assignment is excellent for explaining the difference between a research paper and a research report. A report finds all the relevant material written or known about an issue and reports it back, whereas a research paper takes all of the information and then creates a relevant and original thesis statement about it.

RESEARCH FRAMEWORK PAPER

Another approach is to use a similar thesis as described for the internal research paper but now to require outside *Simpsons*-related articles and books (Chapter 1 details excellent resources). For this type of essay, the student's research question will ask how society or scholars, for example, view some element of the show, and the student's argument will place her view within the researched framework (well supported, of course). The essay may also consult theory. An alternate idea is to have the students focus on one particular critical essay or review of the show and use it to practice summary/response.

PROBLEM PAPER

A fourth option is the problem paper, similar to what might be assigned in an introduction to literature course. In a problem paper, the author seeks to answer a question from the text (or in this case, the show) that has no definitive answer. This essay requires a student to make a claim, find support, and engage in counter-arguments. (The question of whether Homer or Ned is the better father is an example of a problem paper, as either side can be argued successfully if properly backed up with evidence.) These papers can be challenging due to the necessity of engaging with a counter-argument that can't be entirely defeated, but they can also be the most fun to write and to grade.

Additional examples of "problems":
- Why doesn't Marge have any friends? Or, similarly, who is Homer's best friend? (Both of which would require all of the above strategies, plus defining "best friend" first.)
- Why is Springfield not located in any specific state or region of the United States?
- What does the show say about the United States' relationship with the rest of the world?
- Why don't the characters age or change in any substantial way?

A Note About the Viewer's Journal

Any viewer of *The Simpsons* can learn something new just from the show. (Because of an episode, Denise asked her father who Steve and Edie were, for example, in the days before Wikipedia). In a viewer's journal, students should write down any question that pops up. (This journal should be separate from the course notebook.) For example, such questions as "What are the Stonecutters based on?," "Why do so many episodes have monkeys?," "Who is Rory Calhoun?," or "Why does Troy McClure have such a thing for fish?" are all fair game. Students may also be inspired to jot notes in their viewer's journal if there are references to the show on the news, in other television shows, or if they observe others discussing some element of the show. After some easy research (Internet, library, or simply personal, by asking friends and family), a student can gain the answers to these and other compelling questions, and can then go on to create a customized research assignment.

For the viewer's journal, we recommend a double-entry notebook. On one side of the page, the student should write a question or quote from the show (including an informal citation, as nothing is more frustrating than having the perfect quote but no idea where it came from). On the other side of the page, he should write his purpose for including that particular quote. If a student is considering Marge's feminism as a potential topic, for example, he may quote Marge's feelings about women and sports from "Lisa on Ice," and then jot his feelings about the quote, suggestions on where in the essay the quote may be used, and any other related thoughts that will help as he begins the essay. Students may grumble at first, but they will find having a notebook filled with ideas in front of them immensely helpful when opening a blank Word document. To stimulate extra incentive to keep up with the journal, collect the notebooks several times during the term for credit.

Exercises

The remainder of this chapter consists of some of the activities that we have used successfully in our own classrooms. Keep in mind that you should always have a backup plan if the activity relies upon classroom technology and always be armed with a few relevant free-writing prompts.

Rhetorical Analysis of Sources

The best resource for teaching students about choosing and using sources is a librarian. We recommend scheduling a library visit early in the term. A librarian at your institution knows which databases your library has, which databases are best for certain fields, and the keywords and Boolean terms preferred by each. We use several in-class activities to augment the librarian's teachings, or even to replace a librarian-taught class if one cannot be scheduled.

Activity #1: Grade Potential Sources
(Rhetorical Analysis of Source)

Place the students into small groups. Give each group a nonfiction book, magazine, or one of each. Be sure to use selections that have an agenda: books and magazines that lean to the left or the right or that are designed to appeal to men or to women, and books by creationists and paleontologists, for example. After the students have had a few minutes to flip through them, pass out a worksheet that offers questions to help with rhetorical analysis. We allow Internet searching, if possible.

1. What is the source? (Book, professional or academic journal, magazine, etc.)
2. Who is the author? What do you know about his or her credentials?
3. What is the publisher? What genres do they usually publish?

4. When was this text published? Was it written in response to a particular event or another text?
5. Who is the intended audience for this text?
6. What is the overall reliability of this source? If peer-reviewed sources are required, does this source provide that?

After the students have graded the reliability of their sources, have each group introduce the source to the class and offer their findings.

Activity #2: When Can I Trust Google?

If your classroom has Internet access and a screen, this works well as a whole group activity. First, ask the class for someone to Google: a musician, actor, athlete, whomever. When the search results appear, take that opportunity to explain about pay-per-click and site optimization. (I often ask them to look up those terms online and call on someone to explain them to the class.) You might find, for example, that Amazon or other shopping sites might be at the top of the list instead of articles. Discuss why that is. You may also want to show the students Google Scholar, as many of them will not know about the source.

Next, do another Google search, this time on a topic that you have tested ahead of time and know for a fact that an unreliable site appears on the first page. Lately for this exercise, we've been using a search on Martin Luther King, Jr. At the time of this writing, "Martin Luther King: A True Historical Examination" appears on the first results page (martinlutherking.org). This site touts itself as a "valuable resource for teachers and students alike," and the authentic-sounding URL suggests it is, but a quick glance at the site shows its slant. At the bottom of the homepage, click "Hosted by Stormfront." This is a white supremacist group. Thus this activity gets students' attention and offers an opportunity to discuss domain names.

A similar activity may be done with Wikipedia entries.

Logical Fallacies

Activity #1: Fun with Logical Fallacies

We have discovered that our classrooms are often the first place students hear the term "logical fallacies." The concept of the slippery slope or the straw man might be familiar to them, but the distinction and classification of such practices are new. The classroom discussions and activities about logical fallacies are often reported as the most entertaining and enlightening for the students. If the classroom is wired, we'll often put the students in small groups, assign each group one or two logical fallacies to Google, and then instruct them to make up sentences using the fallacy.

Examples include:

- ad hominem
- bandwagon
- straw man
- faulty causality
- appeals to humor and pity
- slippery slope
- appeal to tradition
- hasty generalization
- red herring

Students are often able to recite commercials line for line that use these fallacies for comedic effect, and can often remember ways that politicians have used them.

An advanced form of this activity is to require the student to identify logical fallacies within *The Simpsons*. They might see Lyle Lanley distracting Lisa from her question by saying it is the most intelligent one he has ever been asked, or they might see Homer engage in faulty causality when he believes taking a home winemaking course made him forget how to drive.

The Simpsons comments on faulty reasoning too. For example, the absence of bears causes Homer to believe that a "bear patrol," which includes a stealth bomber, is keeping bears away. Lisa calls her father's reasoning "specious": "By your logic I could claim that this rock keeps tigers away." Even though Lisa's analogy is apt, Homer fails to see her logical argument and buys her rock as protection against tigers ("Much Apu about Nothing").

Activity #2: Let "Weird Al" Yankovic Be the Rhetoric Teacher

The short story "The Lottery" by Shirley Jackson, as well as the song "Weasel Stomping Day" by "Weird Al" Yankovic are terrific examples of how appeals to tradition are logical fallacies. The video for "Weasel Stomping Day" can usually be viewed from his MySpace page or, of course, YouTube.

Weasel Stomping Day
Faces filled with joy and cheer
What a magical time of year Howdy
Ho! It's Weasel Stomping Day

Put your Viking helmet on
Spread that mayonnaise on the lawn
Don't you know, it's Weasel Stomping Day

All the little girls and boys
Love that wonderful crunching noise
You'll know what this day's about
When you stomp a weasel's guts right out

So, come along and have a laugh
Snap their weasely spines in half
Grab your boots and stomp your cares away
Hip hip hooray, it's Weasel Stomping Day

People up and down the street
Crushing weasels beneath their feet
Why we do it, who can say?
But it's such a festive holiday

So let the stomping fun begin
Bash their weasely skulls right in
It's tradition, that makes it okay

Hey everyone, it's Weasel Stomping
We'll have some fun on Weasel Stomping
Put down your gun, it's Weasel Stomping Day
Hip Hip Hooray, it's Weasel Stomping Day

Weasel Stomping Day
Hey!
(Reprinted with permission. Written by Al Yankovic,
copyright Ear Booker Music.)

Activity #3: Teach the Students
How to Tell a Witch and a Fallacy

Show the witch scene from *Monty Python and the Holy Grail* (available on DVD and at YouTube). You might want to share the transcript (below) for them to review. A discussion of the fallacies can be followed by more general fallacy questions (below).

> FIRST VILLAGER: We have found a witch. May we burn her?
> ALL: A witch! Burn her!
> BEDEVERE: How do you know she is a witch?
> ALL: She looks like one.
> BEDEVERE: Bring her forward.

They bring her forward—a beautiful YOUNG GIRL dressed up as a witch.

> WITCH: I am not a witch. I am not a witch.
> BEDEVERE: But you are dressed as one.
> WITCH: They dressed me up like this.
> ALL: We didn't, we didn't!
> WITCH: And this isn't my nose, it's a false one.

BEDEVERE takes her nose off.

> BEDEVERE: Well?
> FIRST VILLAGER: ... Well, we did do the nose.
> BEDEVERE: The nose?
> FIRST VILLAGER: And the hat. But she is a witch.
> ALL: A witch, a witch, burn her!
> BEDEVERE: Did you dress her up like this?
> FIRST VILLAGER: ... NO ... Um ... Yes ... a bit ... yes ... she has got a wart.
> BEDEVERE: Why do you think she is a witch?
> SECOND VILLAGER: She turned me into a newt.
> BEDEVERE: A newt?
> SECOND VILLAGER *(After looking at himself for some time):* I got better.
> ALL: Burn her anyway!
> BEDEVERE: Quiet! Quiet! There are ways of telling whether she is a witch.

KING ARTHUR and PATSY ride up at this point and watch what follows with interest.

> ALL: There are? Tell us. What are they? Do they hurt?
> BEDEVERE: Tell me: what do you do with witches?
> ALL: Burn them!
> BEDEVERE: And what do you burn, apart from witches?
> FIRST VILLAGER: More witches!

Second villager shushes first villager.

> THIRD VILLAGER: ... Wood.

BEDEVERE: So why do witches burn?
SECOND VILLAGER *(pianissimo)*: ... Because they're made of wood...?
BEDEVERE: Good.

PEASANTS stir uneasily then come round to this conclusion.

BEDEVERE: So how can we tell whether she is made of wood?
FIRST VILLAGER: Build a bridge out of her.
BEDEVERE: Ah ... but can you not also make bridges out of stone?
FIRST VILLAGER: Oh, yeah.
BEDEVERE: Does wood sink in water?
FIRST VILLAGER: No, no. It floats. Throw her in the pond!
BEDEVERE: Wait. What also floats in water?
ALL: Bread? Apples ... very small rocks ... cider ... gravy ... cherries ... mud ... churches ... lead...

ARTHUR: A duck. *They all turn and look at ARTHUR. BEDEVERE looks up, very impressed.*

BEDEVERE: Exactly! So ... logically...
FIRST VILLAGER: *(beginning to pick up the thread):* If she ... weighs the same as a duck ... she's made of wood.
BEDEVERE: And therefore?
ALL: A witch!

WITCH-HUNT FALLACY QUESTIONS

1. What is the primary fallacy in the logical proposition that if a woman weighs the same as a duck, she's made of wood, and therefore a witch?
2. What logical fallacy are the villagers engaging in physically when they dress up the woman as a witch before they present her to the local leader?
3. What is the fallacy in the proposition "She's a witch because she looks like one?"

The scene makes fun of the logic of the European witch-hunts, which ended with approximately 100,000 people executed. Unfortunately for those accused, the logic is not much of an exaggeration. Two common tests were as follows. A person (usually a woman) was thrown into water. If she did not drown, the judges concluded she was using magic to save herself and put her to death. If she drowned, she was innocent, but the judges had done their duty and sent her pure soul to God. In some countries it was believed that witches made pacts with the devil, who left a mark on the witch's body. "Witch prickers" were employed to look for such marks — they would strip a woman, shave her hair off, and prick her with needles. If the witch pricker found a mole, callus, or something that did not bleed when pricked (or did not bleed much), he'd found the mark. Witch prickers knew, though, that devils sometimes took marks off the body to confuse the witch prickers and to cause doubt in the populace, so the absence of a mark was not evidence of innocence.

4. King James wrote *Daemonologie*, a book about the danger of witches. When some of his nobles suggested that there were no such thing as witches, James offered the following two possibilities: Doubters were either deluded by the devil or in league with him. Which logical fallacy is this?

At this point, students might be thinking "Okay, but we're not witch hunters." The next step is to show them that fallacies are all around us and that we have all made them and fallen victim to them — but as critical thinkers, we must do the best we can to not let it happen again. (If you are not a master of your language, it will master you.) Especially important is to be aware of fallacies in political language and advertising, as their job is to persuade us, not to educate us.

Have the students identify the fallacies in the following examples:

1. From *The Simpsons*, when Homer forms a vigilante group and is interviewed by Kent Brockman:

    Kent: Mr. Simpson, how do you respond to the charges that petty vandalism such as graffiti is down eighty percent, while heavy sack beatings are up a shocking nine hundred percent?

    Homer: Aw, people can come up with statistics to prove anything, Kent. Forty percent of all people know that.

2. Say a parent wants to remove a Harry Potter book from the library to "protect the children" and "defend family values." Say I fight this initiative using the same language — after all, I want to protect the children's right to read and defend the values of my family, which are that *I* get to police my child's reading. What logical fallacies are we both engaging in?

3. I propose: Since liver failure is more common among people over forty than under forty and since liver failure is sometimes caused by excess alcohol consumption, we should impose a prohibition on alcohol sales to those over forty.

4. Your friend looked up a professor on RateMyProfessor.com. Two people left negative comments about the class having a "lot of work," so she suggested you should not take it.
5. There is no evidence to suggest that the new wrinkle cream would hurt an infant's skin, so it must be perfectly safe.
6. Jessica Simpson is in an ad for a new adult diaper — even though she does not use the product herself, she's hot, so I believe her.

Audience Analysis

Any lecture or discussion on audience analysis should begin with demographics and how a quick survey of an audience's population can help predict its general disposition towards a topic. However, overgeneralization is a danger, and basic demographics (age, gender, religious affiliation, cultural background, and socioeconomic status) can fill in only part of the analysis: Attitudes, beliefs, and values vary substantially within demographically similar groups. Following are some useful terms and concepts for lecture or discussion:

- power distance
- masculinity and femininity dimension
- uncertainty avoidance
- ethnocentrism
- collectivism/individualism

In the following activities, we generally participate. It is arguable that the teacher is also a peer in that she is a member of the audience.

Activity #1: Demographic Hat

To get value-related ideas flowing, start with a free-write, such as, "What family traditions will you continue should you have children, and why?" or "If you win $500,000 but you have to give it to charity, which would you choose and why?" While they are writing, pass out sticky notes and ask them to jot down the top three things they value in their lives and the top three things they value for their society. (On the board, you might write a simplified definition of "value," such as "an enduring quality that makes life good.") Encourage the students not to overthink, and tell them not to put their names on the sheets. When they have finished, collect them in a hat. Be sure to have another free-write prepared so they keep busy while you are picking up the sheets. Make two columns on the board, one marked "personal" and one marked "societal." Then ask the students how they *think* their classmates answered. Jot their responses under the appropriate columns, then, using the sticky notes, write their actual responses under the columns in a different color. Open the floor for discussion based on the differences and similarities of how they predicted or perceived the values to be versus the actual responses. Also, ask them to look for patterns. End with asking if anything about their peers' values surprises them.

Activity #2: The Characteristics Treasure Hunt

Create and hand out a sheet of characteristics, then set the students loose to fill in the categories with classmates' names. Sometimes this is a race (including a prize), or we might add rules, such as each person can fulfill only one category per sheet, but usually we just let it go freely. This activity is not only great for sampling the demographics, it's also a great ice-breaker for the first week of the term. Some sample characteristics to use on the sheet:

- has traveled to Europe
- parents married to each other
- speaks more than one language fluently
- is the youngest in her family
- grew up in small town
- has tattoo
- already misses his dog
- was home-schooled
- loves to cook
- rides motorcycle
- has met someone famous
- bites his fingernails

Use what you know about your classes to create an interesting characteristic list. For example, for night classes attended by working adults, we might add some geared specifically towards these students, like "has a son" or "owns own home." Karma currently teaches in California, and she might use "Has never seen snow." Denise teaches in Milwaukee, and might include "Has gone sailboating on Lake Michigan" and "Doesn't like the Packers."

In addition, we encourage students to make surveys or questionnaires to gather information before a major assignment, if they so choose. (We generally even allow them a small amount of class time to state their case and distribute questionnaires, or even to administer the survey, if it is brief.) In a short lecture about effective questionnaires, be sure to include the differences and benefits of different types of questions (closed-ended, fixed alternative, and open-ended) and discuss how a smart design of the questionnaire can help with quick results tallying.[15]

Counter-Argument

Students are often reluctant to engage counter-argument in their arguments, although any argument worth making will have valid counter-arguments. There are several ways to help students through this challenge. First, students should be encouraged to identify places where authors engage with counter-arguments in their readings for the class. This can be done as part of a search for warrants or as part of a discussion of audience awareness. If the author does not engage with counter-argument, students may be asked why — after all, if the author did not feel the need to address other sides, assumptions were certainly made.

Second, students can help each other see counter-arguments in draft workshops. (A more time-consuming way to do this is to take up your students' drafts and to point them out yourself, but students need the practice more than you do.) We advise having an in-class activity first to model the search for counter-argument. Karma uses the following as an example: She once received the draft of an education proposal that argued teachers should be on-call to their students 24/7. She wrote a note to the student about engaging with counter-argument. The student added one sentence to the final draft, which began, "Of course, some teachers may be too lazy...." She tells this story to the students and then they work as a class to make a list of other possible counter-arguments on the board.

Third, students may be asked to brainstorm a list of counter-arguments in conjunction with a thesis workshop (or on the day a thesis statement is due). Thinking through possible counter-arguments can aid students in moving further into the drafting phase, as counter-arguments can appear anywhere in the essay. We often teach students that writers can put counter-arguments in basically three positions — they can open with the other side and then spend the rest of the paper refuting; they can bring up logical counter-arguments and refute as they go along; they can end with the possible objections to their argument. The latter choice is often unwise, however, as it can leave the reader with a list of weaknesses, especially if the author is not successful in refutation.

Integrating Quotations/Citing/ Avoiding Plagiarism

Handout #1: Basic Quotation Rules

Feel free to use the following 10 rules, making adjustments as needed for your particular class. This handout also includes sample paragraphs and questions about citation practices.

1. You must cite (give credit to) all sources you use, regardless of the degree to which you use them. If you quote, summarize, paraphrase, or refer to someone else's ideas, you MUST cite them.

2. If you are working in MLA or similar format, you need to cite your sources within the essay (with parenthetical references) and then list your parenthetical references on a Works Cited page. Whatever citation style you are using, make sure you are consistent.

3. You must introduce your source when you first use it. Tell your reader what source you are using. Give the full name of the source, the title of the work, and any additional relevant information about who the writer is.

4. You do not have to cite if something is "common knowledge." Even if you do not know a fact, if every source you consult references it, you can deem it common knowledge.

5. If you do not remember where you learned something, own up to it. For example, you might say, "I can't remember the exact episodes, but "Weird Al" Yankovic has been mentioned on *The Simpsons* at least three times."

6. Online sources and encyclopedias must be cited. (Wikipedia is

the "author" of its entries, as is CNN when a reporter is not listed, the Centers for Disease Control, and the like. Consult your style manual for how to cite corporate authors.)

7. Turning in work to one class that you have turned in to another class is considered academic dishonesty and can be charged as plagiarism.

8. Your sources must be documented in such a way that the reader can clearly see which ideas are yours and which are the source's. Introducing your sources helps this. Do NOT paraphrase too closely to your source. If you use a significant word or phrase, put it in quotation marks.

9. Simply putting an author and page number at the end of a paragraph does not signify which ideas in the paragraph belong to the source.

10. Statistics must be cited. If you cannot find a source for a statistic, suspect it.

Take a look at the following paragraph, from "So Television's Responsible!" by William J. Savage, Jr.:

> One hint Matt Groening and the team of Trey Parker and Matt Stone, the creators of *The Simpsons* and *South Park*, respectively, give that indicates their audience should attempt to read their texts seriously is the satiric ways in which the two shows depict cartoons within their fictive worlds. When novelists or playwrights include novels-within-novels or plays-within-plays in their works, sophisticated readers usually take that as an authorial hint regarding what (or how) to think about their medium.... In the cases of both *The Simpsons* and *South Park*, the cartoons-within-cartoons are clever satires, not just of the media in general but of the content and culture of animation in particular. On *The Simpsons*, *The Itchy & Scratchy Show* mocks the violent and nonsensical generic conventions of cat-and-mouse cartoons such as *Tom and Jerry*, but it also touches on other issues as well [198].

Questions about using the above paragraph:

1. Can you consider the fact that Matt Groening is the creator of *The Simpsons* common knowledge?

2. Is the following paraphrase too close to the source? Savage, in his essay "So Television's Responsible!," argues that having cartoons within cartoons in the fictive world of *The Simpsons* "indicates their audience should attempt to read [the] texts seriously" (198).

3. What happens if you read this source and it gives you the idea to talk about a different cartoon within a cartoon, *The Happy Little Elves*? Do you need to cite Savage?

4. If so, how do you keep your ideas distinct? See the following: Savage goes on to discuss how *The Itchy & Scratchy Show* satirizes shows such as *Tom and Jerry* (198). His ideas could also be applied to *The Happy Little Elves*, however.

Handout #2 Meet Three New Friends: The Paraphrase, [*sic*], and the Ellipsis

In the same or a new handout, supply the students with a paragraph from a nonfiction text. We have supplied a sample, but use anything you find useful and relevant. Allowing them to use a style guide, instruct them to answer the prompts that follow the excerpt. Karma uses the following passage and questions:

The following quote is from Luis Alberto Urrea's book *The Devil's Highway* (New York: Back Bay Books, 2004).[16]

What we take for granted in the United States as being Mexican, to those from Southern Mexico, is almost completely foreign. Rural Mexicans don't have the spare money to drown their food in melted cheese. They don't smother their food in mounds of sour cream. Who would pay for it? They have never seen "nachos." In some regions of the south, they eat soup with bananas; some tribal folks not far from Veracruz eat termite tacos; turkey, when there are turkeys, is not filled with "stuffing"—but with dried pineapples, papaya, pecans. Meat is killed behind the house, or it is bought, dripping and flyblown, off a wooden plank in the village market. They eat cheeks, ears, feet, [page break is here] tails, lips, fried blood, intestines filled with curdled milk. Southerners grew up eating corn tortillas, and they never varied in their diet. You find them eating food the Aztecs once ate. Flour tortillas, burritos, chimichangas—it's foreign food to them, invented on the border [39–40].

Exercises

1. Write a paragraph that uses this quote. You should have your own point to make, so I can check to see if you can keep the ideas straight. Paraphrase at least one sentence and quote at least one fragment or phrase. Assume that this is the first time you have mentioned anything from this text.

2. Pretend Urrea's text had a typo — that it reads "its foreign food to them" — and write a sentence in which you quote this phrase correctly.
3. What if you wanted to quote the first, second, and third sentence, but your editor has a very strict word limit and you cannot use every word, though you want the specific ideas? What are at least two ways you could solve this problem? Write out one of them.

The Thesis Statement

Handout #1: Creating Strong Thesis Statements[17]

WHAT IS A THESIS STATEMENT?

The thesis statement is the most important sentence in your paper — it is the main idea of your paper. As such, it controls the paper by providing a clear, specific focus and helps you discover and define what you really want to say. A strong, well-crafted thesis statement is absolutely necessary for a strong, well-crafted paper. The following points and guidelines will help you create a strong thesis.

WHERE DOES THE THESIS GO?

The thesis is usually in the first paragraph of your essay — remember, the thesis is there to direct your paper and guide your reader — though in some assignments the thesis may come later. It is essential to make this statement early, or at least to give the readers their map early if the paper will lead to the thesis statement.

The thesis statement should be (1) *unified*, (2) *narrowed*, and (3) *clear*. In addition, a good thesis statement will have two parts: a *statement* and a *reason*. That is, it will not just assert that something is so, it will also give a reason why (this "why" will give the readers the direction they need). Your thesis must be *provable* and *defendable*. If there are no arguments against your reason, then there is no reason to write the paper. For example, a thesis stating that child abuse is abominable isn't workable — no one will disagree. However, a thesis arguing about what constitutes child abuse can be quite arguable.

The thesis statement should have one focus. Any more will weaken your argument. Try to avoid connecting two loosely related statements with a coordinating conjunction (and, but, or, for, nor, so, yet) because this leads to an unclear, uncoordinated thesis. If there is a relationship between the two sentences and together they make a strong thesis, a subordinating conjunction (through, although, because, since) will help to signal this.

> Original: *The Simpsons* set the tone for later prime-time cartoons and was largely responsible for introducing the dysfunctional family to America.
>
> Revised Thesis: As it was largely responsible for introducing the dysfunctional family to America, *The Simpsons* set the tone for later prime-time cartoons.

The thesis provides a narrowed or limited focus for your essay. Narrow the field of your discussion to a specific line of reasoning/argumentation within a broad topic area. Your thesis should be limited to what can be accomplished in the specified number of pages. Shape your topic so you can get straight to the meat of it — do not settle for three pages that just skim the surface. The opposite of a focused, narrow, crisp thesis is a broad, sprawling, superficial thesis.

> Original: There are serious objections to the content of *The Simpsons*.
>
> Revised: Though it was critically praised, many parents objected to *The Simpsons* when it premiered due to Bart's behavior.

A clear thesis avoids both vagueness ("interesting," "exciting") and abstractions ("society," "culture"). If necessary, define any terms you are using in an appropriate place in the paper (usually in the introduction or second paragraph) and make sure that any potential confusion in the statement is eliminated.

> Original: Society should not censor *The Simpsons* when there are so many worse shows out there.
>
> Revised: A Venezuelan television channel deemed it appropriate to take *The Simpsons* out of the Saturday morning line-up, yet they replaced it with *Baywatch*— ironically, since neither is meant for children.

A thesis is also analytical. Your thesis needs to do more than merely announce your topic — it should reveal what position you take in relationship to that topic and how you plan to analyze or evaluate the topic. The specificity and originality of your take on the topic should be apparent. Avoid oversimplifying or merely stating facts. Your argument should take into account the complexities of your topic. Virtually every argument has more than two sides.

> Original: In this paper, I will discuss the relationship between *Itchy & Scratchy* and *The Simpsons*.

> Revised: While funny in its own right, *Itchy & Scratchy* critically comments on the nonsensical violence perpetuated in children's cartoons, which stands in stark contrast to the content of *The Simpsons*, a cartoon for adults.

> Original: Don't download television shows from the Internet.

> Revised: If a DVD of your favorite show is available, buying it is both more honest and more supportive of the artists who created it than downloading the show illegally.

A thesis is original and dynamic. Generic or formulaic statements and words are the quickest way to lose the reader. Look for ways to make your thesis specific, active, and concrete. Use your own words and ideas; they are always superior to parroting another's.

> Original: There are advantages and disadvantages to Marge's parenting style.

> Revised: While aspects of Marge's parenting style may be questionable, she is loving and supportive, making her a fine role model overall.

When searching for the theses of published authors, remember that many theses are implied. That is, they are not stated directly. Until you are really comfortable with your writing, you should stick to concrete, direct theses. Of course, not everything you write will have an *arguable thesis*, but you should still have a *main point*.

Although some classes/teachers require or encourage the following, you should generally avoid them in humanities essays (and definitely in this class): (1) a three-point thesis; (2) an underlined thesis; (3) "announcing" what the essay will accomplish.

Handout #2: Thesis Exercises

Rewrite each of the following theses. Each thesis should be unified, clear, narrow, and argumentative. Additionally, each thesis should have two parts (statement and reason). Some of these will take a major rewrite to make them work.

1. I believe that the Reverend Lovejoy is wrong when he won't listen to Marge's argument in support of gay marriage.
2. Dumping waste in the ocean is bad for the environment.
3. Why do people constantly blog about how *The Simpsons* isn't funny anymore?
4. Many people have different opinions on whether *The Simpsons* is respectful of religion.
5. We need to do something about counterfeit *Simpsons* merchandise.

Of course, once you have a thesis, you need to know what to do with it. It is often difficult to confront the blank screen, even armed with a thesis statement. Here is a lesson in mining that thesis statement for the start of your body paragraphs. Let's take the following thesis:

As "Whacking Day" illustrates, some students benefit more from home-schooling than from the public education system; thus, we need to revise aspects of the public education system to imitate the advantages of home-schooling, especially for problem students.

There is a clear statement and reason here, but much of the content of the essay can be determined by questioning our thesis further. Here is a list of questions that would almost *have* to be discussed and or defended within an essay developed from this thesis:

1. How does "Whacking Day" illustrate this argument?
2. What aspects of homeschooling are beneficial?
3. Why doesn't the current public education system provide these advantages? In what ways does it sometimes discourage learning?
4. Which aspects of the current education system should we change?
5. Which aspects of a homeschooling system should we imitate?
6. How are we defining "problem students"?
7. Who is going to make these changes?
8. How will these changes be implemented and paid for?
9. How will we determine if these changes were successful?
10. Why should we be taking educational lessons from a television show?
11. Are all homeschooling situations equally effective? Are all public schools equally ineffective?
12. What are some other reasonable proposals to solve the problem identified?

Take a look at these theses (from the Creating Strong Thesis Statements sheet). What are the questions we would have to answer for this
essay to move forward?

> As it was largely responsible for introducing the dysfunctional family to
> America, *The Simpsons* set the tone for later prime-time cartoons.
> While funny in its own right, *Itchy & Scratchy* critically comments on
> the nonsensical violence perpetuated in children's cartoons, which stands
> in stark contrast to the content of *The Simpsons*, a cartoon for adults.

If you have problems generating questions, try the following general
questions:

1. What are the terms or concepts I will have to define for this to
   make sense to the reader?
2. What is the evidence I can give to back up my point?
3. What background information do I need to give so that my
   reader understands my argument?
4. Am I making any assumptions about what my audience already
   knows or believes?
5. Are there any valid counter-arguments to my argument?

Questioning your thesis helps avoid the common problem of feeling
the need to create a three-point thesis. Often, we believe that we can have
a longer paper with a three-point thesis (leading to the problematic five-
paragraph essay), but this leads to an awkward, forced format. None of
the three points can be developed fully. There is no room for counter-
argument, for defining terms, or for connecting ideas.

Diction

Handout #1: The Middle Path

Instructors see two main problems with "voice." One is when students "write like they talk." Few people should write like they talk. Most
of us do not use complete sentences and tend to say "um" a lot. In college, unless you are writing a paper about spoken language or slang, you
should not employ it. Here are some examples:

> Nowadays students feel put down by their teachers when they do not get
> *A*'s.
> So, I feel we should have more student parking spaces!

Fixing these sentences may result in the opposite problem: pretentious diction. This is when students try to sound like they naturally speak in "clichés, trite fad words, unnecessary jargon, solemn mystical mumbo-jumbo, or parrot-like repetition of polysyllabic pseudo-profundities" (Binky, aka Matt Groening). The students get out their thesaurus (or hit Shift F7)[18] and revise their "voice" to sound like the following:

> In the contemporary society of today's modernism world, receivers of educational expertise can experience the sensation of low self-esteem on occasions that include grading that is not exceptional.
>
> Thus, a decision has been reached: an increase in student vehicular storage is needed forthwith!

This is NOT an improvement. Many of the above words are not even used correctly.

I propose a middle path. Buddha realized that moderation was the key to life, so I feel safe applying that to writing. Even our nation's leaders understand that writing should be clear. When President Johnson was trying to get an understanding of Vietnam, he asked Robert McNamara for a two page memo with "Four-letter words and short sentences, several paragraphs so I can read it and study it and commit it to memory." In 1998, the Clinton administration encouraged clarity by holding a monthly award (the "Magyars Gallopavo Garrulitas Terminatrix Encomium," or Gobbledygook Elimination Prize) for the employee who found the best example of bad writing.

Remember that there is a middle ground between the Cookie Monster's "Me Want Cookies" and an idiot's "Currently, a desire exists for baked delicacies with minuscule derivations of cacao."

Also, remember that bureaucrat-ese does not make it onto bumper stickers. People remember clear things. Martin Luther King, Jr., had a dream, not a "recurring nocturnal vision for the duration of standard R.E.M. state."

What is the middle path for the two arguments above?

Handout #2: Avoiding Pretension

Some people still insist that long sentences full of big words are impressive. These people are not paying attention to the ideas.

To these people, I say: The usage of verbose verbalization, conceivably due to the actuality of innate loquaciousness and multifarious concerns à propos a deficiency of security pertaining to the individual's own mental acuity, results in the consequence of the opposite of ingratiating the individual with those who possess actual aforementioned acuity of the mind.

I can talk like this. Aren't you glad I don't?

Look at the following — both are pretentious rewrites of common proverbs. What are the proverbs?

> In order to facilitate the lack of professional contact with a trained medical physician, it would behoove the individual to consume no less than one proverbial Edenic fruit (excluding the stemic appendage and internal reproductive systems, as a matter of course) per terran revolution.
>
> When one facilitates the process of the nocturnal regeneration in an apparatus designated for its use and/or function (in a timely manner), as well as the termination of said facilitative process (similarly in a timely manner) the procedure creates for one a healthful biological effect, increased financial and fiscal ability, and a heightened perception of the self and surroundings as pertaining to culture, society, or self.[19]

Would you remember these proverbs if they were always stated as above?

Try your hand at this. Choose a proverb or well-known quote and ruin it.

Choosing a Topic

Handout #1: The Unexpected Topic

You've already heard the advice — choose a topic that matters to you. You've also been told to be original. It is one thing to say it, one thing to hear it; it's very hard to do it, especially in a rushed quarter. You barely have time to write, right? How are you supposed to have time to come up with a good topic?

Unfortunately, I do not have a good answer to that. However, here are some tips.

1. When you get a paper prompt, read it and tell your brain to start thinking about it. It will. It will come up with ideas for you. When you are in other classes, watching TV, or reading, it will be making connections between your prompt and the other parts of your life.

2. Make a list of the first few ideas that come to mind when thinking about your topic. Note that these are probably the first ideas that are coming into everyone's mind. Get them out of the way and think about how to approach the topic from another angle. For example, if you're asked to talk about politics, the first thing that might come to mind is to talk about which candidate you'd vote for or to choose a current debate (stem cell research or universal health care) and then say whether you're for or against it. This is not going to be all that original, though it may be useful as it may force you to define and/or change your position. Aren't there other things you could talk about, though? What about an essay on your dream candidate, outlining what she or he would stand for? Perhaps, instead of saying you are for or against stem-cell research, you might argue that it should not even be a campaign issue. You might write a paper about an issue YOU care about and try to explain why the candidates are not discussing it (for me: the elimination of the Electoral College; comprehensive sex education; paying ALL our UN dues).

3. Think about new ways of looking at the prompt and run them by your professor. For example, one teacher I had gave us a list of the main characters in a novel and said, "Pick one and write an essay about him/her." The character I wanted to write about was not on the list. Therefore, I asked him if I could write an essay arguing that she should be considered a main character. Most teachers are thrilled by these questions because it means they will get an essay that you are invested in and they might get to read something new for a change. Of course, do not go outside the limits/expectations of the essay prompt without talking to your teacher first.

Proofreading Rant

(The following is Karma's handout/rant. Feel free to use all or parts of it, as the ideas and messages are useful to get students thinking about proofreading and showing pride in any work that has their name attached.)

Before I start, let me give you an example of a common problem. I once had a student write the following after reading an article about the importance of proofreading: "I personally don't really need this chapter usually I am pretty good about being able to sit down and write a articulate piece of work." Yes. Sure you are.

My frustration stems from the fact that my students don't seem to think I should be grading them on their ability to write at the college level. Instead, they turn in work with mistakes my high school child would spot. Some of these mistakes are from ignorance; some are from a failure to proofread. Either way, if they aren't acceptable in the pre-college essays my son writes, they aren't acceptable in college. I'm not sure why so many college students seem content to write at an elementary school level. Unfortunately, too many students believe that if their reader is able to work out what it is they were trying to say, even if they have not said it correctly (or even managed to say the opposite), they shouldn't be held accountable for their writing. This is bullplop. We don't consider someone a competent musician when she hits the wrong notes, even if we can still tell what the song was supposed to be. (To any objectors who say the analogy doesn't hold true because they, as business majors, aren't pretending to be writers, I say: Yes, but you are supposed to be competent in the language in which you work.)

I should also note that I was once accosted at my son's school by the father of another boy. This father was a scientist and wanted to know why the applicants fresh out of college couldn't write well (or at all). This was an accusation. I told him that students simply didn't believe me when I told them that most companies in any industry would rather hire a person who could communicate well than a brilliant and experienced person who can't. What some students don't get is that people can't see your brilliance or benefit from your experience when you can't communicate through writing. They also won't take you seriously.

The fact is, you are judged by other people every single day in several ways. Some people judge on shoes (these people tend not to respect me); others judge on beauty or race or hair length. Everyone, on some level, judges you on how well you express yourself. You wouldn't trust a brain surgeon who said, "Well, what we'se gonna do is cut that open and I'll see if I can't gets those neutrons a-firing." As much as you may say we shouldn't judge others (after all, he could be a brilliant brain surgeon), we *do* judge people this way. It's likely that the only people who don't care about your grammar are other people who make the exact same mistake.

If that person knows even one more comma rule than you do and they're in a position to judge you based on your writing, they will view you (fairly or not) as lesser. If you don't mind that, you can stop reading. If you want to be judged for the smart and wonderful person you are, accept the fact that you will have to express yourself in writing to other people for the rest of your life. And then read on.

I sent out an email (1 February 2005), asking friends and family all over the world for examples of how important it is to proofread your work. Here is a sampling of the responses (quotes are in italics).

Getting Out of College

One of my sisters was getting a Ph.D. in chemistry and was told that if she didn't learn to write better, her dissertation director (also a chemist naturally) would not approve her dissertation. She quickly learned to care about the "niceties" of prose.

Getting a Job

Most people had something to say about resumes and cover letters. Everyone who responded said that if an applicant had an error (just one, mind you) on the cover letter or resume, that candidate's application would go into the "circular file." Education, experience, letter of reference from the pope — none of these mattered when there was even one error on a page (apparently, this includes hourly-wage jobs at places like Starbucks). This holds true for getting into graduate-level education as well. There are two reasons that people care. First, basic literacy is considered important. Additionally, even if you actually want a job where you'll never have to read or write (I don't know of any), people want to know that you care enough about the job you're applying for to proofread. It's attention to detail. One teacher had an ex-student come by for help with his cover letter: *My ex-student wished that he could tell all students how important English class really is. His big goal when he was taking English was simply to get through it* ("Thanks," I said), *but now he wishes he had paid more attention.* You should also know that *some firms have their interviewees take a spelling/punctuation test. A company vice president wrote, (Need I even mention that career-minded and Internet-savvy applicants should really consider creating a basic email address rather than listing toohot4u@yahoo.com on a resume).*

Keeping a Job/Keeping Your Credibility

Another of my sisters was working as a writer/editor for an engineering firm and went to the lead engineer/owner of the company to tell him that she was having trouble editing some of the material. She assumed that what made no sense to her probably made sense to someone who knew more engineering than she did. But the lead engineer told her that the problem was not with her (lack of) engineering knowledge; it was with the field engineers' inability to write. He went on to rail against the young engineers' poor writing skills and told her, as he had apparently told them, that if they didn't learn how to write better they would soon be out of a job.

I have two little stories (very short) that illustrate the importance of editing. One is a spelling error, one is a factual error that I let slip while editor-in-chief for my college newspaper (by the way, I would discuss slips in spelling and grammar as of the same species of problem as slips in fact: they both indicate to the reader that you wrote in haste — give the intelligent reader a good reason to dispense with what you've written). My first story: I misspelled the banner headline (about a play called "Murder in the First"). The headline looked like this: "Thespian Homocide Hits the Big Stage" (or something like this). The point is "homocide" is a particularly bad misspelling of "homicide." In another mistake, I wrote up an ad commemorating the "birthday" of the Marine Corps with the incorrect date ... oops. People get touchy over things like this. Again, to my readers even small mistakes of this kind undermined my credibility (and why shouldn't they have? The same kind of editor who can't spare the time for a dictionary, can't spare the time to double-check a reporter's facts, right?).

If you aren't persuaded by the following example, you must hate America.

As a sergeant in the United States Army, I would be seriously limited if I could not write my ideas clearly. I could be a dumb private and be as illiterate as they come (although my leaders would most likely have me doing physical labor instead of tasks that require basic literacy and intelligence), but as a sergeant, I need to know how to put my thoughts into words. I work in supply and periodically have to write reports of survey to account for lost or damaged property. It takes basic writing skills to be able to express what happened in each particular situation. Some situations are more complicated than others and if my report isn't totally clear, it gets rejected by my higher command and I have to write another one. Commanders also get very irritated if there are any typos or glaring grammatical errors. I also often write memoranda on behalf of my commander and it behooves me to get it right the first time with proper grammar and spelling. I have many important tasks to accomplish in my workday and I don't have time for drafting and rewriting reports and memos. I also don't need any cocky captain ripping me a new one because I can't spell things right the first time.

For the Monetary-Minded: Saving Money and Lives

Scientists have to write to get grants, and have to get grants to have any kind of career (including college teaching). Bad grant-writers don't get grants.

My current employer sent out a proposal for work to a company that already told us they would give us the work, just to send them a proposal. He misspelled the name of the programming language we would be using for the project. The company reasoned that if we couldn't spell the name of the language correctly, then we didn't need to be doing the work. We lost a $6,000 deal over it.

Miscellaneous (Sex and Housing)

My middle-aging friends and I have had hysterical fits of laughter over the bad writing in online personal ads. It is not fair to think that these writers might be stupid, especially when English might not be their first language. But with a lack of any other kind of information about a person, that's what comes across—that the writer is an idiot. Good writers, on the other hand, meet lots of people online, whether for dating or for more mundane purposes.

One friend was online, chatting with his girlfriend, when she *expressed concern that she was gaining weight. As a good, sensitive boyfriend, I attempted to relieve the matter with some comforting comedy, responding with the statement, "Well I haven't noticed a double chin." While writing the statement, "I haven't noticed a double chin," I had mistakenly left the n't off the word have—leaving simply the statement, "I HAVE noticed a double chin." My quickness to type and my careless dismissal of detail resulted in two weeks of groveling, the purchase of three dozen roses, and my physical love life becoming a solitary event for a painfully long time.*

In California, if you want to buy a house, you have to write a statement *about why you are the ideal buyer, effectively selling yourself to the seller. I got my house for cheaper than the highest bid, because my letter was well written and the seller liked it the best.*

So Basically...

Many of the people who responded mentioned McDonald's (in reference to where you must want to be if you never want to get better at self-expression). A sample: *Writing isn't a self-serving enterprise. In the "real world," it's about communicating solutions to problems. Of course, then, if your students prefer to work at McD's for the rest of their careers, that's fine, too. Just tell them not to expect any promotion from the salad station into management— because managers have to write performance reports for employees, and those reports are also being read by their bosses.*

Remember that sometimes a comma isn't just a comma. Sometimes a comma is a lot of money (when there are lawyers around, that is). *In legalese, a last will and testament could read: "I hereby bequeath my entire estate to John, Dick, and Harry." or "I hereby bequeath my entire estate to John, Dick and Harry." In the first sentence, John, Dick, and Harry each get one third of the estate. In the second sentence, John gets half of the estate, and Dick and Harry each get one fourth.* Small dots make a big difference, too: *What really concerns us is, if this isn't caught early, what happens to nurses who give 1 mg of some medicine instead of .1 mg? If the medicine is strong enough, might that be enough to kill the patient?*

Don't forget that it's possible to make mistakes even if your grammar is perfect. I once stopped a boss from signing a contract that misstated the number of shares involved in a corporation going public. *I* think there's a big difference between 60,000 and 600,000, even if that difference is only one zero on a piece of paper.

If you want to improve, here's how you do it:

- Read more. That's how most of your teachers learned grammar; it works better than a dry grammar book.
- When you proofread your own work, read it out loud, slowly. Your tongue will catch things your eyes may miss.
- Use spell and grammar checks, but don't trust them. Some examples of interesting "corrections": *My roommate was writing*

a history paper and attempted to reference Pontius Pilate. Unfortunately, what her spell checker wound up with was: Panties Pilot. In one essay, a student attempted to say high school was monotonous, but the spell checker informed me that high school English was more "monogamous" than college English. While this is probably true, it wasn't what she meant to say. The student who confused me the most was one who somehow ended up with the verb "rape" when he meant "wrap."

- Use your dictionaries, your friends, and the handbooks we make you buy. Use the tutors you've already paid for with your tuition. Have them actually teach you to correct your mistakes rather than asking them to fix your essay for you. Finally, if your teachers make any mark on your paper that you don't understand, ask them what it means. It's their job to tell you.

My final word: You may be thinking to yourself, *I'll proofread when something's important, but I don't need to proofread everything.* Fine. But most of you have expressed interest in getting an *A* in my class. You won't even be able to *pass* if you can't write at the college level, so you might want to start proofreading your work for me. And in my experience, you need to get into the habit of proofreading early so that it comes naturally. Otherwise, you end up sending out resumes with mistakes. And your potential boss isn't thinking, *I'm sure they'll pay attention to detail once I give them this job, even if they don't care about it now.*

Draft Workshop Form

(This is an example of the kinds of prompts we supply our students for in-class workshops.)

Answer these questions as thoroughly as possible on a separate sheet of paper. You may answer in list form or letter form. Please address all of the questions. The quality of your responses makes up a large portion of your participation grade.

1. What are the strengths of this paper?
2. Does this paper sufficiently address the topic?
3. What is the focus of this paper? Is the thesis sufficiently narrowed? Is it an arguable, original, defendable thesis?
4. Is this argument convincing? How might the author alter the

paper to be more convincing? Does the writer have specific examples from the text to back up each claim?

5. Does the writer defend assumptions? Does the writer engage in counter-argument? Does the writer define terms when necessary?

6. Where might the writer want to add more detail or explanation?

7. Is this paper organized well? What could be changed to improve logic or flow?

8. If there is summary, does this paper merely summarize other texts? Where can some of the summary be cut down? Does the author summarize in present tense?

9. Does the author integrate quotations smoothly, explaining how the quotes should be used in the argument?

10. Is there anything about the writer's argument that you don't understand? Does he/she need to clarify any points for you?

11. Check out the introduction and conclusion. Are they functional? Are they good?

12. Is there a title? Is it a good one?

13. Is this paper formatted correctly (does it follow MLA format and academic conventions)? Is there a Works Cited page in MLA format?

14. Is the tone appropriate and consistent?

15. How would you rate this essay in terms of style? Take another look at the essay. Are all of the words accurate, connotative, and necessary? Identify ten words that can be cut. (The easiest way to do this is to look for passive voice—often signaled by "by" or a version of the "to be" verb [am, is, was, were, etc.].)

16. Do there seem to be recurring grammar problems? Be specific—you might want to make notes on the actual paper.

Chapter 3

A Noble Spirit Embiggens the Smallest Man, or *The Simpsons* and Linguistics

English? Who needs that? I'm never going to England. — Homer
Simpson

Linguistics is a complicated but fascinating field of study. With so many definitions and concepts to understand and memorize, it is dreaded by English and anthropology majors and considered the "math" of their fields. But as with many disciplines, the concepts and theories of linguistics can feel less intimidating when approached through a familiar medium, such as *The Simpsons*. There are many subfields of linguistics, including phonology, morphology, language acquisition, psycholinguistics, neurolinguistics, historical linguistics, semantics, syntax, grammar, sociolinguistics, and evolutionary linguistics (and some of these subfields have sub-subfields).

Like many of the principles discussed already in this book, *The Simpsons* has introduced a number of linguistic lessons to a generation of unsuspecting students. Beyond the popularity of its catchphrases ("d'oh"; "mmmm ... donuts" [or "unexplained bacon" or any number of things]; "don't have a cow, man"; "eat my shorts"), the show has had an additional robust impact on its viewers. Intentionally or not, the show regularly presents myriad issues related to linguistics. Thus, consciously or not, viewers engage in sometimes heated discussions of linguistic issues prompted by storylines (or even throwaway lines) in *The Simpsons*. The following sections are intended to demonstrate how *The Simpsons* engages its audience in learning about and discussing linguistics, including some of the subfields mentioned above, including phonology, morphology, language acquisition, semantics, syntax, and grammar.

Phonology

One of the first concepts a student of linguistics must understand is phonology. Phonology refers to the use of sound to create language, and phones (or "segments") are specific speech sounds. Each phone found in language is represented by a symbol, and all symbols are found in the International Phonetic Alphabet.[1] When a word is spelled phonetically, brackets are put around the transcription. For example, [lif] is the transcription for the English word "leaf."

There are two main areas of phonetics study, articulatory phonetics and acoustic phonetics. Acoustic phonetics refers to the study and analysis of the sound waves produced when we speak. Articulatory phonetics refers to the physiological mechanisms that produce different sounds — how all parts of the mouth and air work together to create a segment of speech. Sounds of language fall into three main classes: vowels, consonants, and glides. Most vowel sounds form a syllable or the nucleus of a syllable, whereas consonants are nonsyllabic sounds. Glides (or "semivowels") have characteristics of both vowels and consonants; their sounds move quickly to the next articulation, as in the beginning of the word "yellow," or they end quickly, as in the ending of the word "cow."

There are numerous places of articulation (dental, alveolar, and palatal, to name a few) and manners of articulation (stops, fricatives, and affricates) — far too many to get into here. For our purposes, we will simply consider one of our favorite catchphrases of Homer's, [m], which is a nasal, voiced, bilabial phone.

Any student of English as a second language can attest to the English language's reputation of being difficult to spell and pronounce. Because language is fluid and because English has been influenced by many other languages, its letter combinations are not necessarily pronounced the same way in every word. This complexity of English becomes a throwaway joke in the episode "Apocalypse Cow," in which Homer believes he is entering a "laughterhouse" because the *S* in slaughterhouse is covered. Linguist Susan Wolfe explains the conditions that make these differences possible: "In Old English, the 'h' in 'laughter' designated a velar fricative (like that found in the [Hebrew] pronunciation of '*Ch*anukah' or the German 'ach'). In some words that evolved into a labiodental and in others it disappeared."

Grammar

The word "grammar" refers to the logical and structural rules (or the study of such rules) that govern the sentences in a language. The word "grammarian" is a loose term for a person whose specialty is grammar. It is possible to consider oneself a grammarian without formal training, however. It simply requires dedication to learning and adhering to the rules.

The Simpsons plays with grammar and the English language frequently and often playfully, as in "Lemon of Troy" when Milhouse announces that they've "squozen" their whole supply of lemons at his lemonade stand. "Squeeze" does, after all rhyme with "freeze." In the episode "Trilogy of Error," Lisa makes a grammar robot named Linguo for a science fair. Lisa's feelings about grammar are exposed when she describes Linguo's purpose: "If you misuse language, he'll correct you." Interestingly, she uses the word "language," not "words." Linguo eventually corrects Lisa's incorrect use of "lay" when she should say "lie," which she accepts gracefully enough, but when he criticizes her use of a sentence fragment, her patience has worn thin, and she exclaims, "'Sentence fragment' is also a sentence fragment!"

Linguo never makes it to the science fair because he meets his demise when he has a back alley run-in with some of Fat Tony's goons, whose conversation causes a "bad grammar overload." Linguo has not been programmed to comprehend stereotypical Italian-American (Mafia) speech, unlike most members of the audience, who are familiar with mafia movies and television, thanks to American pop culture's interest in that subculture.

Each of the residents of Springfield has a speaking style; some speak with excellent grammar (such as Lisa, Apu, and Sideshow Bob), and others, such as Cletus and Brandine, do not. The division is not always social or economic; oftentimes, the attention paid to grammar is shown as a personal choice. The characterization of Moe suggests that he knows he's speaking poorly, but he simply can't be bothered to care. One of his oft-quoted lines is in "Lisa the Skeptic." In an archaeological dig, Lisa has found a skeleton that resembles a human, but with wings. The townspeople are convinced the bones are that of an angel, but Lisa expresses skepticism. Moe responds with the demand: "If you're so sure what it ain't, how 'bout telling us what it am!" The blatant use of "ain't" aside, it's as if Moe feels that using some form of the verb "to be" is sufficient.

In the episode "Much Apu about Nothing," Mayor Quimby has scapegoated immigrants as the blame for a recent tax hike, prompting a ballot referendum to boot all illegal immigrants out of Springfield. Apu Nahasapeemapetilan, an immigrant from India who runs the Kwik-E-Mart, is affected. His English is impeccable, in contrast to the poor English of Moe and Homer:

> **Moe:** You know what really aggravazes me? It's them immigants. They wants all the benefits of living in Springfield, but they ain't even bother to learn themselves the language.
> **Homer:** Hey, those are exactly my sentimonies.

Beyond the clear social and political issues raised by this exchange, it raises an opportunity for linguistic discussions. While Homer is not known for his impeccable grammar and language usage, this exchange in which Homer uses a fake word shows how grammar misuse can be contagious.

Linguistics, in general, is not about judging grammar and usage, but rather about *recording* usage. Still, if an argument about whether or not someone deserves to live in Springfield (or the United States, for that matter) is based on their use of the English language, what does that say about citizens who misuse the language?

Words

Morphology

The term "morphology" refers to the makeup of words; a morpheme is defined as the smallest meaningful unit of language. Affixes (prefixes and suffixes) can thus be defined as morphemes, discussed poetically by Homer upon visiting the Knowledgeum, the new science museum in Springfield, in "This Little Wiggy": "Good things don't end with -eum, they end with -mania or -teria." In this case, "eum" is a bound morpheme, which means that it is not a word by itself. "Mania" is a free morpheme, as it can be used by itself or attached to another morpheme. Homer's lament shows that he comprehends the concept of the morpheme, those tiny parts of words that contribute so much to the joy (or non-joy) in inference. A word is considered the smallest free form in language. Free forms can exist in isolation and in multiple places in a sentence. In the sentence "Homer loves pork chops," the word "chops" appears at the end. It could also appear towards the beginning, such as "Pork chops are Homer's favorite." The word "chops" could appear on its own, as in the answer to the question "What is Homer's favorite cut of pork?" This allows the word "chops" to be a free form. If the "s" is removed from "chops," "chop" remains a free form (or word), but the "s" is not. In the sentence "Homer's eating pork chops," if the "'s" is removed from "Homer's," it cannot stand alone either, as words with an apostrophe (as a contraction connecting a subject with a verb) are made up of two parts, the host (Homer) and the clitic ('s).

The words that make up a speaker's mental dictionary are called the lexicon. Much humor occurs in *The Simpsons* when speakers use words that are unexpected (words that the audience wouldn't expect the character to know or a word that isn't commonly used by that character). For example, in the episode "Homer vs. Patty and Selma," Marge asks Homer if they are "in some sort of fiduciary trouble."

In "'Tis the Fifteenth Season," Nelson taunts Ned with his traditional "Ha-*ha*!" but then continues on in an unexpected manner: "Your position has been usurped. Usurped! You heard me."

This type of surprising lexicon humor is the basis for many of the jokes in "Bart's Friend Falls in Love." It is foreshadowed when Milhouse shows Bart his Magic 8 Ball, to which Bart responds, "Cool! An oversized novelty billiard ball." In the secondary story of the episode, Lisa decides to help Homer lose weight by ordering subliminal tapes for him to listen to in his sleep. The company sends them a vocabulary-builder instead; thus, in his waking hours, Homer has the same appetite but his vocabulary has grown. Humor is added by the fact that he seems unaware that his lexicon has expanded. When Marge asks if his appetite has decreased, Homer answers, "Ah, lamentably, no. My gastronomic rapacity knows no satiety." Later, Marge remarks that he ate three desserts, to which Homer replies, "Forbearance is the watchword. That triumvirate of Twinkies merely overwhelmed my resolve."

Neology

WORD MANUFACTURE (COINING)

Neologism is the act of creating or coining of new words (the term can also refer to the newly coined word itself), and we have *The Simpsons* to thank for many neologisms. "Woo hoo" and "d'oh," for example, were coined by *The Simpsons* through Homer. "D'oh" is used often on cable news networks in headlines. Homer's mispronunciation of "Jesus" as "Jebus" has caught on with fans. In several episodes, the word "meh" is used (to mean so-so), and its popularity has since taken off. In fact, the word is now included in some dictionaries (including Dictionary.com) with *The Simpsons* cited as the source.

Notably, the writers of the episode "Lisa the Iconoclast" also created the words "embiggen" and "cromulent." In the following scene, two teachers are chatting at the back of a classroom during a film about the town's founder, Jebediah Springfield:

> **Jebediah Springfield** [*on film*]: A noble spirit embiggens the smallest man.
> **Edna Krabappel:** "Embiggens"? I never heard that word before I moved to Springfield.
> **Miss Hoover:** I don't know why. It's a perfectly cromulent word.

Although "cromulent" and "embiggen" are not yet included in any standard dictionary, they are everywhere, frequently used by fans and nonfans alike. Many pop culture and encyclopedia sites, including Aintitcool.com and Flickr, invite users to click small images in order to "embiggen" them, and Tech Digest used it in a headline in May 2009: "Embiggen Your iPod to 240GB and 42,000 Tracks." A bookstore and art gallery called Embiggen Books is located in Queensland, Australia. The website for the Cromulent Shakespeare Company of Minneapolis, Minnesota, announces the company's goal to "embiggen the Bard."

The word "d'oh" was recently added to the *Oxford English Dictionary* (OED) with the Dan Castellaneta–coined definition. (The scripts merely read "annoyed grunt," and it was Castellaneta, the voice of Homer, who interpreted it as "d'oh"). In the episode "The Itchy & Scratchy & Poochie Show," Comic Book Guy states "Worst. Episode. Ever," carefully articulating with pauses between each word. This construction of this phrase has become part of American slang, with "worst" sometimes replaced with "best" and "episode" replaced with any number of words. One neologism, "learning juice" (Homer's pet name for beer in "See Homer Run"), hasn't quite caught on yet.

Clips, Blends, and Acronyms

Just about every episode of *The Simpsons* features examples of clips and blends. Clipping is the process by which new words are created by dropping one or more syllables. This commonly occurs in names ("Marge" from "Margery," for example). Many clipped words are so common that many speakers are not aware of the original, longer word (our students usually do not know the longer form of sitcom, for example). The humor on *The Simpsons* does not usually occur with the use of clipped words, but rather with Mr. Burns, who insists upon using older, longer versions, such as "telephone machine" (from "Homer the Smithers") and others that are probably pseudo-archaic, such as "bumbled bee" ("Goo Goo Gai Pan") and "dungeonarium" ("Mommie Beerest").

A blend is a word created by combining two words to make one. The blend "brunch" is described in "Life on the Fast Lane," but many new blends have been created by *The Simpsons*, including "craptacular" (from "Miracle on Evergreen Terrace"), which was used in *The Wall Street Journal* by journalist David Gaffen in September 2008.[2]

Some others haven't exactly caught on to regular usage yet, but we are on the lookout for them. In the 1999 episode "E-I-E-I (annoyed grunt)," Homer grows a hybrid plant he fittingly names "tomacco." In actuality, crossbreeds of the two plants (tomato and tobacco) have occurred several times, most recently in 2003 by a fan named Rob Baur, who was inspired to do so by the episode. Perhaps the term will live on in botany circles. Some other *Simpsons*-created blends that we think have a future in American English are "Euroific" ("Bart Carny") and "traumedies," Dr. Hibbert's word for comedy traumas ("Faith Off"). Chief Wiggum expects to be shot just days before retirement, saying that in the business it's called "retirony" ("Homer vs. Dignity").

An acronym is a word created by the first letters in a phrase or title pronounced together as a word. Acronyms are not the same as abbreviations, in which the letters are pronounced individually, such as NYC.[3] Most acronyms maintain their capital letter status, such as COBRA (Consolidated Omnibus Budget Reconciliation Act) or AIDS, but some acronyms have become so common in usage that the word is no longer written in upper case (examples include radar and laser).

In the episode "Marge vs. Singles, Seniors, Childless Couples, and Teens and Gays," a new organization called SSCCATAGAPP (Singles, Seniors, Childless Couples, and Teens and Gays against Parasitic Parents, pronounced as an acronym) is revealed in Springfield, to which Old Jewish Man comments "Catchy name." His comment is ironic, of course, since it is long and awkward. Marge responds to this group's agenda by creating an organization of her own, PPASSCCATAG (Proud Parents against Singles, Seniors, Childless Couples and Teens and Gays, also pronounced as an acronym, and equally long and awkward).

Close viewing of *The Simpsons* is rewarded by subtle jokes found in the background (King Toot's music store appears frequently, as it's right next to Moe's Tavern, but our favorite is Teenage Pasteland), but in the situation of Springfield Heights Institute of Technology, the reward lies in discovering the acronym of the school's name ("Much Apu about Nothing").

Semantics

The term "semantics" in the realm of linguistics simply refers to the study of meaning. The meanings of words change over time. This is called semantic change, and can be positive, negative, or neutral. Amelioration is the semantic change of a word to a more approved or more respectable meaning; pejoration is the semantic change in a word to a lower, less approved, or less respectable meaning. The word "dork" is an example of amelioration, as it used to be a vulgar term for penis, but it now mainly refers to a nerdy or geeky person.[4]

"Suck" and "blow," which traditionally have had opposite (but both neutral) meanings, both have become pejorative in their slang usage, and interestingly have adopted the same meaning. Bart displays this in the episode "Marge Simpson in Screaming Yellow Honkers" when he remarks about the faculty talent show: "I didn't think it was physically possible, but this both sucks and blows." Also in the same episode, Bart tells Marge, "You the man, Mom!" which also displays a semantic change in the word "man."

Connotation and Denotation

The term "denotation" refers to the explicit or direct meaning of a word, whereas "connotation" refers to the associated or indirect meaning of a word. Writers and speakers continuously, often not consciously, select specific words to convey the correct mood and meaning to suit their purposes and goals. In writing, word choice is the biggest element of style, and in *The Simpsons*, even more is at play: humor and satire. For example, in "Papa's Got a Brand New Badge," the townspeople loot the town during a blackout, and when the police arrive, Marge states, "Finally, some oppression."

A colorful extended example of connotation and denotation used on *The Simpsons* is their word choices regarding having sex. In "One Fish, Two Fish, Blowfish, Blue Fish," Homer is told he may die from improperly prepared sushi, so he creates a bucket list. One of the items on the list is to be "intamit with Marge." His choice to use this Marge-approved term on his list is perfect: it accurately depicts his stupidity (through the misspelling) while simultaneously demonstrating the tenderness he feels for Marge as he faces his own mortality.

Marge frequently refers to "snuggling" with Homer, which serves the show well. Marge's personality is well suited for euphemisms, and she frequently seems scandalized and even shocked at language,[5] as seen in "The Last Temptation of Krust" when Marge does a spit-take when Janeane Garofalo remarks in her standup routine that she got her period. In "Two Dozen and One Greyhounds," when Bart refers to Santa's Little Helper's new girlfriend as his "bitch," Marge is convinced that "bitch" couldn't possibly be the right word. Of course, Bart's correct use of the word "bitch" is a clever joke and rife with connotative discussion potential. In addition to demonstrating Marge's propensity for pussyfooting, the euphemism is one of the ways that *The Simpsons* is able to work on several levels, with jokes that appeal to adults without being overly crass.

Of course, occasionally particularly surprising and funny dialogue is included, such as this, another example of sexual terminology. In the episode "Mother Simpson," Abe Simpson sees his fugitive wife for the first time in decades:

> **Mona:** Oh, Abe, you've aged terribly.
> **Abe:** What do you expect? You left me to raise the boy on my own!
> **Mona:** I had to leave! But you didn't have to tell Homer I was dead.
> **Abe:** It was either that or tell him his mother was a wanted criminal! You were a rotten wife and I'll never, ever, forgive you! [Pause] Can we have sex? Please?

Clearly in this situation, Abe would not be inclined to use a romantic term, such as "make love," but he also is a resolute old man, and isn't likely to use slang terms more suited to younger people, such as "do it."

Wordplay

It would be impossible to include all the wordplay in *Simpsons* episodes. Like Shakespeare, *Simpsons* episodes use many varieties of word-play, including some of the Bard's favorites, such as puns and mala-propisms, for humorous effect.

Chief Wiggum is the source for many of the language-oriented jokes, including spoonerisms (slips of the tongue in which words or word por-tions are scrambled). Examples include Wiggum yelling "Scum, freeze-bag!" ("Moe Baby Blues"). Not surprisingly, Homer provides our favorite spoonerism when he states, "I hope I didn't brain my damage" in "*El Viaje Misterioso de Nuestro Jomer.*"

Malapropisms appear frequently, sometimes to show the ignorance of the speaker, and other times to show Freudian slips on the part of the speaker. Examples of the former include Homer complaining that someone is "borgnining" his sandwich ("I'm Spelling As Fast as I Can") or when he announces that he shares the town's "xylophobia" (meaning xenophobia), and as a result, both Ogdenvillians and xylophones are banned from Springfield ("Coming to Homerica"). An example of the lat-ter also features Homer (alone in the elevator with Mindy, a woman he's attracted to) when he says he'll "just push the button for the stimulator" instead of elevator ("Last Temptation of Homer"). Of course, in the case of Homer, it is arguable that he is simply too lazy to be concerned with the correct word. In "Barting Over," when Tony Hawk uses skateboard-ing terms that Homer doesn't know, he confides that he makes up words too.

The episode "Eight Misbehavin'" features an exchange between Homer and Apu, in which Homer uses popular expressions in triads to a ridiculous degree:

> **Homer:** Whoa, too much information! Thanks for the mental picture! Why don't you tell me what you really think?
> **Apu:** Stop spouting those hackneyed quips.
> **Homer:** Could you be any more — hello? Ew, thanks for sharing! More than I wanted to know!

Double meanings create an extended joke in the episode "Hello Gut-ter, Hello Fadder." Homer is on the brink of bowling a perfect game, but Lenny's ill-timed and hilariously phrased interruptions should cause Homer to choke. Luckily, they don't:

> **Lenny:** Miss! Miss! Sorry, I was calling the waitress. Ah, this split you sold me is making me choke!
> **Homer:** Lenny!
> **Lenny:** What? I paid $7.10 for this split!
> **Carl:** Will you at least call it a banana split, you dumbwad?
> **Lenny:** Spare me your guttermouth!

As a charming addition to the bowling-themed double meanings, later in the same episode, Kent Brockman calls Homer a "local pinhead."

Of course, writers of *The Simpsons* are not above toilet humor, but at least in the following exchange from "Last Exit to Springfield," the main reason it is funny is because Burns, of course, has no idea of the double meanings in the words he is saying:

> **Burns:** Now, let's get down to business.
> **Homer** [thinking to himself]: Oh, man. I have to go to the bathroom. Why did I have all that beer and coffee and watermelon?

> [Water drips in the background and Smithers pours a cup of coffee]

> **Burns:** Now Homer, I know what you're thinking. I want to take the pressure off. Now, it doesn't take a whiz to know that you're looking out for Number One. Well, listen to me, and you'll make a big splash very soon.

Double meanings are products of the language's propensity for homophony: words that are pronounced the same and possibly even spelled the same, but which have different meanings, as in the Miss/miss example above. This should not be confused with polysemy, which refers to words that have multiple related meanings. The word "bank," for instance, has many meanings and functions as several parts of speech, but all connote ideas of saving, paying bills, trusting,[6] and financial institutions. The word "hand" is also an example: the hands on the clock, the hands we use to type, the act of giving someone an object (as in, "Hand me the remote control") and the act of "giving a hand," as in helping or applauding.

Syntax and sentence structure create a subtle moment of humor that often sneaks past viewers on their first viewing of "Lisa on Ice." In a showdown game between Bart and Lisa's opposing hockey teams, fans for both sides are chanting the same two words: "kill" and "Bart." The side rooting for Bart's team, however, includes an aural comma in their chant, so that "kill" is a command and "Bart" is the recipient of the command: "Kill, Bart!" Meanwhile, the crowd rooting for Lisa is instructing Lisa to kill her opponent in their slightly different chant: "Kill Bart!" This example displays the complexity of the thematic roles in the English language that can lead to ambiguity. In this case, there is a difference in agent between Bart and Lisa (the agent performs the action).

Jargon

The term "jargon" refers to the specialized language used by people in a specific profession. Jargon is an element of writing style and is discussed in greater detail in the composition chapter. In the episode "The Itchy & Scratchy & Poochie Show," many business buzzwords and jargon are satirized. Commenting on the idea of adding a third character to *Itchy & Scratchy*, one writer says "I don't want to sound pretentious here, but Itchy and Scratchy comprise a dramaturgical dyad." The executives press on, insisting that adding a dog to the show is a good idea for ratings:

> **Network Exec:** We at the network want a dog with attitude. He's edgy; he's "in your face." You've heard the expression "let's get busy"? Well, this is a dog who gets "biz-zay!" Consistently and thoroughly.
> **Krusty:** So he's proactive, huh?
> **Network Exec:** Oh, God, yes. We're talking about a totally outrageous paradigm.
> **Writer:** Excuse me, but "proactive" and "paradigm"? Aren't these just buzzwords that dumb people use to sound important? [backpedaling] Not that I'm accusing you of anything like that. [pause] I'm fired, aren't I?

British Humor vs. American Humor

In the episode "A Star Is Born: Again," Helen Fielding appears as herself when she unexpectedly attends a Springfield book club. When it is clear that the book club members have not read her book and the club is merely a social drinking event, she is not offended, explaining that Americans don't understand British humor. She then spins away in *Benny Hill* fashion.

British humor is typified through many common tropes, such as the absurd, smut, the macabre, the class system, stereotypes, sarcasm, likeable villains, and the socially inept. Many of these rely heavily on language. Some examples of British humor, such as the parodies in *Absolutely Fabulous*, for example, may make it easier for American audiences to find the humor, but the harsh sarcasm and bullying from a show like *The Young*

Ones might be harder for American audiences to enjoy, as a portion of the jokes will be missed without a knowledge of the nuances of the dialects.

To Bart's amazement, Homer finds a British sitcom that he enjoys in the episode "Missionary: Impossible."

> **Bart:** You're watching PBS?
>
> **Homer:** Hey, I'm as surprised as you; but I've stumbled upon the most delicious British sitcom.
>
> **Bart:** *Do Shut Up?*
>
> **Homer:** It's about a hard-drinking yet loving family of soccer hooligans. If they're not having a go at a bird, they're having a row with a wanker.[7]
>
> **Bart:** Cheeky.

Watching this sitcom has affected Homer's vocabulary, and Bart playfully plays along by responding in British vernacular with "cheeky," which extends the joke.

An interesting exercise in comparing and contrasting language and humor between British and American English is watching an episode each of the British and the American versions of *The Office*.

Language Acquisition

After numerous discussions about Maggie's silence, questions continue to linger. She has spoken, but overall, Maggie's utterances are limited to sucking sounds. However, babies like Maggie are actually learning a grammar, which in this context refers to the mental system by which people are able to learn and speak a language. In his book *The Stuff of Thought: Language as a Window into Human Nature*, Steven Pinker explains how young children analyze language:

> When listening to their parents and siblings, they can't just file away every sentence and draw on that list in the future, or they would be mindless as parrots. Nor can they throw together all the words they have found in any order they please. They have to extract a set of rules that will allow them to understand and express new thoughts, and do it in a way that is consistent with the speech patterns used around them [29].

In the tradition of Pebbles Flintstone, Maggie is watching, absorbing, and analyzing everything around her, although we have not *heard* evidence of Maggie expressing new thoughts. Maggie's facial expressions and use of toys, especially blocks, are frequent tools used by the show to alert the audience that Maggie is not a passive member of the Simpson family. For example, in "НОМЯ," Maggie laughs at Homer's joke. Also, in "Bart the Genius," Maggie spells "EMC2" with her blocks. (These actions and communications are much more subtle than those of Stewie Griffin, Maggie's derivative and the baby on *Family Guy*). In the episode "Smart and Smarter," Maggie is thought to be brilliant (already able to teach at Florida State University, according to Henry at the pre-nursery school). Although it is revealed that Lisa had been helping Maggie, the viewer knows Maggie is able to spell words, and the fact that she can pick up on cues from Lisa shows her analytical abilities. The grammar children learn during language acquisition enables them to soon create and understand an unlimited amount of sentences.

Language acquisition is also displayed through Bart and Lisa, who have learned additional languages. Second-language acquisition has its own field of study because the pedagogical concerns are different; learning a second language creates an interlanguage grammar to consider, which is a mental system that is influenced by both the first and the second language. In speaking a second language, transfer occurs when a rule or logic is carried over from the speaker's first language to the second language. Age, cognitive, and affective factors also complicate second-language acquisition. Affective factors include such emotions as motivation and anxiety. Cognitive factors include the mechanics of learning, such as considering if the learning style matches the teaching style in which the student is learning. Bart has less motivation than Lisa, but the full-immersion style works for Bart to learn French ("The Crepes of Wrath") when he is sent to France in an exchange program. When Skinner first poses the idea to Marge and Homer, Marge is concerned about sending Bart to France because he doesn't speak French:

> Skinner: Oh, when he's fully immersed in a foreign language, the average child can become fluent in weeks!
> Homer: Yeah, but what about Bart?
> Skinner: I'm sure he'll pick up enough to get by.

Bart does eventually become fluent. While talking to himself in English, he shifts to French without realizing it at first: "I'm so stupid. Anybody could've learned this dumb language by now. Here I've listened to nothing but French for the past *deux mois et je ne sais pas un mot. Eh! Mais, je parle français maintenant. Incroyable!*"

Bart has unknowingly been using his "built-in analyzers of language," as Pinker describes them. He explains:

> Language itself is not a single system but a contraption with many components.... There are components that assemble sounds into words, and words into phrases and sentences. And each of these components must interface with brain systems driving the mouth, the ear, one's memory for words and concepts, one's plans for what to say, and the mental resources for updating one's knowledge as speech comes in [30].

In "Last of the Red Hat Mamas," Lisa studies a second language through much different means than Bart's experience with French: Lisa takes lessons in Italian. However, the main factor in Lisa's learning is affective. In general, Lisa is enthusiastic to learn, but she has an additional motivation to learn Italian: she must speak Italian to qualify for a summer program in Rome.

Psycholinguistics

Related to language acquisition is psycholinguistics,[8] the study of how the mind processes language. The spoonerism phenomenon discussed above (under "Wordplay") provided researchers some of the first proof that entire sentences are planned in a speaker's brain before they are spoken. Whether the error entails scrambling whole words in a sentence (as in "brain my damage") or if just the first letters of words are placed on the wrong words,[9] the entire sentence must exist in the mind of the speaker, or the errors would be nonexistent or random at best.

In order for psycholinguists to study the lexicon and an individual's mental dictionary, they must use lexical experiments. While such experiments are beyond the purposes of our discussion, the concept of the mental lexicon is demonstrated through *The Simpsons*. We have all experienced the "slip of the tongue" phenomenon. Everyone has a preferred method to attempt to come up with the elusive word (mentally going through the alphabet, asking "Does it start with A? Does it start with B?") or asking the person next to you, or simply talking around it, such as when Homer cannot find a particular word, and asks Marge for the "metal dealie you use to dig food" ("Bart's Friend Falls in Love"). The regularity with which this phenomenon occurs shows the fluidity of the mental lexicon and how it must prioritize words, deciding which words will be easily retrieved and which are stored in a sub-bank.

Historical Linguistics

The 19th century saw a new interest in linguistics. Scholars began to accept that language is fluid and dynamic. In fact, European linguists began to concern themselves with reconstructing Proto-Indo-European, a mainly hypothetical language from which all European languages stemmed. Linguists realized that the majority of changes were regular and not arbitrary, meaning that if one word changed in pronunciation, most or all similar words would change as well. (This may explain the Great Vowel Shift, a major catalyst in the change from Middle English to Early Modern English.) If such an enormous, complicated process can occur in fewer than 200 years in England, it is understandable that comparatively minor changes occur quickly among regional dialects in English. To clarify: a dialect is a variety of language, whereas the term "accent" only refers to the usually regional pronunciation of words. A dialect that is held by a particular socio-economic group is sometimes called a sociolect, and a regional dialect is often referred to as a regiolect.

As stated earlier, linguists are not concerned with right and wrong, proper or improper, so they would not argue whether a certain dialect is correct English, but in general among the American population, "newscaster" English (free of any obvious regional accent or dialect, and spoken with current correct grammar) is considered Standard American English. We have heard arguments that British English should be considered "correct" English because England is the homeland of English. This is faulty logic in many ways, notably in that there is not *one* English dialect in England, and also that English has changed as much in England since it was brought to North America (and other areas of the globe) than is has in North America since the first English speakers arrived.

Language and dialect change is affected by a variety of factors. The phonology and syntax of settlers' previous languages, technology, and culture all have roles. Individuals may change accents and usage by imitation, either "from above" or "from below." "From above" refers to imitation above the conscious: when a speaker unintentionally picks up habits from his or her surroundings. "From below" refers to a conscious decision to change habits. Examples could include something small, such as intentionally switching from "pop" to "soda" depending on the desired regional term, or something grander, like picking up a southern accent in hopes of blending in.

An example of "from above" imitation is found in "Coming to Home-rica," in which residents of the nearby town of Ogdenville flood Springfield to find work after their main industry, barley production, is damaged by bad press. Ogdenville, it is revealed, had been settled 100 years prior by Norwegians, and the accent of the Ogdenvillians is a stereotypical Minnesota accent (à la *Fargo*), complete with frequent uses of "ya" and "uff da." The Simpson family hires an Ogdenvillian as a housekeeper, and it is through her influence that Maggie speaks in Ogdenville-ese. Marge is horrified and joins the mob rule set to remove all the Ogdenvillians from Springfield.

The viewer may be surprised at Marge's reaction, but the desire among parents for their offspring to mirror them in many ways, not to mention a futile desire for purity in language, is not new. This example opens the door for a discussion of how people are relegated to "other" status based on language and various other arbitrary factors.

Activities

Activity #1: Fun with Phones
(can also be assigned as homework)

Have the students locate the IPA on the Internet or allow use of a textbook that contains a phonetic alphabet. Create a handout of words, phrases, or paragraphs (consider the degree of difficulty based on the level of the class) for the students to transcribe (spell phonetically). For beginner level, select single short words and names with a *Simpsons* theme (Moe, bus, school, etc.) Proper names are good to decrease the risks of cheating as students are less likely to locate proper names as phonetic examples. For a more advanced assignment, consider borrowing a passage from the show (transcripts can be found at The Simpsons Archive, www.snpp.com).

Hint: To locate the phonetic symbols in Microsoft Word 2007 go to **Insert > Symbols > Subset > IPA Extensions.**

Activity #2: Everyday Pop Culture Vernacular

Prepare for the students a list of expressions that have been spread through pop culture. In small groups, have the students discuss the origins of the phrases. (If students have laptops and/or the classroom is "smart," consider allowing students to use the Internet to find the answers). After sufficient time, reassemble the class into one group. Designate a writer to collect the findings. Students will be surprised at how much of their vernacular comes from music, television (including commercials), literature, film, and so on. (We include some common expressions from Shakespeare, too). Urban Dictionary and Wikipedia offer lists of idiomatic expressions, but here are some examples of words/expressions from pop culture:

w00t

cool

blues

d'oh

the Man

trash-talk

jump the shark

caps lock voice

redshirt (in sports
or the danger of
wearing one from
Star Trek)

Kodak moment (and,
more recently,
YouTube moment)

peanut gallery

Catch-22

Big Brother

cold shoulder

it's Greek to me

mad as a hatter

Benjamins

ugly duckling

in like Flynn

Spam (meaning junk
email, originated
not directly from
the meat product
but specifically the
wonky *Monty Python*
sketch)

"That's what she said"
(not created by *The Office*,
but definitely popularized
by Michael Scott)

Mickey Mouse (as in a
"Mickey Mouse operation")

any instance of vocalizing
text/IM talk, such as "LOL,"
"sigh," ROTFL," etc.

"Wait for it" (popularized by
Barney on *How I Met Your
Mother*)

Activity #3: Introducing
Amelioration and Pejoration

Assign a slang word or phrase to the full class or to smaller groups. Ask the students to:

List as many definitions for the word or phrase they can.

1. Judge the order in which the meanings came to be.
2. Next, have the students judge whether the meaning is positive, negative, or neutral.
3. Define the terms "*amelioration*" and "*pejoration*" in a mini-lecture and/or write on the board:

Amelioration: semantic change in a word to a more approved or more respectable meaning.

Pejoration: semantic change in a word to a lower, less approved, or less respectable meaning.

4. Have the students determine whether the word or phrase has become ameliorative, pejorative, or remained neutral.

Suggestions for words/phrases:

gay
bitch
punk
"Who's your daddy?"[10]

Activity #4: Dialects and Diction

Using a section from *The Simpsons* that includes a character with a very distinctive speaking style (such as Sideshow Bob, Homer, Fat Tony, or Mr. Burns), require the students to rewrite the set piece in another, very different, character's voice.

Activity #5: Connotation and Denotation

Show an episode of *The Simpsons* and instruct students to record as many words as they can that have different connotations. (Alternately, present a list of words to students that have several different connotations.) Next, instruct the students to give the most common dictionary definition of the word (denotation) and then list the connotations, including those specific to any subcultures, if applicable. Examples:

man
home
lady
paperback
adolescent
television

Essay #1: Language Narrative

Have the students write an essay about their history with language acquisition (primary or secondary). They might also write about their experience in traveling to a place with a foreign language or a time when they interacted with or joined a subculture with its own dialect or jargon.

Essay #2: Word Analysis

The students may write an essay about a particular word or phrase. If they speak several languages, they might compare and contrast the translations. Students should use the OED to look up the complete history of the word; they might think about how the word has changed, or they might discuss denotation and connotation. The students should choose a word or phrase that will allow them to come to interesting conclusions about the significance of the words or the information about the word they find.

Essay #3: Inventing a Word

Have the students invent a word and then write an essay that explains and defends their word. The students will have to be careful to choose a word that does not exist already. Remind them that words and phrases are invented continually. In addition to the words *The Simpsons* has added to our lexicon, *Seinfeld* gave us "close-talker" and "sponge-worthy." Gary Larsen invented "thagomizer," Stephen Colbert graced us with "truthiness," and readers of Dan Savage's sex column created "santorum."[11] Remind students that their word does not have to create something wholly new — they can change an existing word (with an affix, for example) or create a shorter word to replace an awkward phrase (think "juxtaposition" or "anthropomorphize").

Chapter 4

Literature with a Capital *L*:
Fiction, Poetry, Film, Theater

Ah, finally a little quiet time to read some of my old favorites ... [picking up canister]: Honey-roasted peanuts. Ingredients: Salt, artificial honey-roasting agents, pressed peanut sweepings.... — Homer

As *The Simpsons* is a piece of literature in its own right, it is certainly worth discussing as such. Chapter 6 will do so. The show's use of intertextuality[1] and allusions to other texts enable it to be used even in traditional literature, film, and theater classes. Many teachers currently show the occasional *Simpsons* episode in their classes to give their students a moment of levity after working their way through a text. For example, many instructors show "A Streetcar Named Marge" after teaching *A Streetcar Named Desire*, and Denise shows "Whacking Day" while discussing Shirley Jackson's "The Lottery."

There is much more academic potential in *The Simpsons*, however. Its layers of meaning and humor provide the opportunity to have our laugh and learn from it too. Several years ago, Karma's then ten-year-old son attended her world mythology class. She was discussing the hero's journey and attempted to explicate how the journey fit the pyramidal pattern by using the *Hamlet* story. She asked the class if they knew what the crisis moment was — what drives Hamlet to act after his long prevarication. Her son raised his hand.

> **Karma:** You haven't read *Hamlet*.
> **Alexander:** I still know what it is. Hamlet sees the play and knows that his uncle really killed his dad.
> **Karma:** How do you know that?
> **Alexander:** From *The Simpsons*!

While this chapter is subdivided into several sections, keep in mind that *Simpsons* allusions are polyvalent and thus do not always allow for

179

simple classification. For example, while "A Streetcar Named Marge" references the play, allusions to *Cat on a Hot Tin Roof* and *A Streetcar Named Desire* in "Secrets of a Successful Marriage" are specific to the classic film versions.

We will turn our attention first to fiction and follow it with poetry, film, and theater. Each section will include brief discussions of the mainstream theoretical frameworks in the field with illustrating examples from *The Simpsons*. The end of the chapter features exercises and assignments.

While literary discussions often include terms such as postmodernism, parody, satire, irony, pastiche, and so on, these will wait for Chapter 6, where we discuss *The Simpsons* as primary text. The show can be used to discuss a variety of literary terminology and ideas. Fruitful discussions can come from questions about narrative structure: Does Homer have an epiphany in "Homer's Phobia"? What is the denouement in "Homer and Apu?" Is Bart a hero or an anti-hero? Who or what is the antagonist in "The City of New York vs. Homer Simpson?"

"The Telltale Head" begins in medias res. A narrative voice provides closure to "Das Bus" with a deus ex machina. Lisa is Bart's foil, while Milhouse provides comic relief. In "Lisa the Simpson," the television show Lisa appears on towards the end of the episode is seen on the television earlier in the show (though, as a public forum show, it is turned off, ignored just as Lisa's concerns tend to be), providing an example of foreshadowing and narrative economy.

There is not space for a catalog of every literary reference in *The Simpsons*; we discuss only those we consider the most teachable moments. The easiest mistake to make when dealing with *The Simpsons* is to underestimate how smart the show is and how smart it assumes its audience is. For example, Thomas Pynchon, the famously reclusive author, has appeared on *The Simpsons* twice (these are the only times his voice has ever been broadcast anywhere)—with a bag over his cartoon head. The show trusts its viewers, not only to know who Pynchon is, but also why that bag is funny.

Fiction

> **Bart:** Finally—books for today's busy idiot. "Network Programming for Dummies," "Christianity for Dummies," ... "*Moby Dick*"? [reads book]: "Call me Ishmael, Dummy."

An astonishing number of contemporary authors have appeared as themselves on *The Simpsons*: J. K. Rowling, Thomas Pynchon, Art Spiegelman, Alan Moore, Daniel Clowes, Robert Pinsky, and James Patterson, among others. The Springfield Festival of Books in "Insane Clown Poppy" features several authors: Tom Wolfe, Tom Clancy, Maya Angelou, Stephen King, John Updike, and Amy Tan. The final three appeared as themselves. Though the appearances are brief, and though Lisa has to drag her family to the event, this show emphasizes how Lisa, the *Simpsons* writers, and many members of the audience are well read.

In the episode "Husbands and Knives," a comic book store features Art Spiegelman, Alan Moore, and Daniel Clowes — all famous graphic novelists. The episode gives the creators an opportunity to play themselves in a superhero context — Spiegelman declares, "*Maus* is in the house!" when danger looms. It also allows Moore to voice his concerns about the bastardization of his texts and about the state of comics in general.

The following are discussions of specific authors and genres parodied in *The Simpsons*.

Poe: The Tell-Tale Bart

Edgar Allan Poe's classic short story "The Tell-Tale Heart" inspires two *Simpsons* episodes. In "The Telltale Head," Bart decapitates a statue of his town's founder, hoping to impress the bad boys he looks up to. When his guilt manifests, he hears the head speaking to him. In "Lisa's Rival," a new student, Alison, invokes Lisa's jealousy when she appears to be more talented than Lisa in every aspect. The competition culminates in their diorama projects. Lisa is so envious of the new girl's diorama of "The Tell-Tale Heart" that she replaces the project with an actual animal heart. Her guilt is accompanied by hearing the heartbeat — which made the diorama so perfect.

Comparisons of these episodes with the story allow discussions of intertextuality and of character motivation. Poe's story hinges on the narrator's insistence that he is sane. His relationship to the murder victim is not explicated in the text, nor is any reason given for the murder. As Bart and Lisa's sanity are not the focus of these episodes, the stories necessitate clear motives for their actions.

Twain: The Adventures of Bart Simpson

A study of Bart as self-proclaimed "America's bad boy" is appropriate in not only a cultural studies context but also a literary one. Many parents initially objected to *The Simpsons* because of Bart's character — he is not a model child. Good literature, however, is not replete with model children. For those who would cite texts like *Little Women*, be warned that even the author is said to have called the novel "unadulterated pap." Bart arguably continues a tradition in American literature of the adventurous, troublemaking child. The classic representations of this character both come from Mark Twain, in the characters of Tom Sawyer and Huckleberry Finn. *The Adventures of Tom Sawyer* is parodied in an episode entitled "The Simpsons Tall Tales." Twain's characters' placement among such legends as Paul Bunyan and Johnny Appleseed attest to their current role as American icons.

Many of the main events in the text are retold, with Bart as Tom and Nelson as Huck. Allusions are made to events in *Huckleberry Finn* as well.[2] *Showboat*, recognized as the first American musical, is briefly referenced, with Dr. Hibbert singing "Old Man River" aboard a steamboat.[3] Matt Groening has stated that Bart is inspired in part by Tom, Huck, Dennis the Menace, and Groening's brother. Bart's position as one of the most influential people of the 20th century, according to *Time*, allows us to compare and contrast him with Twain's highly influential characters.

A comparison of these texts with *The Simpsons* in general allows for a consideration of what constitutes age-appropriate literature. Although Twain did not write his novels for young adult audiences, today's audiences first experience these texts as children. We believe this is for two reasons. First, there is an assumption that if a text is a "classic" or is out of copyright, it is somehow suitable for children. Second, there is an assumption that any text that focuses on children must be *meant* for them. This second assumption often is cited in reference to *The Simpsons*, with the format of the show furthering the misconception.

Lord of the Flies

William Golding's novel is alluded to in two episodes. "Kamp Krusty" features children rebelling against cruel camp counselors and horrible conditions at summer camp. When a reporter comes to interview the "leader," he must walk past hog heads on sticks to where Bart waits (referencing for a moment the figure of Kurtz from *Heart of Darkness*).[4] However, the episode that more closely parodies *Lord of the Flies* is "Das Bus." In the story, the children set out to a model UN competition, but end up stranded on an island. They quickly pick on one of the weakest among them, Milhouse, breaking his glasses and eventually attempting to attack him. In addition to his irritating weakness, Milhouse is accused of eating the camp's food. Lisa attempts to save him, holding up the model UN charter to stop the attack. In this moment, a wild boar is discovered and Milhouse is declared (mostly) innocent of the charges. The subplot of the model UN is not just a device to get them to the island. Just as the violence of the children's society in *Lord of the Flies* is meant to be contrasted to that of the adults who save them (adults who are at war), the bickering and fighting of the model UN members is echoed on the island. Principal Skinner reminds us, ironically, as he bangs his shoe on the lectern, "Order, order! Do you kids wanna be like the real UN, or do you just wanna squabble and waste time?"

Romance Novels

Marge becomes a writer in "Diatribe of a Mad Housewife"[5] after meeting an author at a bookstore. She begins a romance novel set in colonial times. Biography and fiction become conflated in the plot. The main character, Temperance, at first has an attentive husband who is a whaler. After Homer returns home cranky and tired (after being fired and attempting to find other work), Marge changes Temperance's husband to a drunken, lazy fisherman. Temperance is thus drawn to her neighbor, Cyrus Manly, who resembles Ned Flanders. When Marge completes her novel, *The Harpooned Heart*, she asks Homer to read it. He doesn't, but says he did and that he loves it. The book is a success in the community and Homer endures many insinuations that his wife is in love with Flanders.

This drives Homer to listen to the audio version of the book, read by the Olsen twins. His revenge on Ned is intercut with scenes from the ending of the novel. Temperance's husband harpoons Cyrus Manly, but is caught on the rope, and both are dragged off a cliff. Homer's confrontation on the cliff ends with Homer asking Ned to teach him to be a better husband. Homer and Marge decide to collaborate on a book about JFK's death.

The episode provides fertile ground for discussions of the romance genre, first-time writers, the biographical fallacy, and the power of visual suggestions. Students may be asked to consider why the plot of Marge's novel necessitated an unhappy marriage rather than a happy one. They might be given examples of romance novel conventions[6] and asked to compare them with the show, Marge's novel, and other texts.

One of the many stereotypes about young writers is that first books tend to be biographical — that it is only when writers are forced to leave their lives behind that they find their fictional voice. Students can explore Marge as a young writer — she chooses whaling because of a painting in her living room and peoples her book with familiar personalities. To what degree do young and more experienced creative writers do this?

Any student of literature should be introduced to two logical fallacies germane to the field. The intentional fallacy occurs when readers assume they can read the author's mind, that they know the writer's viewpoints and intentions. The biographical fallacy occurs when the reader assumes that incidents, characters, or beliefs in a work of fiction must come from the author's own life. For example, Margaret Atwood, a famous Canadian author, was asked several times about a work of fiction in which a character had lost a significant amount of weight. The question: How did *you* lose that weight?

Marge's book seems to invite this fallacy, and students may be asked to discuss the implications of our willingness to read in that way. We might also consider how the visuals of the show invite that reading. That is, when we "see" Marge's book, we see Marge as Temperance, Homer as the husband, and Ned as Manly. Thus, the visual representation forces us to see the characters as biographical, however much we might want to resist the temptation. Often, students will find a visual suggestion more compelling than any other textual evidence.[7] The intercutting of the book scenes with Homer's actual confrontation may also be discussed in light of the film convention of cross-cutting.

Children's Literature

Although *The Simpsons* is not for children, it often references contemporary classics of children's literature. "The Girl Who Slept Too Little" features a book called *The Land of the Wild Beasts*, which is a parody of *Where the Wild Things Are*. When Lisa spends the night in the graveyard, a dream sequence is drawn in the style of Maurice Sendak's famous book.

J. K. Rowling appears as herself in "The Regina Monologues" and ridicules Lisa's desire to know the end of Harry Potter's story by saying, "He grows up and marries you. Is that what you want to hear?" The Harry Potter series is referenced in several episodes. "Wiz Kids," part of the "Treehouse of Horror XII" trilogy, features Bart and Lisa attending a school for wizardry. Mr. Burns is the Voldemort character, with Smithers as his snake. The parallel book series to Harry Potter on *The Simpsons* is the "Angelica Button" series. In "The Haw-Hawed Couple," Lisa asks her father to read her the story of the intrepid girl and her wise wizard friend. The audience is treated to several imagined scenes as Homer reads the text. Just as many critics have declared the Harry Potter series too adult for young children, Homer decides (after reading ahead) that he does not want to read the story of the wizard's death to Lisa. He invents an alternate ending for her, which Lisa declares superior after reading the original. "Smoke on the Daughter" begins with the final book in the Angelica Button series coming out. The family participates in a parody of the Harry Potter parties at bookstores that were seen around the world. The fundamentalist Christian response to the text is also referenced, when Flanders ends a story to his children with the following: "...and Harry Potter and all his wizard friends went straight to Hell for practicing witchcraft" ("Trilogy of Error").

Homer's shielding Lisa from the wizard's death may be seen as self-reflexive, as many parents have shielded their children from *The Simpsons*. *The Simpsons* is not intended for young viewers, but its format creates a misapprehension in some viewers' minds.

Cartoons in general have much in common with traditional fairy tales in this respect. The oral versions of fairy and folktales were not for children. They were told to the whole household for an evening's entertainment and around quilting circles and spinning wheels (hence, we "spin" tales). Collections of these tales by Charles Perrault and Giambattista Basile include the sex and violence inherent in the stories of the time. When the Grimm brothers collected the stories circulating in Germany, they altered the tales. As the stories began being read in Victorian-era households, the brothers decided that subsequent editions should be edited with children in mind. Sex disappeared, but the violence remained. (Perhaps this is why disturbing things are often called "grim.")

Critics of American popular culture have long noted our tendency toward the Grimm aesthetic, as we abjure sex in media while glorifying violence. "Scary Tales Can Come True," from "Treehouse of Horror XI," explores the connection between modern media and fairy tales by parodying several traditional tales. The tale begins with Bart watching the fire in an old hut. Marge says she thinks it's too violent. It is, of course, less violent than the world they inhabit, in which parents leave their children to starve in the woods, Goldilocks is mauled by bears, and witches named Suzanne are shoved into ovens. Lisa carries a copy of Grimm's tales while the children journey through the forest.

Matt Groening defended the show's use of violence early in its run, noting that it was in fact gentler than violence in the outside world due to its nature: "With the Simpsons we have the cruelty and violence, but it's not anticipated at all, it's all impulsive, it's all based on people doing things thoughtlessly" (Groening, quoted in Elder 31). This is contrasted, of course to violence in cartoons like *Tom and Jerry* and *Roadrunner*, which are parodied in *Itchy & Scratchy*.

Literary Theory

The following are reductionist definitions of major fields of literary criticism. For more detail, try *A Glossary of Literary Terms* by M. H. Abrams or *Literary Theory* by Terry Eagleton as starting places. Note that these theories can be applied to all literature, not just print fiction.

Formalist Criticism
(New Criticism/Deconstruction)

This is what people refer to when they discuss "close reading." In this type of work, the text itself is the reader's primary concern; the reader is expected to pay very close attention to every word of the text, thinking about how each word (or image) stands on its own and how it relates to its textual context. Diction, syntax, symbols, and figures of speech are central. The basic writing assignment is the explication. As Chapter 6 delves into the text as text (rather than treat the text through intertextuality or allusion), it will demonstrate some formalist concerns.

Archetypal (Myth) Criticism

In this type of criticism, literature is studied in relation to archetypes (the scapegoat, the quest, the savior, etc.) and myths (religions, the Isis myth, etc.). A reading of "Bart as trickster," "Marge as archetypal mother," or "Bart as puer aeternus" (eternal boy) would be examples of the former.

An example of the latter might be a discussion of the mythology in "Lost Our Lisa," in which Lisa attempts to see the Isis exhibit at the local museum. Lisa is unable to see the exhibit on her own, so her father helps her break into the museum. There, they discover that the "Orb of Isis" is an ancient music box. An understanding of some of the aspects of the Isis myth enlightens the story and allows us to consider Lisa's parallels to, and thus attraction to, Isis. Plutarch described Isis as "both wise, and a lover of wisdom," which could also be a description of Lisa. Isis is perhaps most remembered for resurrecting her husband by gathering the pieces of his dismembered body together. She later protected her son, Horus, using the magical, secret name of Re. Lisa's discovery of the secret of the Orb through the dismembering of the Orb could be equated to this tale. Thus, understanding of the myth could illuminate meaning in the primary story for the viewers.

PSYCHOLOGICAL CRITICISM

This criticism uses theories of psychology to illuminate an author, a character, or a work. Note that this does not always have to be Freudian (Oedipal), although "Tennis the Menace" illustrates Homer's Oedipal fears. Psychological criticism means analyzing a character's dreams, such as Lisa's George Washington dream in "Lisa the Iconoclast," for a look into the subconscious desires of the character. Strict archetypal criticism is Jungian. Diagnosing Homer with post-traumatic stress disorder in "The Blunder Years" or with general narcissism disorder would be an example.

GENDER CRITICISM

Traditionally, this has been a consideration of how the sex, gender, or sexuality of the author or reader affects the piece. The newer way to do this type of criticism is to think about the social construction of femininity, masculinity, sexuality, and male/female relations. That is, most modern-day gender theorists do not assume that we are "essentially" feminine or masculine. While we are usually born into one sex (biologically determined), our behavior (what we consider masculine or feminine as opposed to male/female) is greatly determined by our culture. Bart's conflicted relationship with ballet in "Homer vs. Patty & Selma" could be explored using gender criticism. A look at Marge (on the one hand a former feminist, on the other a current traditionalist) could prove fruitful.

HISTORICAL CRITICISM

Critics either use history to better understand the piece or the piece to better understand history. The critic should be careful to distinguish between the historical setting of the piece and the time of composition, if they are different. That is, the episode "That '90s Show" should be considered a product of 2008, although it "represents" the 1990s. A cultural understanding of America in the 1990s would illuminate the episode, allowing the audience to catch references to grunge music, Sonic the Hedgehog, and *Friends*. As a text, it captures the zeitgeist[8] of the 1990s from a 2008 perspective. The following are several often-overlapping fields of criticism that fall roughly under this category.

New Historicism. Scholars are aware that every work is the product of a specific time and place. That is, just as Shakespeare wrote under the constraints, attitudes, and expectations of his time, so do the writers of *The Simpsons*. A consideration of how *Simpsons* texts are changed by censors or of how scenes are deleted in reruns (thus changing the text) to allow for more commercials might be considered "new historical." One might explore, for example, the reluctance of many networks to air "Homer vs. the City of New York" after 9/11; the episode featured Homer's car parked (with a boot) between the Twin Towers.

Sociological Criticism. This is another way to describe historical criticism that focuses on racial or other political overtones of a work. As with historical criticism, you might use the sociological framework to illuminate the work or the work to illuminate the framework. Discussing how nationality and politics influence character decisions in "Much Apu about Nothing" would be one example.[9] Looking at how *The Simpsons* critiques the war in Iraq would be another.

Cultural Criticism. This examines how various aspects of culture fit into a work. This chapter, with its focus on intertextuality and the cultural references *The Simpsons* incorporates, may be classified as cultural criticism. Chapter 5, which focuses on popular culture allusions, gives many examples.

Marxist. You do not have to be a Marxist, socialist, or communist to do this type of criticism. You merely have to analyze social class and economics in the world in which the text was written or the world represented in the text. Thinking about how a character's socioeconomic status affects a character's behavior or obstacles would be typical. The producers of *The Simpsons* might come under attack for outsourcing much of their labor to South Korea. Mr. Burns's longing for an ivory back scratcher in "Simpson and Delilah" might be examined as a class warfare critique. A consideration of Lisa's chances of being able to afford college, given her family's often-precarious finances, would also be effective.

BIOGRAPHICAL

This criticism comprises understanding the work through biography or vice versa. There are two danger zones for in this type of criticism. One is the intentional fallacy — assuming you know the writer's mind and intentions for the work, as in the supposition "That was obviously supposed to be a dig at the pope; the author must be Protestant." The second pitfall is the biographical fallacy. Thus, we should not assume that Homer (or any character) represents the thoughts, feelings, and experiences of his creators.

The controversies surrounding the show (as people label it anti- and pro-family values; anti- and pro-religion) demonstrate the dangers of attempting to oversimplify the message or to conflate a writer/producer with the product.[10] However, responsible biographical criticism can still be done. It may be safely inferred from the body of the text that the creators tend toward the protection of free speech. Similarly, interviews with some writers have revealed that "Lisa the Vegetarian" was created after the conversion of much of the staff.

Poetry: Howl of (and by) the Unappreciated

Although contemporary America is not known for poetry appreciation, *The Simpsons* provides numerous references to classic works. Lisa writes "Howl of the Unappreciated" in "Bart vs. Thanksgiving":

> I had a cat named Snowball...
> She died!
> She died!
> Mom said she was sleeping...
> She lied!
> She lied!
> Why, oh, why is my cat dead?
> Couldn't that Chrysler hit me instead?

While her subject matter is typical of her age (pet death, middle child syndrome), Lisa's poem is a reference to "Howl" by Allen Ginsberg. Lisa's love of poetry is well known. She shares Pablo Neruda's insights with Bart (who says he is "familiar with the works of Pablo Neruda") in "Bart Sells His Soul." She idolizes Robert Pinsky, former poet laureate, in "Little Girl in the Big Ten." She is familiar with various styles and authors, as illustrated by "Moe'n'a Lisa."

"Moe'n'a Lisa" features four famous writers playing themselves: Tom Wolfe, Gore Vidal, Michael Chabon, and Jonathan Franzen. Lisa helps Moe organize his scrap paper rants into Charles Bukowski–esque poetry. The conflict of the episode occurs when Moe does not acknowledge Lisa's help. This creates an opportunity for valuable discussion — to what extent is an editor (an arranger) an author? Is it our egos that reject the idea of collaboration, or is it the product of our individualistic society?

In this episode, Moe is invited to the Wordloaf Literary Conference. This is an allusion to the famous Middlebury Bread Loaf Writer's Conference. Such allusions to poetry and its authors are found throughout many episodes. When Carl asks Dr. Hibbert for a favor and is turned down, Carl protests with "A dream deferred is a dream denied," a line from Langston Hughes ("Moe Baby Blues").

If song lyrics are counted as poetry (and they should be), many characters on *The Simpsons* have written poetry, including Homer. A further discussion of songs and *The Simpsons* will come in Chapter 5's discussion of popular culture.

The first Halloween episode, "Treehouse of Horror," contains the most complete poetry recitation in *The Simpsons*. Lisa reads "The Raven" by Edgar Allan Poe.[11] Although she begins, James Earl Jones's voice takes over.[12] Homer is the narrator; Marge's picture on the wall represents the lost Lenore. Bart is the raven. Homer speaks the dialogue to the raven. The line reading of "Take thy beak from out my heart, and take thy form from off my door" is particularly well done. Viewing this particular reading allows for a discussion of recitation, rhyme, mood, and meter. Lisa and Bart's conversation at the end also reminds us that societies evolve in what they find scary or shocking, though Homer's terror at hearing the tales indicates that we share some primal fears.

Aside from deconstructing or scanning the poetry that *Simpsons* characters write,[13] there are not many instances that call for a training in poetry to enjoy the show. Typical dialogue does not contain the elements of poetry with which most people are familiar: meter and rhyme.[14] We welcome those, though, who would treat the script as free-form poetry, focusing on diction, metaphor, symbolism, dramatic monologue, connotation, denotation, alliteration, stress, and the like — scan at will!

Really Old Poetry: The Iliad and the Odyssey

Although Homer is named after Groening's father,[15] the show has not limited the reference to a biographical one. One of the very first episodes, in which Homer gets his job as safety inspector, is "Homer's Odyssey." In Season 13, the show took the reference into full parody, with "D'oh Brother, Where Art Thou?," part of a trilogy of "Tales from the Public Domain." The title is a reference to the Coen brothers' film *O Brother, Where Art Thou?*, which was a modern remake of the *Odyssey*. The *Simpsons* episode manages to capture much of the plot of both *The Iliad* and the *Odyssey*, moving from the Trojan horse to Odysseus's triumphant return home. While the show references Trojan condoms and has Odysseus kill his wife's suitors, the episode is arguably more child-friendly than the actual text, which includes adultery, rape, and much more violence.

Most Americans no longer regard Homer's works as poetry. This might well be because they invariably read the text in translation, which means that many of the poetic aspects of the texts are lost. Thus, if we remember that we are always engaging with a somewhat corrupted view of Homer's texts, we may not be so hesitant to use the *Simpsons* version as a legitimate retelling. One only has to remember that the surviving texts attributed to Homer were retellings of older tales that had themselves been translated into poetry. One should also remember that "Homer" likely did not exist any more than "Aesop" or "Mother Goose."

Examining the Simpsons family as Odysseus's family provides a rich terrain for a discussion of character. While Odysseus is a hero in the classical sense,[16] he is not consistent with modern definitions of heroism or morality. Certainly, he is clever, though pride causes not only his own problems but the problems of the warriors who sail with him. His leisurely stops at islands with beautiful nymphs and goddesses may provoke questions about his true desire to return home from the war (which he attempted to abstain from attending).

Odysseus is the James T. Kirk of classical Greece. He is essentially an explorer who manages to avoid inter-island (interplanetary) warfare, while sleeping with every attractive woman (human and non-human) who comes along. Kirk may be seen as the better man, as he does not have a Penelope waiting chastely at home.

Marge as long-suffering wife of Homer seems a perfect fit for Penelope. The casting allows us to ask if Penelope may be seen as more than just an allegory for patience. "Homer's" tale does little to show any affection between the couple. We are told that Odysseus leaves for more adventures soon after his return home. When Marge/Penelope starts to talk about daily life with her returning hero, he protests: "Quit suffocating me! I'm going to Moe's!"

Film

> Martin: "This is as boring as *mainstream* cinema!"

The filmic references in *The Simpsons* may be the richest of all literature allusions. The writers do not constrain themselves to contemporary work. They lampoon classics (*Casablanca*[17]), failures (*Waterworld*[18]), and obscure history (Rory Calhoun[19]). While an extensive knowledge of film history is not necessary for enjoyment of the show, people with this knowledge are rewarded with jokes that seem to be just for them.

Since *The Simpsons Movie* was released in 2007, *The Simpsons* now can be taught as film directly, but the television show allows for discussions of many genres, techniques, and theories of film. For example, basic film terms, such as cross-cutting, crane shot, Steadicam, 180-degree rule, and mise-en-scène can be explained using *Simpsons* clips. The fact that the show is a cartoon allows it to recreate many of film's stylistic conventions.

Naturally, certain films and filmmakers are referenced multiple times, revealing their level of popularity in the larger culture. *The Terminator*, *The Godfather*,[20] James Bond, Stanley Kubrick, and Alfred Hitchcock are among those with this honor.

Most of the films the Simpsons see (as they are fairly typical Americans) are mainstream. Action movies in particular seem to be a source of mirth for *Simpsons* writers. Explosions on the show are numerous — there seems to be a policy that whenever there is any sort of crash (no matter what the material or impact force), there will be an explosion. We can see in this convention an exploration of audience expectations.

Arguably, action films still strive for "an aesthetic of astonishment and attraction," described by Tom Gunning as " a series of visual shocks" (116). That is, early film, which was not driven by narrative, attracted its audience through astonishment — how was it possible to capture a moving image? To feel that a train was heading towards you in a dark theater? We currently value action films (which often have narrative problems) if they convey the same sense of wonder — how is it possible to stage that fight scene? To feel that the city was actually destroyed?

The use of explosions in *The Simpsons* does not feed this need uncritically. Often, they are completely unrealistic, as for example when Homer mixes soda and Pop Rocks, creating an explosion we see in slow motion as he is propelled forward by the force ("Homer Badman"). We are also teased into questioning our love of the action genre by the infamous McBain movies we see throughout the series, featuring Rainier Wolfcastle (Springfield's Arnold Schwarzenegger). *McBain*,[21] and the action films we see in the show like it, features lots of violence, crude foreshadowing, pat lines, and forced romantic subplots. One *McBain* feature ends with a sexy woman telling McBain, "You just broke up that meeting," alluding to his throwing people out of a high-rise window. McBain replies, stiltedly, "I'm thinking of holding another meeting ... in bed" ("Oh Brother, Where Art Thou?").

The point about audience expectations is driven home further in "Beyond Blunderdome," in which Mel Gibson (playing himself) screens his remake of *Mr. Smith Goes to Washington*. While the majority of Springfield enjoy the film, Gibson is distracted by Homer's overwhelmingly negative comments and decides to use Homer as a consultant in his revision of the film. The result is a ridiculous parody of an action-film violence orgy in which Gibson's Mr. Smith guns down Congress and the president. When the film executives protest, Homer and Gibson flee in a *Mad Max*–style car. Thus, the episode is able to critique the practice of test screening, violence in film, and one of movies' favorite standards — the car chase.

The horror genre also receives a fair amount of attention in *The Simpsons*. In "Colonel Homer," Bart and Lisa attend *Space Mutants VI*, which features the stereotypical attack on sexy teenagers in a car. Most of the vignettes in the annual "Treehouse of Horror" episodes are parodies of classic horror and sci-fi film, with *The Twilight Zone* thrown in for good measure.

As there are brief film references in every episode, we cannot chronicle them all here. We can, however, illuminate some episodes that directly parody films.

"Marge on the Lam" directly references *Thelma & Louise* when Marge and her new neighbor drive off a cliff in a stolen car. The women have bonded because the divorced neighbor will spend time with Marge when Homer won't. *Thelma and Louise* is remembered as one of the most poignant films of female bonding. Their death was narratively determined once they stepped outside of society's normative boundaries, once they woke to the materialist[22] constraints upon them. It is because *The Simpsons* is a comedy that it is able to have the women live. The episode is thus useful for thinking through genre and gender. Additionally, the question of Marge's friends can be explored. Marge often doesn't seem to have any friends; after this episode, her neighbor is rarely seen. What is it about Marge, her family, or her position that eschews friendships?[23]

"All Singing, All Dancing" is one of the show's many clip episodes. As with the other clip shows, there is a frame narrative. This particular frame features Homer and Bart coming home from the video store with the 1969 film *Paint Your Wagon*.[24] Homer feels cheated when he realizes a film with Lee Marvin and Clint Eastwood is a musical rather than a traditional western. His family tries to explain to him that it's normal for people to break out into song as they remember instances in which they have done so. Although Homer comes to admit that he actually likes musicals, Snake, who has broken into the home, continues to protest, singing through the end credits. The flashbacks show the wide range of *Simpsons* music, from barbershop to parodies of *The Music Man* and Disney films. The episode can be used to teach a subgenre that is often dismissed by critics — the musical. It may also be used to think through circumstantial and incidental music.[25]

"Simpsoncalifragilisticexpiala(Annoyed Grunt)cious,"[26] "The President Wore Pearls," "My Fair Laddy," and "Yokel Chords" parody *Mary Poppins, Evita, My Fair Lady*, and *The Sound of Music*, respectively. "The Days of Wine and D'ohses" references a Jack Lemmon film in which a husband in a co-dependent, alcoholic marriage enters AA: *The Days of Wine and Roses*.[27] Although he loves his wife, he must push her out of his life to stay sober. In the *Simpsons* version, Barney gives up drinking. Homer is unwilling to fully let him go and alternately sabotages and supports his efforts.

One of Springfield's recurring characters comes from Jack Lemmon. Gil is the hapless salesperson whom we first met in "Realty Bites." He is based on Lemmon's character in *Glengarry Glen Ross*, a film and play about real estate salesmen.[28] Gil was able to briefly succeed as a real estate salesman in "Kill Gil, Volume I & II." Lemmon himself voiced a failed sales representative in "The Twisted World of Marge Simpson," but he primarily lives on in Gil, voiced by Dan Castellaneta. The character is pitiable, but often despised for his failure. He represents the victims of changing economies and ruthless capitalism. The original David Mamet character is often compared to Willy Loman in *Death of a Salesman*. The cast of the film *Glengarry Glen Ross* referred to their film as "Death of a Fucking Salesman." Mamet's distinctive voice is lampooned in Homer's response to Lisa when she says she wants to write plays: "You could load it up with lots of swears! That's what David Mamet does" ("Last Tap Dance in Springfield").

No reading of film in *The Simpsons* could be complete without a discussion of two episodes in which *Simpsons* characters make films: "A Star Is Burns" and "Any Given Sundance." The former features a film festival in Springfield, while the latter has Lisa enter the Sundance Film Festival with a documentary about her family.

"A Star is Burns"[29] shows several characters making films — Barney, Hans Moleman, Moe, and Mr. Burns (although Mr. Burns hires "the Mexican Steven Spielberg" to direct). As Homer is one of the members of the jury, we are treated to a discussion of film aesthetics and audience expectations and preferences. Mr. Burns's movie, which steals from several films (*Ben-Hur, Citizen Kane, E.T.*) to convince the audience to love him, receives a few votes because he bribes jury members. Barney's movie, a surprisingly moving film about his alcoholism (based on a black-and-white *Saturday Night Live* sketch by Bill Murray), clearly deserves to win. Homer, however, holds up the jury because he wants to vote for Hans Moleman's film *Man Getting Hit by Football*. This entry, which is reminiscent of *America's Funniest Home Videos* as opposed to a serious contender for a film prize, appeals to the lowest common cultural denominator — Homer. When asked to reconsider, he opines: "Hmm ... Barney's movie had heart, but 'Football in the Groin' had a football in the groin."

In "Any Given Sundance," Lisa films a documentary and shows it at a major festival. Her declaration that film is about "plot, theme, character, language, rhythm, and spectacle" is a reference to Aristotle's belief in six hierarchal elements of drama: plot, character, diction, thought, spectacle, and song.[30] It is her choice of plot and characterization that get her into trouble, however. While her film is critically acclaimed, her family is hurt that she showed them in a realistic, that is to say, negative, light. This raises important questions — who owns a story? Does the rest of the Simpson family have the right to control how they are portrayed? Why is dysfunction always considered more artful and truthful than function? It is not until Nelson premieres his film about his family, which brings even more attention due to his worse conditions, that Lisa is forgiven. The episode is intriguing in its treatment of subject and its depiction of the backstory of films — the editing, the financing, the sound effects, and so forth.

Critics of poetry and film are often able to use the various categories of literary theory listed in the literature section, as most works have character and dialogue. Film, as a visual medium, often incorporates visual theories, however. The pleasure we take in *seeing* is called scopophilia. The term is often used interchangeably with voyeurism, although the latter has a sexual connotation. Comedies such as *The Simpsons* often count on the audience's propensity for schadenfreude (pleasure in watching someone else experience pain or misfortune).

The most significant work on scopophilia in film is Laura Mulvey's 1975 treatise "Visual Pleasure and Narrative Cinema," which popularized the term "the gaze." When we speak of the gaze, we speak of the way the camera treats its subject and how the audience is able to view a film only through that gaze. Mulvey's crucial work argues that cinema employs a (heterosexual) male gaze. That is, the female body is objectified, while the male characters and the camera tend to act as subjects. This becomes problematic for female audience members, who must identify themselves either with the male gaze or put themselves in the "masochistic" position of identifying with an object. Filmmakers and audience members who attempt to curtail this position are said to be "resisting the gaze."

Gaze theory is linked to psychoanalytic theory of power, sexuality, and castration anxiety. It is, like psychoanalytic theory, often dismissed as essentialist and ahistorical. Very few people discredit the central idea of the camera's power over female bodies, however.

It may be argued that Matt Groening has been attempting to resist the gaze throughout the life of *The Simpsons*. He insisted that his animators not draw cartoons that resembled contemporary comic books — no bulging, powerful muscles on the men, no skimpy clothing or large-breasted women. When the show does have characters with these attributes, they are featured either in ads or in movies (like *McBain*) or are shown strictly for those attributes (as gladiators or strippers). One early episode featuring "Princess Kashmir," an exotic dancer, ends with Homer attempting to show Bart that objectifying women is wrong ("Homer's Night Out").

Several episodes refer to the pornographic genre, but two episodes in particular explore it. In "Bonfire of the Manatees," Homer allows the Mob to film "snuggle" movies in his house to repay a debt. In "Home Away from Homer," Ned Flanders takes in college-age boarders, unaware that they have a sexy webcam show. Despite the main characters' resistance to porn being filmed in their home, Homer and Bart have been known to read *Playdude* and Marge watches an erotic video with Homer in "Selma's Choice."

Theater

> **Bart**: This play has everything!

This chapter has already alluded to several plays, but this section will focus on the experience of theater in the Simpsons' world. The world in which the Simpsons live is, after all, highly theatrical.

In the first full-length episode shown, "Simpsons Roasting on an Open Fire," Homer and Marge attend the elementary school's Christmas pageant. Lisa has also acted as Martha Washington to Ralph's George Washington in her school's production. However, Marge has the most investment in theatrical arts. In "A Streetcar Named Marge," Marge decides to audition for community theater because she feels lonely and neglected at home. She wins the part of Blanche DuBois when the director sees her "fragile spirit" crushed by Homer, who does not support her out-of-home activity. The episode consciously parallels Homer to Stanley, with Marge/Blanche trying to escape his brutality. When the play premiers, Homer apologizes because he was able to see himself in Stanley.

Of course, they are not performing Tennessee Williams's version of the play — they have made it into a musical. While having Marge/Blanche fly through the air moaning to symbolize "her descent into madness" seems an odd choice, students of the play will note that Williams included many expressionistic elements in the play that are often forgotten. For example, when Blanche tells the story of finding her former husband with another man, the stage direction reads: "A locomotive is heard approaching outside. She claps her hands to her ears and crouches over. The headlight of the locomotive glares into the room as it thunders past. As the noise recedes she straightens slowly and continues speaking" (95). The use of light, sound, and the character selling flowers for the dead are all expressionistic rather than realistic in nature.

The episode is able to effectively satirize what happens to literature when it is adapted to the musical genre, as musicals seem to demand happy endings. For a real life example, one need only look at *Wicked*— the book ends with the witch's death; the musical ends with her survival and a kiss. Thus, when Marge/Blanche is taken away by the people in white coats and says the famous line, "I have always depended on the kindness of strangers," the full cast breaks out into a song on the theme, ending with the upbeat line: "A stranger's just a friend you haven't met/You haven't met/Streetcar!"

A similar bastardization is enacted when Troy McClure gets the opportunity to star in a musical version of *Planet of the Apes* "as the human" ("It's the part I was born to play, baby!"). The musical version is *Stop the Planet of the Apes, I Want to Get Off!* When the apes realize the human can talk, he announces that he can also sing. The musical incorporates lines from the film and a musical style from Falco's "Amadeus." When the head of the Statue of Liberty appears, Troy drops to his knees and sings:

> Oh, my god!
> I was wrong
> It was earth all along
> Well, you've finally made a monkey...
> Chorus: Yes, we've finally made a monkey...
> You've finally made a monkey out of me
> I love you, Dr. Zaius!

This pandering show proves immensely popular. Even Homer, no fan of the arts, declares that he loves "legitimate theater."

In "The City of New York Vs. Homer Simpson," Marge, Lisa, and Bart attend *Kickin' It: A Musical Journey through the Betty Ford Center* to fulfill Marge's dream "of being in a Broadway audience." We are treated to the song, "You're Checking In," which won two (actual) awards for lyrics and music. This parody of Broadway satirizes Robert Downey, Jr.'s, escapades and the different set of rules that seem to exist for celebrities. A judge sings, "I should put you away where you can't kill or maim us/But this is L.A. and you're rich and famous!"

Sideshow Bob, Krusty the Clown's former sidekick and a homicidal maniac, treats us to several theatrical performances. Bart encourages Bob to sing the score from *H.M.S. Pinafore* in "Cape Feare."[31] Bob also takes over Krusty's lead role in *Pagliacci* in "The Italian Bob." Bob uses the performance to attempt to kill the Simpson family. Viewers familiar with the opera will recognize the intertextuality — in the original opera, there is a play within the opera. The actor playing Pagliacci confronts his wife with violence in front of an audience who assumes the action is part of the show. Similarly, when Lisa asks the audience for help, she is ignored until the audience realizes that what they are seeing is not staged.

We are able to see many characters from *The Simpsons* perform *Hamlet* in a fantasy vignette, "Do the Bard, Man," from "Tales from the Public Domain." Bart is Hamlet, who is told by the ghost of his father to avenge his death and to "take a sweater." Moe is Claudius and has usurped Homer's throne, taking Marge/Gertrude as his wife. Their reenactment includes the play within the play, which finds Claudius objecting that he did not use as much poison as the actor does. When Bart sets up the trap, he uses an actual line from the play: "The play's the thing/Wherein I'll catch the conscience of the King" (2.2.611–12). Claudius points out the strangeness of the soliloquy convention when he overhears. Although the play ends a bit differently, everyone is dead at the finish, including "Rosencarl" and "Guildenlenny."

Many teachers of *Hamlet* show multiple versions to the students to discuss how the same play changes in the hands of different directors. This brief version is no exception. The writers also allude to one particular Freudian reading of the play, popularized by Mel Gibson's version, in which Hamlet's rage at Claudius comes more from his own sense of incestuous cuckoldry than the crime of regicide. When the Simpson family begins to read the play and Lisa gives a brief description, Bart asks if Hamlet would be going out with his mom once his father is dead. Homer replies, "I don't know, but that *would* be hot!" This brief moment might spur a closer reading of the text, as students try to find textual evidence of directors' theories and discuss how they might direct the play, if given the chance.

While "Do the Bard, Man" is one of the show's clearest reference to Shakespeare,[32] students can also be exposed to an intriguing hybrid of *The Simpsons* and *Macbeth* called *MacHomer*. *MacHomer* is a one-man show by Rick Miller, who adapted *Macbeth* with over 50 character voices from *The Simpsons*. As of this writing, the show has been touring for over ten years. While viewing the show is ideal, it is possible to obtain scripts. Reading this alongside *Macbeth* provides great opportunities for discussion about adaptation, casting, genre (blending tragedy and comedy), and time (past and present).

An episode from season 20, "Four Great Women and a Manicure," directly parodies *Macbeth* when Marge relates the story. In her tale, she wants Homer to have the lead role in *Macbeth* and convinces him to kill off the other actors until he has the role. The "Macbeth Curse" is also referenced in "The Regina Monologues," when Ian McKellen suffers accidents when Homer and others say "Macbeth."

The study of theater in a literature classroom requires a combination of literary and film theory, enhanced by an understanding of staging conventions and performance theory. Reading a play is a different experience from viewing a play.[33] Lisa, as we've seen, has referenced Aristotle's aspects of tragedy. In his view, "Tragedy is an imitation of an action that is whole and of magnitude." He further believes playwrights should report what may happen according to probability or necessity and plays should conform to unities of time and place.

Many contemporary works do not follow Aristotle's definitions or expectations, but playwrights are still invested in them. Arthur Miller felt the need to write an essay on why *Death of a Salesman* was a tragedy, despite the fact that it was about a common person, whom Aristotle would not have considered "of magnitude."

The study of both play texts and *The Simpsons* allows for discussion of many theatrical terms and concepts. *Simpsons* characters engage in monologues, dialogues, soliloquies, and even asides, as in "Attack of the 50-foot Eyesores," when Homer turns to the "camera" before a commercial break: "We'll be right back." Episodes require exposition, "stage business," blocking, the fourth wall, suspension of disbelief, and, occasionally, deus ex machina.[34] Characters and plots may be discussed in terms of protagonist, antagonist, major and minor characters, conflict, foils, catharsis, dramatic/tragic irony, and comic relief.

While many experimental plays do not follow the traditional pyramidal pattern, individual *Simpsons* episodes may be mapped onto it as students identify rising action, climax, and falling action (or resolution/conclusion/denouement).

The following terms, which are sometimes confused, may also be elucidated:

climax— the point in the plot towards which everything has been building; the greatest tension is here.

crisis —point in the play at which things are so complicated that the character must make a decision to resolve the conflict.

equilibrium —a state of balance often found at the beginning of plays/works; the action of the text usually involves a disruption of the equilibrium; a hero will restore equilibrium.

image —tangible things that illustrate themes (motifs).

inciting incident —occurs after the point of attack; this is something that happens to drive the protagonist into action.

point of attack —point in the situation where the author decides to start the work/play.

recognition —when the hero/protagonist recognizes a great truth.

reversal —a secret is revealed that changes the course of a character or the play.

spine —often confused with the theme; the spine is a statement made in the infinitive (e.g., to obtain the money); this spine drives the action of the play/work; every character must fit into this spine. Often directors will have different ideas about the spine for any given work/play.

stakes —the importance attached to any moment for a particular character; in other words, what is there to lose? Stakes will change according to the goals, circumstances, obstacles, and tactics of the character.

theme —idea that runs through the text (there are usually several intertwining ones).

touchstone line — most directors choose a touchstone line to guide a production. This is the line the director feels is most important to the play/work, not because it is the line that occurs at climax or because it's the line with the most importance in the dialogue, but because it reverberates through all the characters and scenes.[35]

Conclusion

As promised, this is a very selective list of how literature is intertwined with *The Simpsons*. The opportunities for talking about literature and the show seem unlimited. As the text is multivalent, even the episodes we've discussed can still be mined for more material. For example, although "A Streetcar Named Marge" is primarily concerned with the Williams play, there are numerous other references. When Marge is in rehearsal, she must put Maggie in day care. Maggie ends up in the Ayn Rand School for Tots, which implements Rand's philosophy through refusing to coddle the babies.[36] When Maggie's pacifier is taken away, she leads the other babies on several quests to get the pacifiers back. These moments cast Maggie as Steve McQueen in *The Great Escape*. When she is sent to the play pen for punishment, another baby throws her a ball with which to occupy herself. The music from *The Great Escape* plays as the babies set up elaborate plans. Homer comes to pick Maggie up after they succeed, finding a crowd of babies sucking on their pacifiers, the sound echoing off the walls. The scene is reminiscent of a scene in *The Birds*, which is underscored by a "cameo" of Hitchcock walking a dog past the day care center.

We have included seven assignments for classroom use. Note that all of these handouts depend upon thinking about *The Simpsons* as an adaptation of other literature. Handouts on teaching *The Simpsons* as the primary text can be found in Chapter 6.

The first handout is on comparing and contrasting with adaptations. It is meant to be used by the students when they view or read the adaptation. It can be used as a warm-up exercise for in-class writing, as notes for the final exam, or as a first step in writing a compare/contrast essay, which is our second handout. The third assignment asks the students themselves to produce an adaptation. Assignment four asks the students to analyze their own response to a literary text. Formalist concerns are detailed in the fifth assignment, and integrating other aspects of literary criticism appears in assignment six. A more traditional synthesis assignment is our last addition to this chapter. Any assignment may be altered to fit works other than *The Simpsons*.

Some of the papers and activities in the other chapters are easily adapted for use in a literature class. Finally, we recommend having the students do concise reviews of individual episodes to practice their summary, analysis, and critical thinking skills.

Activities/Paper Assignments

Assignment #1: Comparing/ Contrasting Adaptations

For each of the differences you note, consider why the adaptor (author, screenwriter, director, producer, etc.) might have made that choice (note that directors are generally considered the "author" of films). In other words, ask yourself "why" there was a change when you list "how" there was a change. Think about the intended or unintended effects of the "why" and "how" combined.

Original work(s):   Adaptation:

General Questions:
1. Which characters are added or deleted?
2. What scenes are deleted or added?
3. How does the genre of the adaptation affect the adaptation?
4. How does the specific form of the adaptation affect the adaptation?
5. How do the location and time period affect the adaptation?
6. Is this adaptation also a parody? If so, what is the form or content (or both) of the original being parodied? Would this parody be considered a satire? Of what?
7. What does the adaptation's attitude toward the original seem to be?
8. What lines are edited?

Specific questions for moving from page to visual text:
1. If there is a musical score, how does it affect the piece?
2. How are the actors costumed?
3. Why do you think these actors were chosen?
4. If there are credits, how are they designed?
5. How are the sets designed?
6. How is lighting used?
7. Is there anything else that stands out about this adaptation?

Essay #1: Compare/Contrast

Choose a piece of literature we've encountered as a class and compare it with a *Simpsons* revision. Write a unified essay that discusses the significance of something you observe about the two texts.

You may be tempted to talk about all the differences, but this will not yield a unified essay. Avoid having your essay turn into a list of differences in paragraph form. One way to avoid this is to choose one difference (such as in plot, theme, or form) and explore it fully. The most challenging part is coming up with an arguable thesis. It is not enough to say, "This text says *x* and that text says *y*." This is an obvious and so-what thesis. The trick is to make an argument about these two texts together.

In terms of organizing your thesis, it might be useful to think about it as two sentences. One sentence will be your observation. The other will be an explanation of the significance (what we can learn) from your observation. If you do only the first without the second, you will have a so-what thesis.

You might also think through this by thinking through basic questions. It is not enough to say how an adaptation is different or similar to the original. You must also make an argument about why the choices were made and what effect they had.

An example: Say you were supposed to write an essay comparing the book *Charlie and the Chocolate Factory* by Roald Dahl and *Willy Wonka & the Chocolate Factory*, the 1971 film adaptation. There are numerous differences, even including the title. An essay trying to discuss most or all of them will be disjointed. You also probably can't find significance in each one — why geese and not squirrels? Why one parent and not two for the tour? Yet a discussion of one major difference — for instance, that Charlie is perfect in the book and imperfect in the film — yields the opportunity to think about the effect of this difference in Charlie's characterization. The film Charlie may seem more real to audiences because he acts like the other children, but his sin necessitates the addition of an entire subplot (the Everlasting Gobstopper theft) to redeem him.

In terms of organization, it might seem easier to write first about one text and then about the other. However, this approach is not recommended. When we organize this way, it is too tempting to merely summarize the author's plot, rather than analyze structure, theme, and other aspects.

Grading Criteria

To write a successful paper for this assignment, be sure to:

- Create a thesis that concisely reflects the argument or central idea you present in the paper.
- Provide clear and careful analysis of specific examples from the texts.
- Successfully engage with counter-argument and warrants.
- Organize your writing in a clear and logical manner with coherent, unified paragraphs.
- Have a strong title, introduction, and conclusion.
- Quote and paraphrase accurately.
- Correct any grammar, punctuation, and spelling errors.
- Follow the format and citation guidelines on your syllabus.
- Integrate ideas of style (concision, diction, and the like) into your work.
- Make a point that goes beyond what we discussed in class.
- Avoid the intentional and affective fallacies (assuming you know the author's intention or how the text affects all audience members, respectively).

Assignment # 2: Synthesizing Through Adaptation[37]

You may rewrite a scene from one work. There are several ways to do this. 1. You may rewrite one author's story in another author's style. This can include cross-genre rewrites. 2. You may also rewrite a work from another point of view (change first to third or change character perspective). You must stay in the original author's voice for this option.

These options have the possibility of being fun and they should be, but you should take it seriously. Each rewrite needs to be accompanied by a brief explanation of your rationale. What decisions did you make to make the change? What stylistic effects from one author did you try to bring into another's idea? Taken together, the rewrite and the rationale need to make the word count. If your rewrite meets the word count by itself, that does not mean you can skimp on the rationale. *You cannot just rewrite a scene in your own voice*— that would not be synthesizing.

Essay #2: Self-Analysis[38]

This paper may be different from any other literature essay you have ever written. Instead of focusing on the text, I will be asking you to focus on yourself and your response to the text.

Choose one of the works we have written or viewed. Write an essay that analyzes your response to the text. Don't just tell me what your response is — analyze yourself. What assumptions, biases, knowledge, or beliefs lead you to respond to the text in the way you do?

You may be tempted to stray into a critique of the text in your self-analysis ("As this text is stupid/smart, I felt x"). Avoid this as much as possible, or you'll end up with circular reasoning. You also want to avoid being general and superficial ("I didn't like it because it was boring; I liked it because I could relate to it"). The text is probably not inherently boring, confusing, or relatable, so what does it say about *you* that you found it to be so? Refer to specific points in the text when necessary. Refer to yourself as specifically as possible. Remember that you are not a blank slate — you are constructed to think in certain ways by who you are. Consider nationality, sex, sexuality, age, education level, race, religion, and so on. Don't forget that your training as a reader — the works you've read before — affects your reading as well.

Although this is a self-reflective piece, it should still take the form of an essay with a title, introduction, conclusion, coherent body paragraphs, and so on. As this will reference at least one piece of literature, a Works Cited page in MLA format should be the last page of your essay. (I will also accept your Works Cited entry on the bottom of your last page, if there is room.)

Essay #3: Argument About Form

Choose one of the following options. The questions following the directions are meant to give you ideas — you do not have to answer them in your essay.

1. Write an essay that analyzes a character or characters. To avoid having an overly obvious thesis, I encourage you to work on minor characters (or even absent characters). How do they affect the primary relationship? How do they serve to flesh out the main characters into round characters?

2. Choose one symbol to explore in depth. Symbolism may be found in names, objects, repeated ideas, imagery, music, or almost anywhere else. Note the difference between cultural and contextual symbols. Also note the difference in these two terms: theme — the idea or ideas that run through the story (there are

usually several intertwining ones); image — tangible things that illustrate themes (motifs).

3. Choose another formal aspect of the text (the character's diction, allusions/intertexts, foreshadowing, point of view, and so on) and analyze it in relation to the overall meaning.

4. Write a problem-paper. A problem-paper is a paper that attempts to answer something unanswerable. While there is no definitive answer, an argument can be made based on evidence in the text. You must deal with counter-evidence to your point, however. You must acknowledge competing theories.

Grading Criteria

To write a successful paper for this assignment, be sure to:

- Create a thesis that concisely reflects the argument or central idea you present in the paper. **This thesis will relate to the work as a whole and will be defended by textual evidence.** Note that the thesis should primarily be **about the formal element**, not about a theme, however. No three-point theses.
- Provide clear and careful analysis of specific examples from the text.
- Successfully engage with counter-argument and warrants.
- Organize your writing in a clear and logical manner with coherent, unified paragraphs.
- Have a strong title, introduction, and conclusion.
- Quote and paraphrase accurately.
- Correct any grammar, punctuation, and spelling errors.
- Follow the format and citation guidelines on your syllabus.
- Integrate ideas of style (concision, diction, and so forth) into your work.
- Make a point that goes beyond what we discussed in class.
- Avoid the intentional and affective fallacies (assuming you know the author's intention or how the text affects all audience members, respectively).

Essay #4: Literary Criticism Essay

For this essay, you will analyze a piece of fiction using a form of literary criticism. You will choose both the work and the critical apparatus.

Once again, your argument will be judged on how well you make it, so be careful when gathering evidence for your thesis.

Certain works will seem to suggest certain types of criticism. Remember that it may be more challenging and rewarding to use a non-obvious type of criticism with a work. That is, if the theme of a certain work is masculinity, it may be a bit obvious to do gender criticism on it — try class criticism instead (every character belongs to some social class, after all).

Literary Criticism[39]: Choose from one of the following options: formalist criticism (New Criticism); archetypal (myth) criticism; historical criticism; sociological criticism; cultural criticism; Marxist criticism; biographical criticism; psychological criticism; gender criticism.

There are hundreds of essay opportunities here. You will be graded on the same criteria as your last essay. Your evidence may take other forms, however. You may have to research a fairy tale, biography, or aspect of psychology. If you do so, make sure you integrate your research into the essay smoothly and that you cite all sources according to MLA conventions. Even if you do not do any outside research, your essay must still have a Works Cited page. (The Works Cited page does not count toward your page count.)

Remember that your essay must be based on a clear, arguable, original thesis. This thesis should integrate literary criticism with an analysis of the work or an aspect of the work. Your essay should relate this analysis to the work as a whole (if only in the conclusion).

As you may have noticed, your literary criticism may be hard to define, as the various modes of criticism tend to overlap. If you're looking at constructions of gender, for example, you will probably be looking at how a certain historical period defined gender. You will also notice that masculinity and femininity are often defined differently by different races, classes, and nationalities. Don't be worried about overlap; the real mistake would be to discuss one of these issues in a vacuum — that is, assuming that one aspect of your identity is not informed by all the others.

Hints: Don't start your essay thinking about literary criticism. Think of a thesis — something you want to argue. THEN think about what type of literary criticism you're doing. This assignment is only to make you conscious of what you are already inclined to do. The questions you generate for class should be a great place to start working toward a thesis.

We will be using the same grading criteria as in earlier papers.

Essay #5: Synthesizing Ideas
(The Traditional Way)

For this essay, you will choose your text, your synthesizing texts(s), and your approach to synthesizing them.

There are many different ways of synthesizing a text. Choose from one of the following options below, or discuss your own ideas with me.

Option 1: You may make an argument about your chosen primary text, using at least one piece of literary criticism from another source. There are many different ways to use outside literary criticism. You will be expected to do more than just apply someone else's ideas to the text. *You must have your own point.* Interacting with another person's ideas will build your own argument. You must turn in a photocopy of whatever sources you use with your final draft.

Option 2: You may study a particular author in depth and make an argument about an aspect of his or her writing (themes, techniques, and so on) based on your observation of two or more works. You must include a photocopy of whatever other works you use with your final draft (or check with me to see if I've read it). The important thing, of course, is to choose an author whose work you have enjoyed.

Option 3: You may do a compare/contrast essay about two or more works we have read as a class. If you noticed similar themes or techniques in several works, now is the time to discuss them. Your essay must make an argument that goes beyond simply "one author does this, another does that."

We will be using the same grading criteria as in earlier papers.

Chapter 5

The Simpsons and the Outside World: Culturally Literate and Socially Significant

I used to be with it, but then they changed what "it" was. Now, what I'm with isn't it, and what's "it" seems weird and scary to me. — Abe Simpson

In 1987 (coincidentally the same year the Simpson family first appeared on television), E. D. Hirsch, Jr., published *Cultural Literacy: What Every American Needs to Know*. The book ignited discussions on the state of education, while coining the now common phrase "cultural literacy." Hirsch was a conservator of our shared cultural knowledge, supporting an "anthropological" theory of education — one that would teach every American child our shared cultural terms and ideas.

According to Hirsch, "To be culturally literate is to possess the basic information needed to thrive in the modern world" (xiii). Hirsch's attention to cultural literacy is meant to benefit both students and our larger society. As he explains, "Cultural literacy constitutes the only sure avenue of opportunity for disadvantaged children, the only reliable way of combating the social determinism that now condemns them to remain in the same social and educational condition as their parents" (xiii). To reinvigorate primary and secondary school education in a way that reinforces Hirsch's idea of cultural literacy is to enable students to participate in the larger American community once they graduate: "Only by piling up specific, communally shared information can children learn to participate in complex cooperative activities with other members of their community" (xv). Finally, Hirsch follows Thomas Jefferson's beliefs in the very purpose of mandatory public education, which is to create citizens capable of participating in the democratic process: "Universal literacy is inseparable from democracy" (12).

Although Hirsch is more interested in high culture than popular culture, presumably because children learn popular culture on their own, he does not decry television as antithetical to his pursuit of a better educated populace: "It will not do to blame television for the state of our literacy ... television watching is acculturative" (20). *The Simpsons* may be one of the most acculturative television shows available due to its high level of allusiveness. Jonathan Gray believes the show "should be regarded as one of the key culprits of Americanization" (Gray "Imagining America" 130–131).

In Hirsch's logic, then, *The Simpsons* is educationally progressive, as it is a cross-class educator.[1] Hirsch's logic is still seen today, in the many "cultural literacy" and "bluffer's" guides designed for use in trivia and in business dealings. Arguably, many of the "For Dummies" guides serve the same purpose — to help those adults who feel they didn't achieve full cultural literacy in school or from their parents.

Hirsch identifies a problem with today's students and graduates, that "what they know is ephemeral and narrowly confined to their own generation" (7). Anything that can teach students about the generations before them is therefore valuable. Of course, Hirsch notes that not all information about the past remains relevant: "Although historical and technical terms may follow the ebb and flow of events, and more stable elements of our national vocabulary, like George Washington, the tooth fairy, the Gettysburg Address, *Hamlet,* and the Declaration of Independence, have persisted for a long time" (29). The cultural knowledge presented on *The Simpsons* has ebbed and flowed for over twenty years and, not surprisingly, has alluded to all of these examples.[2]

Due to its own desire to stay relevant as time passes (and possibly complicated by the problem of a significant lag between writing and airing time), writers for *The Simpsons* generally avoid references that will ebb quickly from our cultural mind. They also satirize cultural referents that have passed too quickly, such as when Homer talks about Ray J. Johnson. When the family claims not to know whom he's talking about, Homer sings Johnson's song. Lisa cuts him off: "I'm sick of him already" ("Mom and Pop Art"). Further, the show illustrates both the generation gap and some people's inability to follow the ebb and flow of cultural referents through Mr. Burns, who expects people to understand an oblique reference to Rory Calhoun and who believes that people still deliver mail by autogyro.

Hirsch created (with two other authors) a list of what he feels we should know, omitting things that were too "obvious" to be listed (138). He notes that "very few specific titles appear on the list, and they usually appear as words, not works, because they represent writings that culturally literate people have read about but haven't read" (xiv). Thus, Hirsch acknowledges that even the "great works" do not need to be understood to achieve literacy. Instead, it is only necessary that they be recognized as part of our shared culture. In regard to learning about these things via *The Simpsons*, we might use Hirsch's quote, replacing "have read about" with "have seen about."

Hirsch's List: A Thought Experiment

Hirsch's list is very long, taking up a great deal of his book. As a thought experiment, we have taken one letter, K^3 (not one of the most commonly used letters in the English alphabet), and attempted to show how *The Simpsons* fulfills Hirsch's desire for cultural literacy. The results follow:

Kabul — In "New Kid on the Block," babysitter Laura Powers orders food from a restaurant called "Two Guys from Kabul," explaining that she had lived in Kabul when her parents were still married.

Kafka, Franz — In the episode "Little Girl in the Big Ten," Lisa joins two college girls in Café Kafka. Inside and outside the café there are cockroach paintings referencing *The Metamorphosis*.

Kamikaze — In "Bart the Fink," Krusty goes on a kamikaze mission.

Kangaroo court — While the term "kangaroo court" is not used (to the best of our knowledge), there are examples of kangaroo courts (trials that lack due process), most notably in "Treehouse of Horror VIII" when the Salem witch trials are satirized.

Kansas — In "Much Apu about Nothing," Kansas and Kansas City are panned when Homer and Apu are studying the U.S. map. In addition, Kansas is noted as one of the states where the Simpson family is not welcome in "Kill the Alligator and Run." In "Lisa the Greek," the Kansas City Chiefs are one of the teams on Homer's gambling bracket. Interestingly, creator Matt Groening

has a family connection to a KU scientist, who named a 1997
sperm study after Homer. Groening designed the experiment's
patch.

Kant, Immanuel — Although the show doesn't discuss Kant (to the
best of our knowledge), the topic of enlightenment (about
which Kant wrote definitive works) is used in several episodes,
including "Bart's Comet" and "They Saved Lisa's Brain." Many
scholars have done Kantian readings of the show, notably in *The
Simpsons and Philosophy*.

Kapital, Das (title) — We could not find an instance in which this
title was alluded to, but class and financial issues are pervasive
in the show.

Karachi — One of the booths at the Squidport is called "Karachi
Hibachi" (in "Worst Episode Ever").

Keats, John — In the episode "The Secret War of Lisa Simpson,"
Bart is sent to military school. Lisa decides she wants to be a
student there too when she observes a class discussing the poem
"Ode on a Grecian Urn" by John Keats.

Keep the wolf from the door — this is an idiomatic expression
meaning "to maintain oneself at a minimum level." In "Lisa
Gets an 'A,'" Gil, begging Superintendent Chalmers to give him
a large order of Coleco computers, tells them that "the wolf is at
old Gil's door."

Keller, Helen — To date, the show does not appear to reference
Helen Keller.

Kelvin, Lord — The origin of the name Artie Ziff "may be an elec-
trochemistry pun referencing a well-known part of the Nernst
equation" that takes the universal gas constant (R) and multi-
plies it by the temperature in Kelvin (T). (This information is
found on Wikipedia. At the time of this writing, we had not
gotten confirmation that this is the correct origin of Artie Ziff's
name, although we are inclined to agree because the creator of
Artie Ziff, Al Jean, left a career in mathematics to become a television writer).

Kennedy, Edward — Mayor Quimby is a composite of several
Kennedys.

Kennedy, John F. (JFK) — Mayor Quimby is a composite of several
Kennedys. References to Kennedy's assassination are made in

"Mayored to the Mob" and "Diatribe of a Mad Housewife."
John Kennedy is also seen in "Duffless," "Grampa vs. Sexual
Inadequacy," "Simpson Tide" and several other episodes.

Kennedy, Robert F. (RFK) — Mayor Quimby is a composite of several Kennedys.

Kent State University — "The Girls of Kent State" are on the cover of
one of Homer's old *Playdude* issues in the episode "All's Fair in
Oven War." In "D'oh-in in the Wind," Homer puts daisies in the
police officers' guns, like antiwar protestors did in the 1960s.

Kentucky — the narrator in "Behind the Laughter" calls the Simpsons a "Kentucky family," although it should be noted that
another state was used for the reruns. In addition, George
Washington makes a jab at Kentuckians in "Lisa the Iconoclast."

Kentucky Derby — Kentucky Derby winner Secretariat was referenced in "The City of New York vs. Homer Simpson." Also,
Springfield Downs plays an important role in "Saddlesore
Galactica."

Kepler, Johannes (founder of scientific method) — Many science
teachers have taken examples from *The Simpsons* to teach the
scientific method in their classes. We have included some in
Chapter 1.

Kettledrum — In "Lisa the Skeptic," Principal Skinner says his
heart is beating like a kettledrum (in anticipation).

Key, Francis Scott — Francis Scott Key was referenced in the
episode "Lisa on Ice."

Keynes, John Maynard — To date, the show has not referenced
Keynes, although economic issues are central to the show.

Keynesian economics — See above.

KGB — In *"El Viaje Misterioso de Nuestro Jomer,"* Homer's call is
tapped by the KGB.

Khomeini, Ayatollah — Homer pushes an Ayatollah T-shirt in the
neighborhood rummage sale in "Two Bad Neighbors."

Khrushchev, Nikita — In "Das Bus," a model UN is held at
Springfield Elementary. A row ensues, and Skinner takes off a
shoe and raps it on the table to silence the students. This banging alludes to the same action done by Soviet leader Khrushchev.

Kibbutz — Writer Mike Reiss has remarked that the writers' room
is like a kibbutz.

Kidd, Captain — Sea captain McAllister is a composite of famous and stereotypical sea captains.

Kidney — Grampa receives Homer's kidney in "Homer Simpson In: 'Kidney Trouble.'"

Kiev (capital of Ukraine) — Kiev isn't mentioned directly, but Ukraine is mentioned through references to Chernobyl ("King Sized Homer" and "The Last Temptation of Homer").

Kilimanjaro — In "Simpson Safari," Homer tells Bart to go to the top of a hill to get a better view, to which Bart exclaims, "Mount Kilimanjaro?"

Kill with kindness — While this idiom is not stated on the show (to our knowledge), Ned Flanders may certainly be said to kill with kindness.

Kilometer — Lisa shows her ability to convert miles into kilometers in "Homer and Apu."

Kilowatt-hour (kWh) — The word "kilowatt" has been used, but not "kilowatt hour" (to our knowledge). "Kilowatt couch" was used as slang for electric chair in "I Don't Want to Know Why the Caged Bird Sings."

Kinetic energy — Perhaps displayed most prominently in *The Simpsons Movie*, where Bart and Homer ride a motorcycle in the dome over Springfield. Science bloggers have enjoyed explaining kinetic energy to describe if that ride was possible.

King, Martin Luther, Jr. — In the episode "Mypods and Broomsticks," people prepare to celebrate MLK Day.

King Arthur stories — It is revealed that Burns owns King Arthur's sword, Excalibur, in "Rosebud."

King James Version (Bible) — In "Home Sweet Homediddily-Dum-Doodily," Ned invites the kids to play "Bombardment of Bible questions." Todd requests the "St. James" version, and there is some debate about whether it's a mistake that he says "St. James" instead of "King James," or if it's an inside joke.

King Kong — In "Treehouse of Horror III," one segment is a parody of *King Kong* called "King Homer."

King Lear (title) — In "Guess Who's Coming to Criticize Dinner," the Simpson family sees Krusty the Clown perform (terribly) in Shakespeare's play *King Lear*.

Kingdom come — *Kingdom Come* is the title of one of the *Left*

Behind books, which was satirized in the episode "Thank God,
It's Doomsday."

Kingdom was lost, For want of a nail the — this proverb is not spoken (that we know of) but is displayed several times. It is better
known as "the butterfly effect": small actions have a huge effect
on other people and events. The episode "Trilogy of Error" is an
excellent example, as is "Much Apu about Nothing," in which a
harmless bear traveling outside of its normal range ultimately
causes much heartache and stress on the town.

King's English, speak the — To our knowledge, this phrase is not
stated in the show.

Kinsey, Alfred — No direct mention of Kinsey, although the sexol-
ogy demonstrated in "Grampa vs. Sexual Inadequacy" may refer
to Kinsey and/or Masters and Johnson's research. Also, Liam
Neeson appeared in *Kinsey* and *The Simpsons* in the same year.

Kipling, Rudyard — In the episode "Old Money," Grampa Simpson quotes several lines of Kipling's poem "If—."

Kissinger, Henry — Upon a visit to the Springfield Nuclear Power
Plant, Henry Kissinger loses his glasses (which Homer finds and
wears) in "$pringfield (Or, How I Learned to Stop Worrying
and Love Legalized Gambling)."

Kitty Hawk — The Wright Brothers' plane and Kitty Hawk are
discussed in "Sideshow Bob's Last Gleaming."

Kleptomania — In "Mom and Pop Art," Jasper Johns is portrayed
as a kleptomaniac.

Klondike Gold Rush — In "Lady Bouvier's Lover" Grampa acts out
Charlie Chaplin's fork antics from the 1925 movie *The Gold
Rush*.

Knee-jerk reflex — In "The Springfield Files," Homer's knee-jerk
reflex is tested.

Knesset — Although several episodes reference Jewish heritage and
religious practice, the Knesset itself is not referenced.

Knights of the Round Table — In "Maximum Homerdrive," the
steak Homer eats is called "Sir Loin-a-lot."

Knock on wood — In "Lisa the Greek," Homer says "nothing bad
could come of this" but doesn't knock on wood, so of course
bad things happen.

Knowledge is power — Lisa certainly believes in this ideal, as evidenced in "Yokel Chords," when she tutors underprivileged children.

Koran — Homer mistakenly refers to the Koran as the "Corona" in "Mypods and Broomsticks."

Korea — *The Simpsons* frequently discusses that much animation is done in Korea.

Korean War — In "Dog of Death," Skinner expresses a desire to have history books at Springfield Elementary that "know how the Korean War came out."

Kosher — Springfield's Lower East Side houses a kosher meats and produce store ("Like Father, Like Clown"). A frustrated Ned says he "even kept kosher to be on the safe side" ("Hurricane Neddy"). In "Lisa the Beauty Queen," Lisa's biggest competition holds the crowns to the "L'il Miss Kosher" pageant (and, ironically, "Pork Princess").

Kremlin — In "Springfield Up," Burns says he once scored the vending machine contract for the Kremlin.

Ku Klux Klan (KKK) — In "Krusty Gets Kancelled" his comeback special is abbreviated "KKK." When he sees the initials, he realizes those aren't the letters he wants behind him at the Apollo Theater.

Kuwait — In "Sweet Seymour Skinner's Baadaasssss Song," Skinner is talking with a colonel who remarks on the medals he earned by securing a Montgomery Ward's in Kuwait City.

Of all the entries for the letter *K*, *The Simpsons* potentially lacks just a few of them (we say "potentially" because it's possible that we may have missed some, or some could have been used between the writing and publishing of this book). Indeed, the cultural richness found in *The Simpsons* is unprecedented in American television.

Cultural Shifts and Social Issues

We use *The Simpsons* frequently to discuss social issues, in courses with or without a *Simpsons* focus. For example, Denise teaches a humanities overview course to freshman-level students at an engineering university. Her text considers several common themes of the humanities (morality, freedom, love, happiness, death and life affirmation),[4] and

Denise frequently uses *The Simpsons* early in the unit as a way to encourage discussion and critical thinking. The same is true of composition classes with an argument essay focus; there are *Simpsons* episodes to complement virtually any controversial topic.

In our "Writing about *The Simpsons*" courses, we found it useful to divide the semester by paper assignments and three or four themes frequently examined by the show, such as sexuality/gender issues, religion, community, family, and politics. At the start of each new unit, we recommend an in-class viewing of an episode heavy in that unit's topic, and several focused free-writes around that topic.[5]

The remainder of this chapter will discuss some of the social and cultural issues we have discussed often in our classrooms with *The Simpsons* as our copilot. Next, we will cover the top pop culture topics discussed in our classrooms. Third, we will offer suggestions for applicable Simpsons episodes to use in class, and fourth, we will close with some related activities and assignments we've used in our classes. The issues, episodes, and activities that follow can be used in a wide array of classes, from American studies to cultural studies to sociology to women's studies.

The Simpsons *and Sexuality*

In the early days of the family sitcom, married couples did not have sex with each other, implied or otherwise. Most early sitcom couples had twin beds. While many dramas (especially those on HBO) tackle issues of infidelity, very few contemporary sitcoms address marital sex, sexual problems (besides cheap throwaway lines), or infidelity.[6] *The Simpsons*, however, addresses all of these issues in believable and respectful ways. Homer and Marge have almost split up (or have temporarily separated) on several occasions. In "The War of the Simpsons," a frustrated Marge signs them up for a couples' retreat. Homer makes a bad situation worse by doubling the retreat as a fishing trip. In "The Cartridge Family," Marge packs up the kids and moves to a cheap motel when Homer refuses her demands to give up his gun.

Both Homer and Marge have been tempted to have extramarital affairs, but neither of them was able to follow through. The circumstances that led to these almost-affairs were compelling enough that less committed spouses could have successfully justified the affairs to themselves. In

"Life on the Fast Lane," Marge feels unloved and unappreciated by Homer, who has presented to her the bowling ball (for her birthday) that he has bought for himself (it even has his name on it). When Marge meets a man who clearly wants to devote his attention to her, the audience empathizes with her temptation. In the episode "Colonel Homer" (in season 3), Homer discovers a cocktail server, Lurleen Lumpkin, with a tremendous singing talent. She is very attractive and attentive to Homer, but he doesn't seem to notice and is only concerned with recording her music. In contrast, in "The Last Temptation of Homer" (from season 5), Homer is unexpectedly smitten with Mindy, a new coworker at the power plant. Homer's attraction to Mindy is immediate, involuntary, and out of his control. He fights his attraction and ultimately does not give in. The audience realizes Homer's attraction to Mindy at the same time Homer does, and recalls the fact that he previously had had a chance to cheat (with Lurleen) and wasn't tempted for a moment, but the fact that he finds himself in this situation through no fault of his own creates deep empathy with the audience.

Homer and Marge have also grappled with problems in their sex life. In "King-Size Homer," Homer's plan to gain 60 pounds to get on disability has an unintended side effect: Marge finds him less physically attractive. She tells him as much, injuring his pride. In "Natural Born Kissers," Homer and Marge find the solution to a slowdown in their sex life when they realize they are turned on by the fear of getting caught having sex outside their home. The depiction of a problematic sex life, as well as an exploration of what they do to get their sex life back on track, is poignant in "Grampa vs. Sexual Inadequacy." Marge is shown to be the instigator of sexual relations for the duration of this episode, challenging Victorian ideas about sexuality and gender. Homer's excuse for his waning libido can also be used to discuss the role of stress on sexuality: "Marge, there's just too much pressure. What with my job, the kids, traffic snarls, political strife at home and abroad. But I promise you, the second all those things go away, we'll have sex."

The Complicated Issues of Gender

Before we discuss at any length how *The Simpsons* deals with issues of gender in the complexity such a rich issue deserves, we must first define gender. For our purposes, we will put it plainly: "Gender" does not refer to biology (being born with male or female parts is denoted by the word "sex"). Rather, "gender" refers to the performance of femininity and masculinity.[7] Although students often see gender differences as innate, they need only be reminded that masculinity and femininity change over time and across geography. Decisions to act (or not to act) within the societal constraints of gender are made continuously in *The Simpsons,* notably through Lisa, of course, but also through Marge, Homer, Bart, and secondary characters as well.

Oftentimes, Bart's bad behavior is depicted as innate (such as the episode "Bart vs. Thanksgiving," for example, in which he destroys Lisa's centerpiece, later stating that he doesn't know why he hurt her and he doesn't know why he'll do it again), but more often, he seems to be acting in way that he thinks "America's bad boy" should behave. On several occasions, Bart wants to impress the bullies, such as when he refers to his "tummy" but quickly corrects himself, becoming more and more vulgar until he gets an approving nod from Nelson: "I mean stomach! Gut! Crap factory!" ("Das Bus"). In "The Telltale Head," Bart chops the head off the statue of the town's founder to gain status with the bullies. In "Bart the Mother," Bart does not want to shoot a bird, but Nelson's peer pressure convinces him to take the gun. Although he intends to miss, he shoots and kills the bird. As the title of the episode suggests, Bart chooses to perform the role of mother to the bird's eggs, even telling them, "You can call me Mother. No, wait, that sounds kinda fruity. Just call me Mom." This is one of the times when Bart's status as Marge's "special little guy" (a designation which simultaneously pleases and embarrasses him) is challenged, but not destroyed. Perhaps the occasion that challenges Marge and Bart's relationship the most is in "Marge Be Not Proud," when Bart shoplifts a video game from Springfield's megastore, "Try-n-Save," which disappoints Marge tremendously.

The Simpsons often follows familiar family sitcom tropes and storylines, but because of the medium, it is able to subvert and satirize the familiar. The brother/sister relationship is explored frequently on the show, often providing the most poignant moments. In "The Secret War of Lisa Simpson," Bart is sent to military school, and Lisa decides to attend the same school because she desires higher academic standards than Springfield Elementary offers. But the military school has never had a female cadet, and with Lisa's presence all the boys are removed from their dorm, to their dismay. The cadets haze both Bart and Lisa, but especially terrorize Lisa, forcing her to do many muddy pushups and heckling her as she attempts the final obstacle, called the Eliminator, "a 150-foot hand-over-hand crawl across a sixty-gauge hemp-jute line with a blister factor of twelve. The rope is suspended a full forty feet over a solid British acre of old-growth Connecticut Valley thorn bushes."

However, Bart sneaks out for late-night training sessions with Lisa and ultimately shouts his words of encouragement over the voices of the taunting boys, who are chanting "Drop! Drop!" Bart's words of encouragement drown out the others' voices. He says, "You can make it, Lisa. I know you can! Come on, I know you can do it! Just get your hands back on the rope! Just a little further!" His words inspire her to triumph over the Eliminator.

Although Bart does occasionally enjoy stereotypical big brother duties such as protecting and encouraging Lisa, when his role as the son is threatened he sees Lisa as an equal rival and not as his little sister, as in the episode "My Sister, My Sitter." Homer and Marge decide that Lisa is mature enough to be in charge while they go out on the town, even though Bart is two years older. Bart is infuriated that Lisa is deemed more trustworthy; meanwhile, Lisa becomes a bit drunk with power. Bart does his best to thwart Lisa's authority by pulling numerous pranks, feeding Maggie coffee ice cream, and instigating a physical struggle with Lisa that causes him injury.

In "Lisa on Ice," Lisa is required to join a sports team to avoid failing gym, and her talent at goaltending is discovered, making her a bigger hockey star than Bart. He tries to outdo her scholastically, but when that fails, he confronts Lisa in her room: "Lisa, certain differences, rivalries, if you will, have come up between us. At first I thought we could talk it over like civilized people. But instead, I just ripped the head off Mr. Honeybunny." Lisa then informs him that Mr. Honeybunny was actually *his* cherished childhood toy. The episode ends on a very tender note as Bart and Lisa, in the final tense moments of a tied game, throw down their gloves (literally) and hug.

Gender and sports issues appear also in "Homer vs. Patty and Selma," in which Bart feels conflicted about his love for ballet. At first, he has no desire to do ballet (and only signs up for it because he's late to school that day and all the other activities, including pull-ups and lap running, were full), but he ends up embracing it and excelling. When the audience (even the bullies) is captivated by Bart's beautiful performance, he removes his mask to reveal his identity. Of course, the bullies, still being who they are, chase after him. In "Bart Star," Lisa shows up for football tryouts, saying, "What position have you got for me? That's right. A girl wants to play football." When she sees that there are already several girls there, tossing the football around, and that the coach, Ned Flanders, is genuinely happy to see the girls there, Lisa backtracks, saying, "Well, football's not really my thing — after all, what kind of civilized person would play a game with the skin of an innocent pig?" Clearly, Lisa has no interest in actually *playing* football; her motivation was simply to subvert the status quo. When her attacks on the game are foiled (it turns out that the footballs are not actually made of pigskin and that for each one sold, a dollar goes to Amnesty International), she runs off, confused and upset. Although it is tempting to make an argument about a deeper meaning behind this scene, the truth here is probably that the writers thought it would be funny. Occasionally, the audience does need to be reminded that Lisa is an eight-year-old girl (with a touch of middle child syndrome) and does sometimes act like one.

The Simpsons frequently ponders with its audience the validity of homemaking as a profession. Marge has tried different occupations (such as police officer, pretzel maker, and real estate agent), but none of these lasts longer than its episode. However, Marge excels in her position as a police officer and in fact, it is her experience as a homemaker who has shopped for her "full-seated husband" that gives her a good detective eye (in "The Springfield Connection" Marge is able to get to thwart the blue-jeans bootlegging operation because she recognized the shoddy stitching).

Lisa feels homemaking is an easy job until she takes it on in "Little Big Mom." When Marge suffers a broken leg, Lisa assures Marge that she will keep the house and care for her father and brother while Marge is in the hospital, saying, "Oh, Mom, I've seen what you do around the house, and I can handle it. Maybe I can even make things more efficient." The house quickly becomes a disaster, and Homer and Bart are impossible for her to manage. No one is happier to have Marge back than Lisa.

Marge's parenting can be contrasted with Homer's, but more engaging issues of parenting can be seen when we think through other characters' parenting styles, such as those of Homer's parents. Several episodes reference Abe Simpson's inability to provide emotional support for his son. In "Grampa vs. Sexual Inadequacy," Homer and his father become estranged until Abe is able to provide one compliment — he's proud that Homer is "not a short man." In "Bart Star," Homer becomes overbearing in his support of Bart as quarterback because of his memories as a high school gymnast — Abe yelled, "You're gonna blow it," while Homer was executing a beautiful floor exercise routine.

Homer's relationship with his mother is even more strained. Mona Simpson became a social activist in the 1960s, and her involvement in a sabotage of Mr. Burns's germ warfare laboratory caused her to flee from the police. In "My Mother the Carjacker," Moe tells Mona, "When you took off, you left a hole in Homer's heart that he's been trying to fill with alcohol for years." Mona's abandonment of Homer was not motivated by a lack of motherly affection, but students often have difficulty accepting the idea of imperfect mothers. A discussion of the difference in societal expectations regarding fathers, mothers, and responsibility can be fruitful. We often ask, for example, why "single mother" has a negative connotation, while "single father" has a neutral to positive one.

Friendship on the show also seems to hinge on gender. Much speculation has been made about why Marge and Lisa rarely have friends. Marge has no best friend, and references have been made to it. In "Marge on the Lam," Marge laments to Homer that it's hard for her to make friends. The accompanying flashback reveals one reason why: Homer bursts in with a spraying skunk while wearing a T-shirt that reads "No Fat Chicks" — just another example of the negative effect Homer has on Marge's happiness.

Homer and Bart suffer no friend shortage — Homer spends much time with Moe, Barney, Lenny, and Carl, and Bart's best friend is consistently Milhouse. But is there a grand issue to be made about gender and friendships? After all, the reason that Homer spends so much time with Moe, Barney, Lenny, and Carl is that they are all often together at Moe's Tavern. Milhouse is largely comic relief. Perhaps the reason that Marge and Lisa lack best friendships is that female friendships simply aren't seen as funny. When the show emphasizes female friendships, it's generally regarding competition and backstabbing, two very common circumstances in television and film. In classroom discussions, female (and male) students will talk about how they find girls and women to be rougher on each other than boys and men, which we have used to start discussions in our classrooms regarding feminism, abjection, and how to prevent or curtail such "girl on girl crime."[8]

Although we can't think of a time when "slut" has been used by a female character[9] towards another female character on *The Simpsons*, there is definite "girl on girl crime." For example, Marge is kicked out of the female investor's group in "The Twisted World of Marge Simpson" for being too conservative, and they treat her harshly. Marge dives into female friendship in "Marge on the Lam" when she makes friends with a new neighbor, Ruth. Marge is happy to have someone to accompany her to the ballet when Homer refuses, and soon Marge is swept up in Ruth's drama (including a high-speed chase, *Thelma & Louise* style).

When Terri and Sherri make fun of Lisa for being vegetarian, Janey (Lisa's sometime best friend) asks her if she's going to marry a carrot. The ridicule is so powerful that even sweet, mild Ralph joins in, saying, "I can't believe I used to go out with you" ("Lisa the Vegetarian).

Competition brings out the worst in Lisa in "Lisa's Rival." After Alison, a new student, is named first chair in saxophone, Lisa turns to Bart for help and together they devise a plan to take Alison down, replacing her diorama with one that surely won't win. In the end, while Lisa doesn't confess to the sabotage, she does "discover" the real diorama in time for it to be considered in the contest.

Homer often struggles to understand his daughter, who is in many ways a little girl but who is also smarter than he is in that she is capable of critical thinking. In "Much Apu about Nothing," Lisa, while trying to explain a logical fallacy to Homer, ends up with his cash by selling him a rock that she has just explained is "just a stupid rock." In "Lost Our Lisa," Lisa uses verbal gymnastics to trick Homer into saying she may ride the bus to the museum to see a special exhibit on its last day in Springfield after Marge had already said no. Although she is capable of tricking Homer, she is not worldly enough to understand the intricacies of the city transit system and winds up on the wrong bus. In "Lisa the Vegetarian," Homer apologizes to Lisa about their fight, working under the assumption that she is right, although he doesn't understand why. (He is surprised when she admits partial fault.) Homer stands by Lisa in the episode "Lisa the Iconoclast" in which she uncovers the truth about the town's beloved founder, Jebediah Springfield. Homer is the only one who believes Lisa, and he chooses to attract attention to Lisa so that she can share her news with the crowd.

In "Make Room for Lisa," Lisa and Homer's relationship is badly damaged when Homer allows Lisa's room be turned into a cell phone tower. She begins to experience stress-related stomachaches and, after a trip to Dr. Hibbert, Homer and Lisa wind up visiting Karma-Ceuticals, where they enter sensory-deprivation tanks. Lisa has several hallucinations, including one in which she becomes Homer. This experience shows her not only what it's like to be inside Homer's head but also how she appears to Homer. She realizes that her treatment of him is hurtful and that he does many things for her that he dislikes. The episode closes with Lisa asking Homer to do something they'll "both enjoy," a demolition derby. And Lisa actually does enjoy it, because she is spending time with Homer.

Feminism

Just as it's necessary to define terms like gender before a productive conversation can begin, we must define feminism, an equally, if not more so, misunderstood word. Jill Dolan's 1988 book, *The Feminist Spectator As Critic*, is a useful source in defining the various major forms of feminism today, two of which are perhaps the most useful to distinguish between here. Dolan refers to "radical" feminists as cultural feminists, explaining that they base their analysis on "a reification of sexual difference based on absolute gender categories" (5). In other words, radical (cultural) feminists believe there are intrinsic qualities in being a female or a male, and this system "gives rise to a formulation of femininity as innate and inherently superior to masculinity" (Dolan 6–7). This view of feminism that relies on intrinsically feminine characteristics also presupposes a sisterhood — a unification of the female gender based solely on their sex. Not only is this view essentialist, it also leads to an exclusion of the male sex.

On the other end of the spectrum is materialist feminism, which "deconstructs the mythic subject Woman to look at women as a class oppressed by material conditions and social relations" (Dolan 10). By seeing women as a class, materialism links itself to socialism, especially in Britain. That is to say, women are not defined merely by their sex/gender, but as "subjects who are influenced by race, class, and sexual identification" (Dolan 10). These forms of feminism stand in contrast to a sort of middling feminism that wants equal rights for women (one that grants women fair pay and access to work), rather than disturbing the status quo or changing other fundamental inequalities in the system.

It is also useful to note that many feminist critics agree that we are in what is termed third-wave feminism. First-wave feminism, part of the Victorian era and early modernism, was a movement that saw getting the vote as paramount. Second-wave feminism was part of the civil rights movement of the 1960s and 1970s and is what many picture when they think of feminism and feminists.

Matt Groening came of age during the second wave. He was adamant about his characters being drawn in a non-objectifying way, though a few *Simpsons* characters are drawn in a more objectified style, in a way that draws attention to the fact. Groening explained in an early *Mother Jones* interview, "The rage against women in a lot of comics, and a lot of pop culture in general, is something that I never felt. I could never figure out why cartoonists and rock stars who couldn't get laid in high school felt compelled to get their revenge for the rest of their lives in creative self-expression" (Groening, quoted in Elder 31).

Characters in *The Simpsons* run the gamut of feminist to nonfeminist ideologies, reminding us that neither sexism nor feminism is uncomplicated. On one extreme is Mr. Burns, who has to be forced to hire at least one woman at the plant and who, when Lisa suggests that he is reinforcing society's phallocentric nature, says, "I don't know what 'phallocentric' means, but no girls!" ("Burns' Heir"). On the other extreme is Gloria Allred, "Shrill Feminist Attorney" ("Behind the Laughter"). Most of the other characters are more nuanced. Lisa is an outspoken feminist, but when confronted with her eating disorder, she attempts socially responsible self-analysis. Still, she succumbs to society's expectations of body-thought: "I know this obsession with thinness is unhealthy and anti-feminist, but that's what a fat girl would say" ("Sleeping with the Enemy"). It may be argued that Lisa inherited feminist tendencies from her mother. "The Way We Was" shows a young Marge having her consciousness raised and becoming an outspoken advocate for women's equality in high school. While many episodes reinforce this perception of Marge, such as when she fights for recognition for doing "man's work" ("Please, Homer, Don't Hammer 'Em") or when she fights for the rights of gays to marry in "There's Something about Marrying," others illustrate her move away from feminism into more conservative ideologies. For example, she often does not support Lisa's brand of feminism and seems to have forgotten a few of the core values, such as when she says, "When Virginia Woolf wrote every woman needs a room of her own, she must have been talking about the kitchen" ("All's Fair in Oven War").

Body Image, Appearance, and Plastic Surgery

We frequently chat with friends and students about the sitcom trend of the past decade or so[10] in which very attractive women are married to not-as-attractive men. On shows such as *The King of Queens, Cougar Town, According to Jim*, and *Family Guy*, the husbands are extraordinarily less appealing than their wives. We like to ask our classes why that might be. Generally, students decide that either women are less superficial than men are, or the shows' creators want to *depict* women as less superficial, or (more likely, in our opinion), good-looking women get ratings, whereas men need only be funny. Consider dramas like *Grey's Anatomy*, for example. While there are moments of humor, the show does not depend on the delivery of jokes the way that a sitcom does, and *Grey's Anatomy* has a good-looking male star for every good-looking female star.

Unlike the other sitcoms mentioned, however, we know that the start of Homer and Marge's relationship was based on genuine affection. (We've learned this through flashback episodes, especially "The Way We Was.")

Interestingly, there have been several *Simpsons* episodes that deal with body image and appearance. As is true of many topics, the flexibility of the medium enables the show to do the topic justice. Interestingly, it's not just Marge and Lisa who have grappled with self-image issues; several episodes have featured men dealing with insecurities regarding their bodies and appearance.

In "Bart Star," Bart splits his pants during fitness testing, and a video of the incident winds up on the evening news. He is unconcerned, however, even while Lisa taunts him about the Pop-Tarts he's eating. Still, Bart, Milhouse, Rod, and Todd try out for football, presumably because of pressure by their parents (although in the case of Rod and Todd, it is to keep their minds off girls and other temptations). The remainder of the episode, however, has little (if anything) to do with health and fitness, and focuses on competition and parenting.[11] Because Sherri and Terri tease Lisa about having a big butt, she develops an eating disorder in "Sleeping with the Enemy." Just as eating disorders can be said to have no end, Lisa won't give Homer closure at the end of the episode, telling him that she's still not happy with her body.

"Lisa the Beauty Queen" also deals with Homer and Lisa's relationship, but is particularly compelling as a look at self-esteem and confidence. Lisa's self-esteem takes a hit when she receives a particularly unflattering caricature. Even though the artist is a hack and draws her with roller skates after she tells him she doesn't like roller-skating, she sees herself in the image and moans, "Oh, my God, I'm ugly." In a move of selfless intentions, Homer enters Lisa into a beauty pageant. The winner, Amber Dempsey, is a career pageant contestant who won "Pork Princess and Little Miss Kosher in the same week." Lisa is runner-up and becomes Little Miss Springfield after Amber is struck by lightning. Lisa uses her position to speak up about issues important to her; before she sings the national anthem, she states: "I'd like to say that college football diverts funds that are badly needed for education and the arts!"

The pageant organizers, seeking to find a loophole to take the crown from Lisa, find that Homer had written "okay" in the space on the application that stated "keep this space blank." They strip her of the title, and Homer feels bad, but she tells him, "The point is you wanted me to feel better about myself, and I do." Knowing Lisa, it wasn't that she felt prettier that helped her self-esteem; rather, it was the fact that she spoke her mind and had an audience willing to listen to her.

In "Large Marge," Marge is mistakenly given breast implants in a plastic surgery center as disorganized and busy as a fast-food restaurant. She is angry at first, but as she begins to experience how life is for bigger-breasted women, she becomes interested in keeping them. She is even "discovered" as a model. However, Marge quickly becomes tired of her enormous breasts when her back begins to hurt and they get in the way (literally) of doing everyday things, such as caring for Maggie.

In "Pygmoelian," Moe enters a bartending contest, the winner of which is to be featured on the new Duff calendar. He wins the contest, but when he receives the calendar, he finds that they've covered his face. Fed up with his ugliness, he turns to plastic surgery and becomes a dreamboat, but because he is focused on revenge, he winds up undoing all the positives that his new handsome face brought to his life. The episode ends with an injury, causing Moe's face to revert exactly to how it looked before the surgery.

In "Husbands and Knives," Marge finds success with a gym she has opened for regular women (called "Shapes," a spoof of Curves). Homer is introduced to the concept of trophy husbands, and turns to stomach stapling and plastic surgery when he fears that Marge will leave him for a younger, fitter model. Of course, Homer's fear is unfounded and irrational; Marge will not leave Homer because of his physical appearance (although we have learned over the years and as recently as "Homer the Whopper" that Marge is more attracted to him when he is slimmer).

Culture and Homosexuality

In the time that *The Simpsons* has been on the air, the culture's overall attitude towards homosexuality has become slightly more accepting. In comedy, however, this attitude has changed drastically. In an interview on National Public Radio's *Fresh Air*, filmmaker Judd Apatow describes a current wave in television comedy, on shows such as *The Colbert Report* and *The Daily Show*, in which intolerance is mocked. According to Apatow, the message is simple: "Don't be a jerk." Thus, *The Simpsons* and other shows offer an interesting way to approach how the overall culture's attitude towards homosexuality is changing.[12]

Will and Grace debuted on NBC in September of 1998. In its eight-year run, it won seven GLAAD[13] awards and was considered the gateway for other gay-friendly television shows, such as *Queer Eye for the Straight Guy*, *The L Word*, and *Queer as Folk*. *Will and Grace* seemed filled with gay stereotypes and didn't do much to dispel myths about gays, but to its credit, it did put gays on television screens across middle America. Still, an overarching message like the one that Apatow describes was lacking on *Will and Grace*.

On April 30, 1997, the main character on *Ellen* (played by Ellen DeGeneres) came out, shortly after DeGeneres herself did. Leaks of DeGeneres's negotiations with ABC to out her character led to bomb threats and harassing phone calls to the show's writers. It seems insufficient to say that this was a big deal, causing a much bigger hubbub than the infamous kiss between Roseanne and Sharon (Mariel Hemingway) on *Roseanne* in 1994.[14]

A year and a half before *Will and Grace* debuted, and a couple months before the notorious *Ellen* episode, on February 16, 1997, without much fanfare or controversy, an episode of *The Simpsons* entitled "Homer's Phobia"[15] first aired. Fox censors originally wanted all references to homosexuality removed, but executive turnover occurred and the episode was resubmitted, cleared with no problem, and ultimately won Emmy and GLAAD awards. In the episode, Homer becomes friends with a gay man named John (voiced by John Waters). When Marge tells him that she thinks John is gay, Homer has a meltdown, suddenly deciding that he hates John and doesn't want him in the Simpson home. Irrationally, he believes that spending time around John will make Bart gay. Marge and the children largely ignore his childish intolerance and remain friends with John, and in the end, John ends up saving Homer's life. All of the homophobic, irrational, and intolerant characters (Homer, Barney, and Moe) end up looking ridiculous in the end (Moe in fact appears to be masking homosexual tendencies with his professed intolerance[16]), which suggests that *The Simpsons* (along with *Roseanne* and *Ellen*) were on the upslope of the trend that Apatow speaks of, that current comedy recommends that we not be jerks.[17]

The lack of reaction to *The Simpsons* doing a gay-themed episode is thanks to many factors. For example, the gay character presented in the episode was new and voiced by a guest. In addition, the storyline isn't about the character coming out and there is no romance or kissing in the episode. Nevertheless, arguably the biggest factor was that the show had had a gay character from the beginning; it seems that since the show has never hidden the sexual orientation of Waylon Smithers, but has never made an issue of it either, the audience was guided to feel the same.

In a similar manner to the show's treatment of sexual orientation (gays and possible gays, such as Patty Bouvier and Lenny and Carl, respectively) are simply present without any commotion (which is common in real life), as are non–Christians and other "non-mainstream" individuals. *The Simpsons* seems to reserve judgment for extreme and unlikely sexualities — such as Troy McClure's fish fetish. While any sort of extreme and unreasonable viewpoint is mocked on *The Simpsons*, the show tends to show respect and tolerance for the diversity of humankind.

Perhaps the most intriguing way in which the show illustrates the fluidity of gender and sexuality is in its depiction of Homer. Below is a list of times when Homer moved along the sexuality spectrum[18]:

1. In "Little Big Mom," Homer tries to remember what the skiing instructor said to do in an emergency, but his thoughts go to Flanders flexing in his tight ski suit and Homer thinks to himself, "Stupid, sexy Flanders!"

2. After Springfield wins a football game against Shelbyville, Homer kisses Flanders.

3. When Homer becomes president of the union at work, Mr. Burns invites Homer over to try to negotiate. Homer, however, misinterprets what Burns is saying and believes that Mr. Burns is coming on to him. His response is "Sorry, Mr. Burns, but I don't go in for these backdoor shenanigans. Sure, I'm flattered, maybe even a little curious, but the answer is no!"

4. At the end of "Three Gays of the Condo," Homer lives with two gay men for a short time. Upon reconciling with Marge, she kisses Homer and he says, "Wow! That has to be the best kiss I had all night." Pause. "Or was it?" He is referring to a kiss he received earlier from one of his gay friends.

5. In "Blame It on Lisa," Homer is kidnapped in Brazil while the rest of the family is at Carnival. Marge laments that Homer isn't there because he would have loved it: one of her reasons is all of the "ambiguous sexuality."

6. In the steam room with Rainier Wolfcastle, Homer has to resist the urge to look at his "famous wang."

7. Apparently, Homer sometimes wears Marge's underwear, though he says it's "strictly a comfort thing."

8. In *The Simpsons Movie*, Homer almost kisses a pig. He later refers to the pig as his summer romance.

9. Homer sometimes bends his knee when Marge kisses him.

10. Homer attends the "mustache parade" (gay pride parade) Springfield has every year. Lisa has also had him march in the parade.

11. Homer apparently shares Lisa's crush on the level five vegan — he gets lost in his eyes. Homer also seems entranced by the man who saves manatees.

12. When trapped with other tow truck drivers in a basement, Homer campaigns to be their leader. He promises, "I will determine how far we can go without being gay."

13. In "The Burns and the Bees," Moe tries to tell Homer how to get bees to mate. Homer asks, "You and me?" When Moe explains that he means the bees, Homer seems dejected and says quietly, "I have no inclination."

14. In "Monty Can't Buy Me Love," Mr. Burns approaches

Homer and pleads, "I want to be loved." Homer's response: "I see ... well, I'll need some beer."

15. In "Brother's Little Helper" Marge suggests a night out: "We can try that bar where men dance with other men. Doesn't that sound adorable?" Homer replies, "Well, sure, if it's true."

16. Homer's description of Oliver North during his trial: "He was just poured into that uniform."

17. Homer's favorite jukebox song is "It's Raining Men."

18. In "Mom and Pop Art," Homer sketches Lenny and Carl in the showers. Lenny reassures Carl that it's for art's sake. Homer replies, "Oh, yeah ... art."

Religion,[19] Diet, and Other Personal Choices

Apu's Indian heritage and Hinduism are omnipresent, and the one time Hinduism is a spectacle, it is Homer who is behind the production and ends up making an idiot of himself ("The Two Mrs. Nahasapeemapetilans"). Judaism is present and treated with respect, notably in the episode "Like Father, Like Clown," in which the Simpson kids help reunite Krusty with his estranged father, Rabbi Hyman Krustofsky. The episode was well researched, and two rabbis, Harold M. Schulweis and Lavi Meier, were hired to consult on the script. Critics praised the episode for its emotional depth, and Schulweis said of the overall episode: "I thought it had a Jewish resonance to it. I was impressed by the underlying moral seriousness" (quoted in Pinsky 150).

In 2001, in the episode "She of Little Faith," Lisa discovered that Buddhism was a better fit for her than Christianity. Richard Gere makes a guest appearance as himself in that episode, which is fitting as he is a Buddhist and supporter of Tibet. In the episode, Gere is a spokesperson of sorts for Buddhism. He tells Lisa, "Buddhism teaches that suffering is caused by desire," and gives her a pamphlet that explains the virtues of his philosophy to Lisa and the audience. This comforts and inspires Lisa, as she now has a term to use that defines beliefs that she'd held all along. Lisa's conversion (for lack of a better word) is not forced upon her. This is contrasted by the way that Marge tries to win Lisa back to Christianity with trickery (including a fake pony) and bribery (this is a Christmas episode, after all).

Lisa went vegetarian in 1995 ("Lisa the Vegetarian"); she was obnoxious and doctrinaire at first (like many people we know who are fired up when discovering something new, such as religion, feminism, or politics. Denise was definitely guilty of it when she went vegetarian in college), but through the examples of Apu and Linda and Paul McCartney, Lisa learned how to hold firm in her beliefs but not push them onto others. Through the examples of "Lisa the Vegetarian" and "She of Little Faith," *The Simpsons* demonstrates that bullying and tricks are poor substitutes for leading by example.

Stereotypes

The Simpsons has played with numerous stereotypes of ethnic groups, subcultures, races, nationalities, and members of various socioeconomic classes, to the anger and offense of some. However, the group that has the most right (if any) to be offended is the group that is being satirized by the depictions of these stereotypes: the oftentimes clueless Americans who believe and perpetuate such stereotypes.

While many of the stereotypes depicted on the show exist within Springfield, many countries have shared the stereotype spotlight on *The Simpsons*, including Japan, Canada, India, Brazil, France, and Australia.

In the DVD commentary, the creators said they were purposely nasty but overtly inaccurate in their depiction of Australia. Because *The Simpsons* is very popular in Australia, the writers "thought [Australians would] enjoy a roasting." Some members of the Australian audience were not amused, but it was a warm reception compared to Brazil's response[20] regarding the episode "Blame It on Lisa" in which the family visits Rio de Janeiro to look for a missing orphan. In Rio, Homer is forced to wear Speedos (instead of trunks) on the beach, he is kidnapped and develops Stockholm syndrome, and Bart is captivated by a children's show called "Teleboobies." Several episodes have since referenced Brazil in an equally snarky way.

The biggest stereotype of Japan depicted in "Thirty Minutes over Tokyo" is its supposed reputation for cruelty and harshness. Living cats are processed into Sanrio products at the Hello Kitty factory. When the Simpsons lose their money and go on a game show to try to win tickets home, the host of the show (which is called "Happy Smile Super Chal-

lenge Family Wish Show") explains, "Our game shows are a little different from yours. Your shows reward knowledge; we punish ignorance."

There are three categories to choose from in the game: "Ow, that
hurts," "Why are you doing this to me," and "Please let me die." Upon
leaving Japan, Bart announces, "Goodbye, Japan! I'll miss your Kentucky
Fried Chicken and your sparkling, whale-free seas."

In "The Bart Wants What It Wants," when Bart wants the Simpson
family to travel to Canada, Homer says, "Why should we leave America
to visit America Junior?" The episode makes some friendly jabs at Canada,
including its sports (curling and poor Olympic standing), and plays with
Canadian slang (Milhouse calls Bart "hoser.")

France and the French have the distinct honor of being the playful
target of early episodes. In "The Crepes of Wrath," Bart is sent to France
in an exchange program, where his hosts mistreat him and put antifreeze
into their wine. In "Life on the Fast Lane," Marge is wooed by a sweet-
talking bowler who, except for his surprising bowling ability, is a walking
French stereotype.

Brits are also playfully mocked, especially their cuisine. The experi-
ence of eating eel pie prompts Chief Wiggum (as a British inspector in
"Treehouse of Horror XV") to announce, "We British sure eat crap." In
"Lisa's Wedding," a fortune teller predicts Lisa's future courtship with a
British man. When Lisa calls her mother from England, Marge says,
"Remember, an elevator is called a 'lift,' a mile is called a 'kilometer,' and
botulism is called 'steak and kidney pie.'" Unfortunately, Lisa's fiancé turns
out to be quite a snob, and he tells her, "This has been quite trying. You
know, I've attempted to enjoy your family on a personal level, on an ironic
level, as a novelty, as camp, as kitsch, as cautionary example — nothing
works. Frankly, I'll be quite relieved when we get back to England and
we won't have to deal with them."

Perhaps the group that gets the most roasting is Italian Americans.
Despite his thick accent, Luigi the chef doesn't speak Italian; he explains
that his parents taught him broken English. Similarly, Fat Tony's rival
capo in "Moe Baby Blues" says "Oh, bambino. Or is it a bambina? I don't
speak any language so good." Springfield has a mafia run by Fat Tony, but
the group is so sloppy and unsophisticated that it is only allowed to continue operating in Springfield because its stupidity is rivaled only by the
police department's, whose head, Chief Wiggum, is corrupt, lazy, and
ridiculously incompetent. In "Moe Baby Blues," the president of the Ital-

ian American Anti-defamation League also has a gun, and the Mafia stand-off he witnesses "really burns his cannoli."

The excesses and preoccupations of celebrities are frequently satirized, but the show's examination of celebrity and Hollywood isn't a satire on celebrity culture but a satire on how the average American *thinks* of celebrity. For example, the dress that Sara Sloane wears to the concert in "A Star Is Born-Again" shows how outlandish the average person thinks that celebrities must be, marking an interesting contrast to the tabloid magazines that do their best to find stars shopping in jeans or sunbathing with visible cellulite.

For example, in "When You Dish upon a Star," Homer discovers Kim Basinger and Alec Baldwin living on the outskirts of Springfield. Their predicament is understandable: They are people in the public eye wanting some privacy. What average person hasn't felt the need for space at some point? Hopefully the audience sees that Kim and Alec's reaction to Homer's betrayal was not out of celebrity-style self-importance but rather out of simple disappointment and loss of trust.

Stereotypes may begin for a reason, maybe occasionally even for a good reason, but the reliance on stereotypes to make value judgments is pure laziness, and *The Simpsons* demonstrates the flaws in such actions. One such example of the undermining of stereotypes is when we see Nelson giving an informal tutorial on huckleberry preparation. His tender moment is disrupted when he sees the principal and quickly pretends he was talking about bullying ("Lard of the Dance"). We are reminded that our perceptions of other people are often wrong and that our behavior is often partially determined by their expectations of us.

Education

From Springfield Elementary to a variety of universities, educational systems and institutions are mentioned frequently, sometimes as the topic of entire episodes (such as "The PTA Disbands" and "Lisa Gets an *A*"), or throwaway lines (the writers seem fond of the Seven Sisters, and our alma mater, Florida State University, was referenced in "Smart and Smarter").

Advocating the teaching of a show that critiques educational institutions may seem counterintuitive. After all, as George Meyer, one of the principal shapers of the show, says of the one "goal" of the show: "It's to get people to re-examine their world, and specifically, the authority figures in their world" (quoted in Turner 56). We are the authority figures, and thus some may be threatened by this invitation to meta-analysis. However, thinking through the efficacy of the educational status quo is productive. We as teachers can learn from the show as well. As a satire of education, both as a system and its individual practices, the show asks us to reevaluate the success of modern education and of ourselves as instructors. Two scholars, Gavin Morrison and Alan Britton, recently argued as such in the presentation "Images of the Teacher in *The Simpsons*: Subversive, Superficial, or Sentimental" at a 2008 international conference on teaching.

The problems faced by the underfunded and poorly staffed Springfield Elementary are indicative of widespread problems that U.S. public schools face in general. A teacher strike occurs in "The PTA Disbands" due to budget problems. Although the Springfield population gives lip service to their children's future and acknowledges that teacher salaries are related to the issue, they refuse to raise taxes to achieve higher educational quality. In "The President Wore Pearls," Lisa runs for class president on a platform that includes a "French teacher who actually speaks French." When she is tricked into signing an order eliminating music, art, and gym, Bart remarks, "You made this school even worse, and it wasn't exactly San Diego State to begin with."[21]

In "Separate Vocations," Lisa makes cracks regarding teachers' salaries: "You're earning your 18 grand a year" (to Miss Hoover) and on her news show in "Girly Edition," Lisa includes schoolteachers concerned with "cashing their big, fat paychecks" rather than their students as one of the problems with society.

Mrs. Krabappel and Bart's love/hate relationship is occasionally examined with heart, notably in "Bart Gets an *F*." The assumption that teachers love to fail students (or enjoy tricking them) is challenged in this episode. When Mrs. Krabappel grades Bart's test, she is surprised that he is upset, saying, "I figured you'd be used to failing by now." However, she softens when she realizes that he studied in earnest, and finds a way to justify giving him a D- on the test.

Through Bart, the abundance of people with higher degrees is mocked. He tells his mother that he's going to go taunt the Ph.D.'s working at a Barnes & Noble–like bookstore called Bookaccino's. He says,

"Hey, guys, I heard an assistant professorship just opened up (they gather around excitedly) at the University of ... psych! ("Diatribe of a Mad Housewife"). The "overeducated" writers at Itchy & Scratchy Studios and the engineers at Herb Powell's automobile company are mocked as well. University instructors in particular come under fire for pretentious behavior in "Little Girl in the Big Ten," "That '90s Show," and "Homer Simpson, This Is Your Wife."

Community

In "Lisa the Iconoclast," Lisa becomes a pariah in her class for writing an essay in which she reveals the unflattering truth about the town's founder, Jebediah Springfield. She discovers that he was a murderous pirate, even despite the museum curator's attempts to foil her discovery. In the end, though, although she is right, she doesn't share the truth with the town because she realizes the myth of Jebediah adds value to the community and town pride.

Early in the episode "Lemon of Troy," the kids learn what community means to them and the audience learns the origins of the Springfield/Shelbyville rivalry. It starts as Bart earns a lecture from Marge when she catches him writing his name in wet cement. She wonders where his town pride is, offering these words:

> **Marge:** This town is a part of who you are. This is a Springfield Isotopes cap. When you wear it, you're wearing Springfield. When you eat a fish from our river, you're eating Springfield. When you make lemonade from our tree, you're drinking Springfield.
> **Bart:** Mom, when you give that lecture, you're boring Springfield.
> **Marge:** Bart, you have roots in this town and you ought to show respect for it. This town is a part of us all. A part of us all. A part of us all. Sorry to repeat myself, but it'll help you remember.

Her words do stick with Bart, and he tells Milhouse that Springfield is a "pretty cool place to live." When the Shelbyville kids steal Springfield's beloved lemon tree, Bart rallies support for his plan to get the tree back, saying, "That lemon tree's a part of our town, and as kids, the backbone of our economy." It takes the adults working with the kids to get the lemon tree back into Springfield, and its return is a source of joy and pride for the town.

Surprisingly, Homer is the voice of logic in "Much Apu about Nothing" when the town has a proposition on the ballot to remove all undocumented immigrants from Springfield. When he finds out that Apu may be sent away, Homer dedicates his time to helping Apu, saying, "Wow, you must love this country more than I love a cold beer on a hot Christmas morning." Having someone he cares about potentially affected makes Homer realize it was wrong for him to support Proposition 24. At a gathering, Homer tries to inspire the townspeople to vote against Proposition 24, with this moving tribute to immigrants:

> Most of us here were born in America. We take this country for granted, but not immigrants like Apu. While the rest of us are drinking ourselves stupid, they're driving the cabs that get us home safely. They're writing the operas that entertain us every day. They're training our tigers and kicking our extra points. These people are the glue that holds together the gears of our society. If we pass Proposition 24, we'll be losing some of the truest Americans of all. When you go to the polls tomorrow, please vote no on Proposition 24.[22]

The Simpsons *and Science*

Math and physics professor Paul Halpern has written a book about science in *The Simpsons* entitled *What's Science Ever Done for Us* (see Chapter 1 for a description of Halpern's book), and since we are not scientists (at least, not beyond our liberal arts educations), we have no intentions of outdoing or even matching Halpern's work. However, discussions of science do arise in our classes. The general aim is not to argue for or against the accuracy of *Simpsons* science; we generally prefer discussions about the presence of science on the show, how science is treated, and how science is the impetus for much of the action. From "Bart's Comet" to Homer's numerous run-ins with robots, our students (especially Denise's students at Milwaukee School of Engineering) enjoy discussing the importance of science on the show.

Lisa in particular is familiar with the scientific method and even poses her science projects in the form of research questions. For example, in "Duffless," Bart destroys Lisa's science experiment, a tomato she enhances with steroids. Inspired by a mental image she has of Bart as a hamster, she changes her project to answer a research question: "Is my brother dumber than a hamster?" In "Treehouse of Horror VII," in the segment called "The Genesis Tub," she creates another research question: "Will cola dissolve a tooth?"

The conflicts between science and religion are examined in "Lisa the Skeptic," in which many of the townspeople rebel against science, trashing the Museum of Natural History, the Springfield Robotics Lab, and, to further show their confusion, the Christian Science Reading Room. Moe's hypocrisy (symbolic of all the rioters') is illustrated when he is injured by a falling mammoth's tusk at the museum, and laments, "Oh, I'm paralyzed; I just hope medical science can cure me."

Job Satisfaction

In humanities courses, a common theme is living and loving life. We tackle such questions as "How important is a career to personal satisfaction?" and "Is it possible to be fulfilled in life with a job one hates?" Joy (or lack thereof) in work is a common theme in the humanities, particularly in American literature (including *The Simpsons*). The issue of Marge's satisfaction was discussed to some degree above in that she frequently takes jobs outside of the home but doesn't keep them for more than one episode. However, she seems happy overall with homemaking because of the creativity she finds there, as described in "Separate Vocations." Lisa is devastated by the results of an aptitude test that recommends she be a homemaker. In attempt to make Lisa feel better, Marge shows Lisa how she arranged the bacon, eggs, and toast into a smiley face on the plate. Lisa asks, "What's the point? They'll never notice," to which Marge responds, "You'd be surprised." (Lisa was correct, however, as Homer and Bart scarf down their food without noticing.) In "Mr. Lisa Goes to Washington," Marge makes "meatloaf men." (This time Bart does notice her special effort, however, because he bites the head off his meatloaf man.)

Perhaps the most poignant episode dealing with job satisfaction is "And Maggie Makes Three." It is told largely in flashback, when the Simpson family consisted of Marge, Homer, Bart, and Lisa. The family's budget allows for Homer to hold his dream job (pin monkey) at Barney's Bowl-A-Rama as long as everything stays exactly the way it is. Homer loves his job, and he's good at it, too. But then Marge discovers that she's pregnant, and Homer must go back to his detested job at the nuclear power plant to sustain a family of five. The end of the episode shows Homer's workspace, covered with pictures of Maggie in the place that he "needs the most cheering up."

Closely tied to the issue of job satisfaction is the larger issue of class. After all, job satisfaction is dependent on two class issues — the ability to make a living wage and the ability to have some choice in one's job, which is often a function of class privilege. Several issues address how job satisfaction and economics are tied, as both Homer and Marge are forced into jobs they would not normally take to support the family. Mr. Burns financially exploits his workers, the government (he once "liberated" a trillion dollars), and the local taxpayers/customers. The system is set up to allow Mr. Burns to continue gaining wealth, with only a few honest politicians and a relatively ineffectual union to temper his greed. Burns even attempts to outsource labor to India to avoid the few restrictions on his labor practices ("Kiss Kiss, Bang Bangalore"). Sprawl-Mart locks in its employees and refuses to pay them fairly ("On a Clear Day I Can't See My Sister"). Medical care is dependent upon wealth, as are higher education opportunities.

"Scenes from the Class Struggle in Springfield" and "A Tale of Two Springfields" are among those episodes that directly address class differences. Yet perhaps the most interesting episode to deal with class is one that exposes the relative lack of reality of the Simpsons' financial situation. After all, Homer is usually able to support and wife, three children, risky financial investments, his alcoholism, and Marge's gambling problem[23] with his job at the power plant, although he is routinely fired and often does not go in to work. "Homer's Enemy" points out how awkward this situation would be in reality by showing a character who has to work much harder than Homer to achieve much less. Frank Grimes resents the ease with which Homer lives, especially when he sees all of the utterly amazing things Homer has accomplished, such as going into space. This episode elicits a discussion of the social contract and the alienation of the modern worker from his labor. It reminds us that there are economic disparities and prejudices, and that hard work does not always equal success. The end of the episode sees Frank die in a mad attempt to imitate Homer's carelessness. Homer falls asleep at the funeral; the others in attendance laugh at his disrespect. As Robert Sloane argues in "Who Wants Candy?: Disenchantment in *The Simpsons*," "Indeed, the final scene of the episode is one of the most disturbing ever shown on *The Simpsons* ... the effect is chilling" (152). The last line belongs to Lenny, who declares, "That's our

Homer!" Just as he and the others are Homer's audience in the moment, so are we — and he's *our* Homer too. We laugh at his disrespect all the time, just as we laugh at his economic and job woes without thinking about how we might feel if he were real. As Sloane states, "Clearly, the world of *The Simpsons* is fantasy, and our attention is explicitly called to that fact in this moment" (151).

The Simpsons *and Popular Culture*

The term "popular culture" (henceforth "pop culture") has gone through an amelioration. Previously, the term "popular" referred to the base, vulgar tastes held by common people (think beer vs. aged scotch). Since the late 18th century, the meaning has shifted to simply mean "widespread." Still, some critics will contend that for something to be liked on a near universal scale, it must be watered or dumbed down in some manner. Pop culture envelopes all trends and tastes in a given culture, including film, television, and music. While historically pop culture tended to refer mainly to a culture's consumption habits, it now can be applied to arts and hobbies, such as cooking, quilting, scrapbooking, and knitting.

The purpose of this section isn't so much to convince anyone that *The Simpsons* is a mirror of pop culture. Anyone who's watched the show realizes that each episode contains at least a dozen pop culture references, and if anyone still needs convincing, Turner's *Planet Simpson* is an encyclopedia of the show's pop culture references. Rather, we seek to demonstrate pop culture's relevance as a course of study and look at the show's active role in that study. A postmodern take on culture is that there is no "high" or "low" culture, and that all elements of culture are combined. As *The Simpsons* is a postmodern show, with purposeful combining of many types of art and culture, it only seems appropriate to think of pop culture in that light.[24] An average episode of *The Simpsons* may refer to other television shows, Shakespeare, an opera, a well-regarded classic film, and Twizzlers, and may feature a gratuitous belch or Homer falling down a cliff, and all within a few minutes.

These references are sometimes simple jokes, but are often satirical. Indeed, analyzing *The Simpsons* is meta. From musicals to cartoons to politics to commercial trends, *The Simpsons* continuously satirizes virtually every element of our culture. In our classes, we enjoy the challenge and the meta joy of actively breaking down and discussing a show that breaks down and discusses our culture.

The Simpsons has much more staying power than other satirical cartoons, such as *South Park* and *Family Guy*. The lag between authoring and airing an episode of *The Simpsons* is considerably longer than *South Park*'s, for example, which enables the writers of *South Park* to tackle recent events and celebrities enjoying their fifteen minutes; the selected trends featured on *The Simpsons* have a stronger resonance than the topical references tackled by *South Park*. In addition, purposely outdated references, such as Bart's adoration for *Mad* magazine,[25] the excitement of yo-yos,[26] and the shows within the show (*Krusty the Clown* and *Itchy & Scratchy*), give the show a timeless quality, and the show's consistent attention to comic books works in its favor as the trend of adapting comics into top-grossing mainstream films progresses.

Occasionally, *The Simpsons* does take cues from *South Park*, such as its MMORPG[27] parody called "Earthland Realms" in the 2007 episode "Marge Gamer." This particular episode may have lacked a bit of bite because *South Park* did it first and because MMORPGs had already been popular for years, but it works because of the self-reference (Marge discovers the game because she finally goes online to get an email address). The show avoids passing fads to ensure the episodes are relatively timeless, and the writers' attempts at engaging with the cultural zeitgeist do not usually fall short. Recently, Lisa encountered a problem when she ordered too many songs for her "Mypod,"[28] and several years ago, "Treehouse of Horror XII" found the Simpson children in a Hogwarts-like magic school.

Chris Turner has written an entire book about the pop culture references in *The Simpsons*; our goal is to discuss how *The Simpsons* has actually changed our popular culture.[29] In our discussion on linguistics, we describe how *The Simpsons* has affected language — not just the lexicon, but syntax as well. However, *The Simpsons* has changed television, making it smarter, which in turn just might be making the audience smarter.

Canadian journalist Alec Ross attributes the seriousness of pop culture studies, beginning in the 1960s in the United States, to the thought held by many scholars that "much of the culture was a direct, wide-ranging and influential response to serious 1960s social issues — civil rights, Vietnam, coming of age of baby boomers, etc.— which are themselves legitimate topics of scholarly study." *The Journal of Popular Culture* was founded in 1967 and continues to be the foremost pop culture journal.[30] The Popular Culture Association (PCA) has held annual conferences since 1971, featuring dozens of panel topics. Recently, panels have included everything from ethnic pop culture (Asian, Brazilian, and German, for example), to Internet culture, comics, Shakespeare on film and television, fat studies, and pop culture in education. Each of these panels is chaired by academics with pop culture specialties. We have found that attending and presenting at PCA/ACA[31] is as relevant as more traditional academic conferences such as the Modern Language Association, and arguably more fun.

Technology and science writer Steven Johnson argues in his book *Everything Bad Is Good for You* that pop culture has "grown more complex and intellectually stimulating in the past thirty years ... demanding more cognitive engagement with each passing year" (xv). Johnson states that since its start, television programming has steadily increased mental demands on its viewers, demands such as attention, patience, and retention (64). Television has changed and grown since Neil Postman decried it in his 1985 book *Amusing Ourselves to Death*:

> I raise no objection to television's junk. The best things on television are its junk, and no one and nothing is seriously threatened by it. Besides, we do not measure a culture by its output of undisguised trivialities but by what it claims as significant. Therein is our problem, for television is at its most trivial and, therefore most dangerous when its aspirations are high, when it presents itself as a carrier of important cultural conversations [16].

Using the complicated storylines and surplus of characters on *The Sopranos* as an example, Johnson argues that television audiences are much more willing and able to put effort into their viewing than they would have in the 1980s (69–71). Previously, Johnson says, the question when watching a drama was "How will this turn out in the end?," but with shows like *The West Wing* and *Lost*, the question is "What's happening now?" (76).

Audiences of situation comedies have also matured. Johnson places *The Simpsons* as the start of this trend, stating that (with the notable exception of *Everybody Loves Raymond*) recent commercially and critically successful comedies have taken "structural cues" from *The Simpsons* (89). Sitcoms used to rely mainly on sarcasm and one-liners, which allowed new audience members to join at any time with no drawbacks. Johnson points out that sitcoms have become more nuanced, requiring audience members have some knowledge of the background of characters, such as Monica's overweight childhood on *Friends* and George's alias Art Vandelay on *Seinfeld* (85). On a show like *Three's Company*, by contrast, the audience just had to remember the basic premise that to continue living in an apartment with two women, Jack Tripper was pretending to be gay (84).

Johnson explains, "The most telling way to measure these shows' complexity is to consider how much external information the viewer must draw upon to 'get' the jokes in their entirety" (Johnson 84). *The Simpsons* is thus more complex than *Seinfeld* or *Friends* because it relies upon the audience's understanding of numerous primary and secondary characters (infrequent appearances of Gil, Sarcastic Man, and Lindsey Naegle, for example), but each episode relies upon knowledge outside of the show even beyond the criteria of complexity offered by Johnson, the numerous film allusions (86). This layering, according to Johnson, enables *The Simpsons* "to retain broad appeal *and* the edgy allure of cult classics" (emphasis ours), plus they grow more entertaining with each viewing (88). Because the episodes have an inside-joke quality to them and because there are so many quick allusions (some of which can be missed by even the most observant viewers), a sitcom built upon one-liners cannot compete. A second viewing of a sitcom with a flat structure is tired and dull.

The Simpsons *and Music*

While in many ways *The Simpsons* is a sitcom, it eschews one of the most annoying and persistent mainstays of traditional sitcoms: the laugh track. Because there is no canned laughter, the show's use of music, which is always well chosen and genuine, is allowed to glow. With a combination of the original score created for every episode by Alf Clausen, the use of existing songs integrated into episodes, and original musical numbers (even in episodes that are not musical episodes), *The Simpsons* uses music in ways that no other sitcom or cartoon has.

Fox Music president Richard Kraft credits the "three-dimensionality" of the series to the fact that *The Simpsons* is "one of the few television shows still scored with live musicians," as most shows now use synthesized music (Donkin). Not only does the music tap into the listeners' emotions, it also keeps the listener connected in a primal way, as Daniel

J. Levitin explains: "Computational systems in the brain synchronize neural oscillators with the pulse of the music, and begin to predict when the next strong beat will occur" (191). Considering music's compelling addition to the witty, surprising dialogue on *The Simpsons*, the way that the show has connected with viewers through sound (in the mesolimbic system of the brain, according to Levitin) is no surprise. It's the perfect equation.

It's a testament, not just to the general quality of the show, but specifically to its use of music, that many musicians have lent their talent and voices to the show. In fact, many artists and groups, among them Michael Jackson and Green Day, have approached the show first. In addition, many artists have been honored to mock themselves on the show, including Elvis Costello, who, upon losing his glasses, cries, "My image!" ("How I Spent My Strummer Vacation"). *The Simpsons* has playfully teased both R.E.M. and U2 for their environmentalism (with their participation, of course), and every member of the Beatles has appeared on the show except John Lennon. Suffice it to say, we don't miss the laugh track.

Episode Lists[32]

Themes of the Humanities

As mentioned above, there are five common themes in the humanities that accompany the study of art and literature: morality, freedom, love, happiness, and death- and life-affirmation. The following list includes episodes that we recommend to supplement the discussions in humanities courses for each of these themes; it is by no means a complete list of appropriate or useful choices.

MORALITY

"Bart the Fink" 3F12: After unintentionally outing Krusty as a huge tax cheat, Bart feels incredibly guilty. He tracks Krusty down to convince him to return to television. Krusty then fakes the death of his alter ego to collect the insurance money. This episode was inspired by celebrities in the news with tax problems, and is a wink towards common stories about celebrities who are believed (by some) have faked their own deaths.

"Bart the Mother" 5F22: When Bart kills a bird, he feels guilty and takes the eggs from her nest to care for them. When the eggs hatch, Bart finds that they are not birds but lizards. He visits the Springfield bird-watching group, where Principal Skinner tells him they are an invasive species of Bolivian tree lizards. Skinner wants to kill them as "quickly and gruesomely as possible." Even though by law they should be exterminated, Marge helps Bart escape with the baby lizards. This episode examines the gray areas of right and wrong.

"Homer vs. Lisa and the 8th Commandment" 7F13: Lisa is upset with Homer when he steals cable TV service. Though he tries to justify it, ultimately her righteousness rubs off on Homer.

"Lisa Gets an *A*" AABF03: When Lisa returns to school after being out sick, she hasn't read *The Wind in the Willows* and, in desperation, goes to Nelson for the answers to the quiz. Her grade is so high that it raises Springfield Elementary's ranking to qualify for a grant. When she tells Principal Skinner that the school cannot accept the money, he orchestrates a ruse so that Lisa can come publicly clean but the school can keep the money.

"The Last Temptation of Homer" 1F07: Homer is instantly attracted to Mindy, a new employee at the power plant. He tries to avoid her, but when they are sent to Capital City together, Homer kisses Mindy in the hotel room. He takes Mindy's advice, however, to follow his heart, and he returns to Marge without committing adultery.

FREEDOM

"Summer of 4 Ft. 2" 3F22: The episode begins with the last day of school (is there any sweeter freedom?) and the Simpson family is on their way to the beach where they borrow the Flanders' vacation house. Bart brings Milhouse along, but since Lisa has no friends, she takes this opportunity to reinvent herself. She "forgets to pack" so that Marge will have to buy her all new clothes. As a seemingly entirely different person, she makes friends.

"Bart-Mangled Banner" FABF17: Issues of freedom of speech and the USA PATRIOT Act are examined in this episode.

"Much Apu about Nothing" 3F20: The idea of America is examined (and satirized, of course) in this episode about scapegoating and immigration. Apu says it best when he refers to America as the land he loves, where he has the freedom to say and to charge whatever he wants.

LOVE

"The Way We Was" 7F12: In flashback, this episode tells the story of how Marge and Homer met and fell in love, including trickery, the prom, a sleazy nerd, and French tutoring.

"Another Simpsons Clip Show" 2F33: After reading a romance novel, Marge gathers the family around to share stories of romance, but all anyone can come up with are tales of heartbreak. In the end, though, Marge shares the story of how she and Homer fell in love (clips from "The Way We Was"). This episode shows the distinctions between crushes, lust, infatuation, and actual love.

"And Maggie Makes Three" 2F10: Homer's stint at as a pin monkey at Barney's Bowl-A-Rama ends when Marge becomes pregnant with Maggie. Before she is born, he is resentful, but as soon as he sees her face, he is filled with fatherly love and keeps her pictures in his workspace at the power plant, the place where he "needs the most cheering up."

"The Secrets of a Successful Marriage" 1F20: Trust in the Simpson marriage is challenged when Homer can't keep quiet about private matters (such as what Marge likes in bed). Homer grovels to get her back, saying that he can offer her what no one else can: "complete and utter dependence." In the end, he convinces her that he cannot afford to lose her trust again. This episode is dense with issues of love, trust, enabling, and dependence.

"Three Gays of the Condo" EABF12: Homer finds an old note from Marge that she never gave him, in which she said she couldn't stay with him because she didn't want a life of watching him get drunk. She didn't leave him (obviously), and Homer thinks it was because she was pregnant with Bart. Homer feels betrayed and hurt, and moves out. After some twists and turns (including a come-on from his new roommate), Homer eventually realizes that she stayed with him out of love.

HAPPINESS

"Homer and Apu" 1F10: Homer's sting operation causes Apu to lose his job at the Kwik-E-Mart. Apu is devastated until he gets his Kwik-E-Mart back. This episode is rich for discussing joy at work, fulfillment, and identity.

"You Only Move Twice" 3F23: When Homer is offered a new job with the Globex Corporation, it seems perfect, especially after the family watches a video about the planned community of Cypress Creek, which is beautiful. Homer's boss, Hank Scorpio, is an affable chap. However, after they move to Cypress Creek, Homer is the only one who's happy. Marge is bored with the house that cleans itself so she drinks wine in the middle of the day. Lisa is allergic to everything. Bart is sent to a special class because he is behind the other fourth graders. The family wants to return to Springfield, and although Homer loves his job and feels that he's good at it, he gives up his happiness for his family's.

"Grade School Confidential" 4F09: Edna Krabappel and Principal Skinner find love, and understand, as Skinner says, "what true happiness can be." However, rumors of their relationship spread wildly and become distorted, and Superintendant Chalmers demands that they choose between their relationship and their jobs.

"Moaning Lisa" 7G06: When Lisa is depressed, her parents can say nothing to help her. When Lisa meets bluesman Bleeding Gums Murphy, he teaches her to express her sadness through her saxophone. Marge encourages Lisa to smile and pretend to be happy, but when she sees the other kids taking advantage of Lisa, she backtracks, saying, "Lisa, I apologize to you. I was wrong. I take it all back. Always be yourself. If you want to be sad, honey, be sad. We'll ride it out with you. And when you get finished feeling sad, we'll still be there. From now on, let me do the smiling for both of us." When Lisa hears this, she smiles out of genuine happiness.

DEATH AND LIFE AFFIRMATION

"One Fish, Two Fish, Blowfish, Blue Fish" 7F11: After hearing he may die from improperly prepared fugu, Homer creates a bucket list to make the most of his last hours of life. He does his best to cross everything off the list. The next day (when he realizes he didn't die), he vows to live life to its fullest.

"Alone Again, Natura-Diddly" BABF10: When Maude Flanders is killed in a bizarre accident, Ned is forced to face life and parenthood without her. He meets a Christian rock singer named Rachel Jordan, and while he is attracted to her, it is clear that he's not ready to date. Still, because he is attracted to Rachel, the audience is hopeful that Ned will make it through the grief of losing Maude.[33]

"'Round Springfield" 2F32: While Bart is in the hospital with appendicitis, Lisa sees her hero there, Bleeding Gums Murphy (whom she had met previously in "Moaning Lisa"). The next day, she is saddened to learn that he has died, and decides a good way to pay tribute to him would be having the local jazz radio station play his album. With Bart's help, she's able to do this, and the episode ends with Lisa playing with Bleeding Gums, even though he has "a date with Billie Holiday."

Social Issues in Writing Courses

Earlier in this chapter, we discussed common cultural/social topics that we use in our *Simpson*-focused writing courses. We generally divide the course by topic, and select the paper assignments that seem to fit most smoothly with those topics.[34] The following is a list of episodes that we have used in our classes.

Sexuality/Gender Issues

"Natural Born Kissers" 5F18: Homer and Marge discover a creative way to speed up the slowdown in their sex life.

"Bart the Mother" 5F22: Bart shoots a bird and, out of guilt, takes her eggs home to care for them. This episode is a terrific examination of the mother-son relationship.

"The Secret War of Lisa Simpson" 4F21: With Bart's help, Lisa succeeds as the only female cadet in military school.

"Lisa on Ice" 2F05: Lisa and Bart become rivals when they play for opposing peewee hockey teams. Marge says that girls should be able to play any sport that boys do, but doesn't want Lisa to play hockey because it is "so violent and dangerous." Marge is guilty of a double standard — she hadn't voiced concern about Bart playing hockey.

"Homer vs. Patty and Selma" 2F14: Bart is forced to take ballet but discovers that he loves it.

"Little Big Mom" BABF04: Lisa thinks homemaking is easy until she takes over the household duties while Marge is in the hospital.

"Marge on the Lam" 1F03: Marge becomes friends with a divorcée who sweeps up Marge into her drama.

"Lisa the Beauty Queen" 9F02: To raise Lisa's confidence, Homer registers her for the Little Miss Springfield Pageant.

"Homer's Phobia" 4F11: Homer has an irrational fear that the Simpsons' new friend, John, will make Bart gay.

"Lisa vs. Malibu Stacy" 1F12: Lisa is horrified at the sexist messages she hears from her new talking Malibu Stacy doll (based upon an actual talking Barbie doll). Lisa tracks down the creator of Malibu Stacy, the reclusive Stacy Lovell. With some persuading, Lovell agrees to work with Lisa to create a doll who will be a better influence on young girls, with "the wisdom of Gertrude Stein and the wit of Cathy Guisewite; the tenacity of Nina Totenberg, and the common sense of Elizabeth Cady Stanton. And to top it off, the down-to-earth good looks of Eleanor Roosevelt."[35]

Religion

"Lisa the Skeptic" 5F05: An angel skeleton provokes a war between science and religion in Springfield, but when the townspeople find out they've been horribly tricked for publicity, Lisa (the only one who didn't fall for the ruse) is the only one who's angry.

"She of Little Faith" DABF02: Lisa discovers that she is a Buddhist.

"Homer the Heretic" 9F01: Homer has a terrific day, skipping church while the rest of the family suffers through a long sermon and dangerously freezing temperatures. Homer decides he's never going to church again, but after a fire, he is convinced to try to regain his faith.

"Home Sweet Homediddly-Dum-Doodily" 3F01: When the Simpson kids are placed in foster care at the Flanders home, Ned finds out that the children were never baptized and attempts to baptize them himself. Homer and Marge feel that Flanders is overstepping his boundaries and get to the river just in time to stop the baptism.

"Bart Sells His Soul" 3F02: When Bart sells his soul to Milhouse for five dollars, strange things start happening and he is desperate to get it back. He goes on an intense physical and emotional journey to retrieve his soul and, with some help from Lisa, he is able to do so.

"The Joy of Sect" 5F23: The occasion of Homer being brainwashed into a cult gives the show a chance to demonstrate the tactics cults use to indoctrinate their subjects. This episode has fun showing the differences and similarities between mainstream religions and cults.

"Missionary: Impossible" BABF11: After Homer calls PBS with a phony pledge, he runs from the pledge enforcement crew to the church, where the Reverend Lovejoy rescues him by sending him on a plane to "Microasia" to be a missionary, despite his lack of religious faith. Homer ruins the natives' lives by introducing them to gambling and alcohol.

"Pray Anything" EABF06: When Homer wins his lawsuit against the church, the Simpson family moves into the house of worship. It becomes a riotous bar. A storm begins, causing a flood. Everyone flocks to the roof of the church. The Reverend Lovejoy returns in a helicopter, leading everyone to pray for forgiveness, and the rain stops.

"Thank God It's Doomsday" GABF14: Because he sees a *Left Behind*-type movie and reads odd events as signs of the rapture, Homer believes the rapture will occur, even giving it a date and a time.

"The Monkey Suit" HABF14: Lisa begins secretly teaching evolution when Springfield Elementary moves to a strictly "biblical science" curriculum. When she is arrested and put on trial, it is Marge who cleverly saves her by making Homer look like a monkey in court.

"Mypods and Broomsticks" KABF20: When Bart befriends a Muslim boy named Bashir, Moe, Lenny, and Carl convince Homer that all Muslims are terrorists. Homer eavesdrops on Bashir's father, only hearing snippets, and thinks that he is planning an attack, but of course, he is wrong.

Education

"That '90s Show" KABF04: Academics and revisionist history are satirized in this flashback episode, which shows Marge in college in the early 1990s.[36]

"Separate Vocations" 8F15: Aptitude tests reveal that Lisa should be a homemaker and Bart should be a police officer, causing them to freak out and swap their typical sibling roles. Bart becomes a hall monitor and Lisa a bad seed, mouthing off to her teacher and stealing all of the teachers' editions of the textbooks. This episode shows how such tests can have negative effects on students, or that they simply don't matter (as depicted through Martin Prince, who chants "Systems analyst, systems analyst" and then is pleased when his test result is "systems analyst").

"Girls Just Want to Have Sums" HABF12: When the boys and girls are separated at Springfield Elementary, the girls are taught nothing useful about math, suggesting that the difference between boys and girls in math and science is more nurture than nature.

"The PTA Disbands" 2F19: The teachers go on strike when the school is unwilling to provide them with a small cost-of-living increase and better materials for the school.

"Lisa's Substitute" 7F19: When Miss Hoover goes on a sick leave, a substitute named Mr. Bergstrom takes over the class and makes a huge impact on Lisa. This is a beautiful and poignant episode.[37]

"Whacking Day" 9F18: When Bart is expelled from school, Marge must homeschool him. The episode illustrates that traditional education does not serve all students and inspires discussion about independent learning.

Community

"Much Apu about Nothing" 3F20: Issues of immigration, fairness, scapegoating, political corruption, and mob rule are examined in this hilarious episode.

"Lisa the Iconoclast" 3F13: Lisa becomes a pariah in her class for writing an essay in which she reveals the unflattering truth about the town's founder, Jebediah Springfield. In the end, she doesn't share the truth with the town because she realizes the myth of Jebediah adds value and pride to the community.

"Lemon of Troy" 2F22: When the Shelbyville kids steal Springfield's beloved lemon tree, the kids learn what their community means to them.

"Hurricane Neddy" 4F07: When a hurricane destroys the Flanders home, the whole town pitches in to rebuild it for them. (Sadly, they do a terrible job).

"Eternal Moonshine of the Simpson Mind" KABF02: The entire town works together to help Marge give Homer a surprise party.

Family[38]

"Any Given Sundance" KABF11: Lisa makes a documentary about her family called *Capturing the Simpsons*, and enters it in the Sundance Film Festival. The film is a hit, but the portrayal of the family hurts and embarrasses them, and Lisa apologizes.

"Mother Simpson" 3F06: When Mona Simpson returns to Springfield after 27 years, Homer is ecstatic to have his mother back and Lisa finally feels some sense of belonging as she sees that she and her grandmother have intelligence and passion in common. Even Bart and Maggie bond with their grandmother, and everyone (especially Homer) is sad to see her go.

"Bart the Lover" 8F16: Bart answers Mrs. Krabappel's personal ad and tricks her into thinking a man named Woodrow is interested in her. When he tells the family, Homer tells Bart to confess to Mrs. Krabappel what he's done, but Marge says no, saying that she'll be humiliated. Instead, they all work together to write Woodrow's last romantic letter in which he tells her he must leave town without meeting her.

Politics

"Sideshow Bob Roberts" 2F02: When Sideshow Bob calls a right-wing radio show hosted by Birch Barlow (who reminds the audience uncannily of Rush Limbaugh), Barlow starts an effort to get Sideshow Bob released from prison. He is successful, and Sideshow Bob runs against Mayor Quimby in the mayoral election and wins by a landslide. Bart and Lisa (with the help of a whistleblower) discover that Sideshow Bob has committed voter fraud, and he is returned to prison. This episode is rich with references to real events and many political films.

"Mr. Lisa Goes to Washington" 8F01: Lisa is a finalist in an essay contest and the family is flown to Washington, D.C., where she is to present her essay. While there, she witnesses a corrupt deal on the part of the congressional representative from Springfield and loses her faith in America. She rewrites her essay and reads the new one, in which she shares what she's learned about the corruption. In the end, the crooked politician is arrested, and, Lisa realizes that despite some corruption, overall the system is good.

"Two Cars in Every Garage and Three Eyes on Every Fish" 7F01: A journalist sees Bart catching a three-eyed fish, and the ensuing media attention sends inspectors to the power plant, which is undoubtedly the cause of the fish's mutation. To avoid spending a huge sum getting the Springfield Nuclear Power Plant up to code, Mr. Burns runs for governor. When Burns's advisers suggest he have a publicity-stunt dinner with an average family, Burns chooses the Simpsons, even though they are a "Mary Bailey family." Inspired to be a good example for Lisa, Marge shows Springfield just how powerful a homemaker can be, and cooks the three-eyed fish for dinner. Burns is unable to swallow his bite of mutated fish and loses the election.

"Much Apu about Nothing" 3F20: Mayor Quimby blames immigrants for the new frivolous tax that has Springfieldians griping, leading to a ballot proposition to have immigrants removed from Springfield.

"Mr. Spritz Goes to Washington" EABF09: When their politicians won't do anything to stop airplane flights over the neighborhood, the Simpsons encourage Krusty the Clown to run for Congress.

"E Pluribus Wiggum" KABF03: When Springfield becomes the city to host the earliest presidential primaries, the media descends upon the town. In disgust, residents write in Ralph Wiggum, which leads both parties to court him as their candidate.

Activities/Paper Topics

Activity #1: Point/Counterpoint

Show the episode "Much Apu about Nothing" to the class. Have the students write two essays, one in which they argue for Proposition 24 and one in which they argue against Proposition 24.

Activity # 2: Gifts from the Humanities

Review with the class the definition of "aesthetics" and the gifts from the humanities (beauty, beautiful movement, language, ideas, deeper sense of the past, and becoming an infinite person).[39] Show the episode "Lost Our Lisa," and have the class discuss how Homer and Lisa's visit to the museum offers them each of these six gifts. Next, have them discuss (or free-write) about a time when they were moved by a work of art.

Activity #3: Count the Pop Culture References

Show the *Simpsons* episode of your choice to the class. We recommend choosing an episode that you know well, or flip through The Simpsons Archive (snpp.com) — each episode capsule contains a very complete (if not totally complete) list of references.

Instruct the students to jot down every pop culture reference as they hear it (including jokes that they don't understand but that they suspect might be pop culture references). Have students form small groups to share their findings, and if the students have laptops, allow them to look up references they don't understand. Ask the class which jokes they thought were the funniest, cleverest, weirdest, and so on. Have each student jot down one thing they learned about pop culture from the exercise (and use it as attendance for that day, if you keep attendance).

Gender/Feminism Discussion or Writing Activity

Any episode can be used to inspire these discussions or writings — after all, you can't see characters without seeing gender roles at play. These are some of the questions that might provoke good responses: Are the characters (male and female) feminist? What about the town in general? The society? What brand of feminism does Lisa inhabit? What about future Lisa? Past and current Marge? How does feminism intersect with politics? Does feminism belong more to one party (of the many) than the other? Does feminism exclusively belong to essentialism? To abortion rights? To gay rights? To being porn- or sex-friendly? To capitalist opportunity? Why might Marge be ambivalent about feminism? Are the gender representations on the show realistic?

Free-Write List

Every teacher should have an arsenal of good free-writing prompts. Not only are free-writes good ways for students to generate paper topics (we use them frequently to warm up the class), but they are also useful when technical difficulties stand in the way of a particular planned activity, if students haven't completed the reading assignment, or the discussion is not flowing for whatever reason. Many of the following prompts are useful for both composition and humanities classes.

1. Write about one of your family holiday traditions. Talk about why you like it or dislike it, if you plan to continue the tradition with your own children (or if you already follow the tradition in your own home), what its origins are, and what details following the tradition entails. If the tradition is religious, discuss the religious components.

2. Does your family have a pariah? What makes this person an outsider? How well do you know him/her? How do you personally feel about this person? Is his/her status justified?

3. What is your family's emigration story?

4. What gives your life meaning?

5. Do you believe in "women's work" or feel that certain professions should be performed by a specific sex? Why or why not?
6. You have won $100,000 but have to give the money to charity. Which charity or charities do you choose, and why?

Research Essay #1:
Ethnography of a Subculture

If not already covered in class, discuss the definition of "subculture," explaining also the definition of "counterculture." A subculture simply refers to a group of people with a culture, covert or overt, that differentiates the group from the larger culture that contains it, whereas a counterculture is a group whose ideologies run against the dominant culture. Discuss elements of culture that make up subcultures, such as shared attitudes, values, goals, language, and practices.[40] (Also, we generally mention that any group that practices hazing is probably a subculture, but, of course, hazing is not required).

Because *The Simpsons* is culturally rich, use the show as a starting point. Have small groups of students compile a list of various subcultures. On the board, create a master list, using it to lead a full-class discussion that will generate student interest. Some of the subcultures will be unfamiliar to some students, so encourage students to share what they know about the subcultures. (Perhaps a student has a relative who is a Shriner or a Harley rider, for example.) Suggested episodes:

"Take My Wife, Sleaze" BABF05: When Homer and his friends start a motorcycle club called the "Hell's Satans" (a play on Hells Angels), members of a motorcycle gang already called "Hell's Satans" come forward to punish Homer. However, the episode has a rather ironic ending as the bikers decide to follow Marge's advice to get normal jobs.

"Maximum Homerdrive" AABF13: When Homer's competitor in a steak-eating contest dies, Homer decides to honor the man by making his final delivery. He brings Bart along, and together they learn the secrets of the truck-driving life.

"Homer the Great" 2F09: Homer joins the Stonecutters, a secret society inspired by Freemasonry. The elements of a secret fraternity are satiric and oddly realistic, including secret signs, peculiar rules, and strange rituals.

"Boy Scoutz 'N' the Hood" 1F06: Bart joins the Junior Campers while under the intoxicating influence of an all-syrup Squishee from the Kwik-E-Mart. The Junior Campers are similar to the Boy Scouts, and while Bart regrets what he's done at first, he likes certain perks of membership (such as having his own pocket knife), and sticks with it until a disastrous camping trip.

"Hurricane Neddy" 4F07: After a breakdown, it is revealed that Ned hates his parents, who were beatniks.

"Mother Simpson" 3F06: In this episode, Homer is reunited with his mother, Mona, who he thought had been dead for 27 years. Mona had actually left because she was a wanted criminal — as part of a radical group (similar to the Weather Underground Organization), Mona had broken into Mr. Burns's germ warfare laboratory, where the group detonated an antibiotic bomb.

"D'oh-in in the Wind" AABF02: When it occurs to Homer that he doesn't know what his middle name is (and Abe doesn't know either), Homer tracks down two old friends of Mona named Seth and Munchie. They hold down jobs but still maintain some of their hippie ways, and manufacture a Fruitopia-type beverage.

"Bart Carny" 5F08: A traveling carnival arrives in Springfield, and Bart and Homer foolishly befriend a carny and his son, who try to steal the Simpson home. The episode plays with the stereotypes regarding "traveler" types and raises interesting questions about people who choose to live off the grid.

"Weekend at Burnsie's" DABF11: This episode deals with the medical marijuana issue, and because Phish performs, the episode also serves as a good jumping-off point to discuss the unique culture of jam band fanhood ("Deadheads," "phans," or "phriends," who follow the bands for weeks or months at a time. Also, jam bands are uniquely known for allowing performances to be freely recorded).

"The Springfield Files" 3G01: Agents Fox and Mulder (from *The X-Files*) appear in this episode, serving as a discussion starter about how the FBI and other government agencies could be considered subcultures.

"Strong Arm of the Ma" EABF04: After being attacked at gunpoint, Marge becomes agoraphobic and begins lifting weights in her basement for lack of anything better to do. She realizes that the muscles have increased her confidence. She becomes a competitive bodybuilder and takes performance-enhancing supplements (and subsequently becomes very unappealing).

"Bart Star" 5F03: In this episode, many of the Springfield Elementary schoolchildren play peewee football. We use this episode to discuss sports culture, gender issues in sports, and parental pressure. Other episodes that focus on sports include:
"Lisa on Ice" 2F05 (peewee hockey)
"The Homer They Fall" 4F03 (boxing)
"Hungry, Hungry Homer" CABF09 (minor league baseball)
"Homer at the Bat" 8F13 (company softball leagues)
This is by no means an exhaustive list of the episodes that deal with sports and other subcultures (see the episode guide in the introduction), but it should offer a good starting point for discussing subcultures.

Position Paper: Making the Argument

You've been working on a specific topic for some time. Take the same topic you've worked on for your Summary/Response paper and write a paper in which you make an argument (for an audience of other students). Be sure to explain the issue briefly in your introduction. Your point must be narrow, unified, and arguable. If you find that you have to do a little research to come up with evidence, make sure you have a Works Cited page in MLA style.

Refresh your memory on the argumentative techniques we have thought about this term: types of claims, qualifiers, audience, warrants, counter-argument, and so on.

Below are some thoughts on organizing your position paper. Please note that the numbers by each section are only for organizational purposes. They should not be taken to represent paragraphs in your paper. You should spend adequate time with each of these sections as you see fit.

1. What is an interesting way to introduce your issue? How can you make the audience care about the condition and costs you describe? How can you set up your ethos?

2. Next, as you locate yourself in the conversation, explain what, precisely, others have claimed about this issue. Or, what are the prominent positions people have taken on your issue? Give an accurate, compressed, paraphrased summary; use direct quotations sparingly. If you're arguing for something to change, you will first have to explain the status quo.

3. After introducing the conversation about your issue, you will then explain in detail how you agree and/or disagree with those positions. Give your claim about the issue and explain how your position differs from others' positions and where you fit with them based on your circumstances. Make sure you fine-tune your claim. If you haven't done so already, connect with your audience here about how important your claim is.

4. Spend the rest of your paper giving evidence and support for that claim. The first part of the paper should not exceed one-third of its length. The bulk should be devoted to your point. Think about where you will put your most powerful evidence. How will you present it? How will you incorporate quotations? Where will other evidence go?

5. Find the best place to deal with counter-argument (as you go along, or all at once somewhere). Remember, if you're proposing something, you have to do all of the following in your essay: defend the fact that this is a problem that needs fixing, propose your fix, and explain why your fix is the best. In other words, a counter-argument may simply be a counter-proposal.

6. How will you end your essay?

Paper length: 5–7 pages, properly formatted

The Proposal: Reform

For this essay, you will write a proposal. A proposal argues that some action should take place and implicitly suggests that there are good reasons why it should. Your thesis should have a clearly stated claim and reason. It should also be a single thesis, not a three-point.

Remember that proposals are action-oriented, focused on the future, and audience-centered. That is, you must be arguing for something to happen. Occasionally, you may argue that something should stay the same, but only when there is a strong possibility that it may change. Otherwise, the proposal would not be relevant. A proposal should focus on what should happen in the future, not what has happened in the past, although past patterns can be used as evidence for future change. A proposal must take its audience into account. Watch your assumptions. Remember that you're trying to be persuasive.

Things your proposal must accomplish:

- relate the claim to a need or problem — why is this change important?
- prove that your solution will solve the problem
- show that your solution is feasible
- deal with counter-arguments and proposals
- use your own experience to illustrate your point

Whether you propose something related to politics, education, commerce, or social behavior, you must propose something that YOU can be a part of. Thus, you can't propose that Senator X vote for Y, but you could propose that there should be a petition for Y, which you could start.

Avoid trying to discuss something global — you have a very restrictive word requirement. You will be more successful with a local or small proposal.

Your essay must include YOU — why do you care? what would you be willing to do?

This essay will be more readable if you're actually passionate about the subject, so try to think about ways you would actually want your world to change.

Paper length: 4–6 pages, properly formatted.

Media Analysis: Gender Representations

For this assignment, you will make an argument about the representations of gender in an episode of *The Simpsons*.

To get started, try to think outside our culture. If you came from a completely different culture (one in which there was no gender, for example) what would you learn about our sex/gender system from watching this episode? What are the messages about gender conveyed in the episode?

Try not to go for the obvious. If an alien watched *American Pie*, it would probably ascertain that guys like sex. I expect you to dig deeper than that. I would argue, for example, that the movie sets up a troubling premise (four guys who gotta get laid at all costs) and then tries to "take the curse off" this premise in various ways. However, all our protagonists are "rewarded" at the end of the film, thus telling us that the premise wasn't so troubling after all.

Every single piece of media tells us something about gender. The more interesting papers may be the ones that discuss media whose focus isn't gender. Think about how the characters in the episode interact with each other, performances of masculinity and femininity, and how characters are taught to perform their gender correctly. Be careful about conflating terms — for instance, male/masculine, female/feminine, sex/gender.

This paper should include a brief summary of the episode. You should summarize only the relevant portions of the plot. What is the minimum information the audience needs to know? Save detail for close analysis of certain scenes.

Page length: 4–5 pages, formatted correctly.

Media Analysis: Stereotypes and Class

Gregory Mantsios, in his essay "Class in America: Myths and Realities," states: "People in the United States don't like to talk about class.... Class is not discussed or debated in public because class identity has been stripped from popular culture" (318, 319). Implicitly or explicitly, however, issues of class permeate our popular culture. Although the characters in our media may not identify themselves with any particular class, for example, one of the aspects of characterization is social class. For this essay, you will choose a piece of media (a movie, series of ads, television show, book, and so forth) and analyze it. More specifically, you will make an argument about how stereotypes/representations about class work in that piece of media. If possible, integrate ideas from the articles on class in our book.

To begin your thinking for the paper, you may wish to consider the following questions. If you find that any of the questions lead to an idea for a paper, please feel free to use them to frame your thesis or develop your argument. How is social class constructed in the piece of media? Are there conflicts between people of different classes? What message might the story be sending about social class? How does class intersect with race? With age? With sexuality? With gender? With nationality? With religion? With education level? What do issues of class have to do with "the American dream"? If the story presents a picture of class not contemporaneous with our own, how is the representation different? Are those characters more or less aware of class boundaries and differences? How might we understand the history of class in America by engaging with this media? What defines social class in the piece of media (blood, race, ethnicity, economic status, education)?

To write a successful essay you will need to demonstrate that you've carefully analyzed (watched many times or reread) the media you've chosen. You should quote from the media when appropriate, but do not overwhelm your paper with many large quotations. I'm interested in reading what you have to say about the piece of media.

Think about stereotypes about class. There will be stereotypes in every single piece of media. Simply identifying them will not make an argument. You must do more than that. Once you determine that stereotypes are present, you need to decide how they are functioning. Sometimes stereotypes are there to make a point. Sometimes stereotypes are there to be undermined. Are the stereotypes you're seeing reinforced or undercut? Is the stereotype necessary or productive?

Try not to go for the obvious. We all know that lower-class white people are often stereotyped as being "white trash." Writing about white trash representations in the movie *Sweet Home Alabama* will not get you a good grade unless you talk about those stereotypes on a higher level of analysis. Coming up with a nonobvious idea is the hardest part. Expect to spend a lot of time on this.

This paper should include a brief summary (about a paragraph) of the media. You should only summarize enough for the audience to follow your argument. What is the minimum information the audience needs to know? Save detail for close analysis of certain aspects of the media.

Remember to define what you mean by "class" in your paper; not everyone defines it the same way. Further, remember that "media" does not just refer to "news media."

Page length: 4–5 pages, properly formatted

Partner Project

Part 1 due to partner: (date)
Part 2 due to partner: one week later
Part 3 due to instructor: one week later
Divide into groups of two. Spend some time talking with your partner. Discover what you agree with and disagree about (some of our class discussions might give you some jumping-off points). Choose *two* topics on which you have at least slightly different opinions that you both want to write about.

Part 1: Write an essay stating your point of view about one of the topics (your partner will take the other topic). Perhaps you're arguing for change, or perhaps you're arguing for your audience to take action, or perhaps you're arguing for your audience to stop change that you see coming. Do not write this directly to your partner — pretend this is a general magazine article. Use your "public voice." Remember that writers know they're already in a conversation about topics — there are people who have argued this before you. What are their arguments and counter-arguments? If you use outside research, cite it correctly. As you're writing this for a general audience, you may want to define terms, address warrants, and situate yourself in the argument. Remember that the best arguments employ logos, ethos, and pathos to varying degrees. Give this essay (no more than five pages) to your partner on the day assigned. If you do not give your essay to your partner on the day assigned, you will lose at least a quarter of your overall grade — that is, you cannot get more than a 75 percent, which is a C. It is unfair to hold up your partner's work.

Part 2: Pretend that you have read your partner's essay in a magazine or journal. Pretend you do not know the author personally. You are going to write a rebuttal essay. You will need to give a brief, coherent, and fair summary of the author's work before you begin to analyze the piece. Remember that you can discuss any aspect of the piece — the evidence, the main claims, the sub-claims, the logos, ethos, pathos, logical fallacies, tone, warrants, organization, bias, and so on. Try not to reproduce any faults you see. Review the guidelines for conceding and refuting in our handouts. Remember that your own essay is persuasive and must have all three appeals operating to some degree. Note that you may also discuss what this essay has NOT said about the issue. If you use outside sources, cite them. I expect you to quote specific passages from the first essay. Give this essay (no more than five pages) to your partner.

Part 3: Read over the rebuttal essay. Remember not to take anything personally. This person is agreeing and/or disagreeing with an essay — it's not a personal attack. Take some time to think about what your partner has said. Write an essay (five pages or less) responding directly to this piece. You may find yourself disagreeing with everything in the rebuttal essay. You may find yourself acknowledging some of the critique. Perhaps you find yourself in a position to say, "X said I didn't do Y, but that's not what I was trying to do in the first place." As you respond, quote or paraphrase from Parts 1 and 2 where appropriate. Give this essay, along with Parts 1 and 2 of this thread, to me. That is, you will turn in Parts 1 and 3 that you wrote, along with your partner's Part 2. Your partner will turn in your Part 2 to me. Everything should be accompanied with a thoughtful "Memo for Out-of-Class Essays." In the memo, try to tell me what this whole experience was like for you.

A plea from the grader: Try to find original topics. Otherwise, I will have to read many essays on abortion rights, gun control, gay marriage, sports controversies, and political diatribes. There are so many more things to have opinions on, such as foreign-language requirements at college, spanking, declawing cats, and if the iPhone is worth the expensive data plan.

Chapter 6

The Simpsons Class:
Satire and Postmodernism

Moe: It's po-mo! [blank stares from all] Post-modern! [more staring] Yeah, all right — weird for the sake of weird.
Guys: Oooh!

["Sideshow Bob's Last Gleaming"] then, ends with a broad parody of Hollywood formula to underscore the futility of a character's efforts to destroy TV on a TV show, and then adds a coda in which another character acts out the same formulaic ending that had appeared on a TV set on this TV show as a paramount example of TV formula. If this is starting to give you a headache, that's perfectly understandable. — Chris Turner [388]

As anyone who's tried can attest, defining the postmodern is challenging. That's why so many instructors of theory are drawn to *The Simpsons* — we can readily use the show as an example when we want to explicate that which defies explication (both in theory and in practice).

Any teacher of a *Simpsons* course must struggle with this term, among others. This chapter will discuss the terms germane to *The Simpsons*, talk about the practicum of a *Simpsons* classroom, and conclude with sample paper assignments and a sample *Simpsons* syllabus.

The Postmodern Moment

There are several ways to think about postmodernism. In terms of time, we are postmodern. That is, if modernism is the time between the great wars, we are now post that time. It's possible that our time will be renamed later, but we're stuck with the term for now.

In terms of artistic movements, we are also in a time that *includes* postmodernism. Discussing movements is more slippery than discussing time. Students often believe that movements completely coincide with time — that all artists stopped being Victorian and began being modern when World War I began. They must be reminded that art doesn't work that way. People still write Elizabethan sonnets, gothic stories, and modernist plays.

As Brenda K. Marshall[1] explains in *Teaching the Postmodern*, "Although our contemporary culture has evidenced enough flashes of the postmodern moment for it to be an increasingly familiar term, we are not living in a period identified 'totally' as postmodern.... The postmodern moment is not something that is to be defined chronologically; rather, it is a rupture in our consciousness" (5). Marshall discusses how difficult it is to define postmodernism:

> One of the results of seeing the postmodern moment as an awareness of being-within a way of thinking is the recognition that such an awareness disallows the speaker (the subject) the comfort of absolutely naming the terms of that moment. Naming must occur from a position "outside" of a moment, and it always indicates an attempt to control. Crucial to an understanding of the postmodern moment is the recognition that there is no "outside" from which to "objectively" name the present. The postmodern moment is an awareness of being-within, first, a language, and second, a particular historical, social, cultural framework [3].

That is, since postmodernism in some sense equals a recognition that we can't always know what we want to know, or define (control) what we want to define, we will always stumble when trying to pin down postmodernism. Marshall sees postmodern awareness as first an awareness of language. She is acutely aware of the limitations of language and of language's potential to delimit a full understanding of what she terms "the postmodern moment." Postmodern theorists see language as that which constructs our identities and our thoughts. In this way, it shares concerns with materialist feminism (defined in Chapter 5). Ultimately Marshall writes, "[p]ostmodernism is about language. About how it controls, how it determines meaning, and how we try to exert control through language" (4).

Marshall contends that postmodernism is also concerned with "a particular historical, social, cultural framework" (3). This issue is one of identity and alterity — how we define our identities through subjective understandings of ourselves and others: "It's about difference. It's about power and powerlessness, about empowerment, and about all the stages in between and beyond and unthought of" (4).

Finally, what's central to Marshall's introduction to postmodernism is the idea of the postmodern moment. In a class on postmodernism, it is not entirely useful to hold a temporal or movement-centered definition unless the class is focused on the idea of "postmodern art." Students must, of course, be taught the temporal and movement definitions before being exposed to the more malleable understanding of the postmodern moment. We do not always use Marshall's term, as students often respond better to the idea of "postmodern techniques." Yet Marshall's term is probably more accurate, as it allows for discussion of both techniques and central ideas (such as epistemological problems).

Marshall holds that the postmodern moment is a mindset — a lens through which to see work. Postmodern moments also occur within works themselves. It is vital to note that postmodern techniques are at play in texts created before postmodernism. Shakespeare uses meta-theater and self-reference to great effect, for example. *Don Quixote* is as postmodern as almost any text besides those of Pynchon. It is equally vital to understand that not all texts created in the postmodern era are postmodern in spirit — in fact, few are. Even those texts that may be deemed properly postmodern may have non-postmodern moments. Marshall explains, "It's a moment, but more a moment in logic than in time. Temporally, it's a space" (5).

This disruption of the distinction between time and space might be labeled as poststructuralist. Many theorists conflate postmodernism and poststructuralism. It is thus necessary to define the latter as we continue discussing the former. Structuralism was concerned with distinguishing between and thus understanding the sign and the signifier, the signifier and the signified. Poststructuralism rejects such dualism, and in doing so resists the structuralist assumption that the signifier is superior to the signified.[2]

This disruption of binaries leads to the disruption of other binaries and, logically, a dismissal of the idea of superiority inherent in the binary model. In practical terms, this means that we conflate the self and the other, rather than holding them as separate (and holding the self as always more valuable than the other). We recognize the intertwining of black and white, light and darkness, female and male, heterosexual and homosexual, thus rejecting the structuralist/modernist model that perpetuates power differences. Note that poststructuralism seeks to explode binaries, creating new spaces and problematizing distinctions/definitions, rather than just reversing the hierarchies that structuralism and the status quo maintain.

In this way, poststructuralism is obviously related to postmodernism, especially in its deconstruction of and attention to language. Additionally, "[w]hereas structuralism's drive is toward closure, poststructuralism resists closure with its emphasis on textuality and intertextuality" (Marshall 7). Yet poststructuralism may also be linked to modernism, as many poststructuralist theorists and the texts they use are modernist, but Marshall believes that "only within the postmodern moment do the questions raised by poststructuralists have currency" (8). For Marshall, and for us as well, poststructuralism is a series of tools — a way of thinking — which aids in discerning the postmodern moment.

This focus on poststructuralism makes the following discourse on postmodernism uneasy (but the awareness of unease may make it more productive), as it discusses postmodernism in terms of its differences to modernism, in an endeavor to make postmodernism comprehensible to students. Postmodernism cannot be understood without understanding its relation to modernism (though this discussion has surely made clear that postmodernism may not be fully understood even with a good grasp of this distinction). An attempt to do so requires the sort of chart Karma made when she was in graduate school (reproduced here without alteration):

Modernism	Postmodernism
*master-narratives of truth, science, progress (in modernity)	*cannot have master narratives because they are ahistorical
*search for epistemology	*non-epistemological (situated)
*metaphysics (presumes self that can be transcended)	*spurns metaphysics due to lack of self
*self-conscious characters	*self-conscious art forms
*draws on tradition and history, while inventing new forms (although no originality, try to make it new)	*parodies previous forms and calls into question stable concept of history (art of the moment)
*colonial	*post-colonial
*multiple perspectives	*multi-voiced characters
*celebrates authenticity	*self-conscious fakery
*theory of relativity	*loss of spatial/temporal coordinates
*autonomy of art (autotelic)	*blurring of boundaries of creator/audience
*experimentation of form/stream-of-consciousness	*new forms about form (metafiction, new journalism)
*alienation as theme and technique (Brecht/Wright)	*still alienated, but there won't be anything coherent made out of the

Modernism	Postmodernism
*machine age makes automatons	fragmentation, there is too much
*elitist	indeterminacy
*central crisis as gender changes/impo-	*information age makes fake people
tent men	*mixing of high and low art
*search for meaning of complex reality	*chance to hear from new voices
*modernist assumption of chaotic	*different realities in jumble
world	*carries modernist assumption about
*impotent, questing hero	world into realm of art
*reaction against machines, war	*if quest, it's in lexical playing field
	*reaction against war, consumerism,
	homogeneity

Karma usually begins her discussion of these distinctions by reminding students of how modernity arose out of the modern period. People had just survived World War I. They were shocked by the extent of the warfare and the power of the weapons they'd created, which allowed them to massacre without seeing the face of the enemy, something that had not been possible before. Many believed that God had either abandoned the world or had never existed in the first place. The Industrial Revolution had reached its zenith, displacing the traditional family structure (that of living perpetually in a very extended family) as people moved into cities, facing pollution and crowded conditions. People were alienated from the products of their labor as they became as mere cogs in the machines that replaced them.[3]

Modernism is thus primarily about alienation — alienation from products of labor, from the family, from God, from each other. Modernist art therefore often has the quest for Truth (with a capital *T*) and for connection as a central theme (which underscores the theme of alienation).

Postmodernism comes from the post–World War II period, when humanity had seen what came after "the war to end all wars" — including forced labor camps, the Holocaust, and nuclear weapons. Shifts in technology now enabled the Information Age, as the first world moved into service industries rather than production, thus further alienating the labor force. The renegotiation of power after the war resulted in a focus on postcolonialism, as many more countries gained independence from colonial powers. This is a proximate cause of postmodernism's attention to the voice of the subaltern, the abject. This attention was furthered by civil rights movements — working toward an end to racial, class, sex, sexuality, and national prejudices. Material consumption became the way we judge success, as we became more and more subject to the whims of corporate interests. Globalization became a central issue at all levels of power.

Poststructuralist ideas come into play, though, as we remind students that the binary of modernism/postmodernism is problematic. Most artists are still working in pre-postmodernism modes. The anxiety of alienation is still with the postmodernists, as the sense of alienation that epitomized the early 20th century has not left us in the 21st century. Indeed, our ability to be and need to be constantly connected (via Twitter, email, cell phone, text messaging, Skype, and the like) can be said to emphasize the lack of connection many feel.

If there is a difference in how alienation is experienced, it may be that in the postmodern moment, there is a sense of play — there is still a search for connection, though we may play with our identities (as we construct and reconstruct our Facebook pages and our avatars). There is still a search for Truth, though the postmodernist acknowledges that there isn't any such thing, so we might as well have fun as we find our smaller truths along the way. Thus, there is more blurring in form, in content (through intertextuality and a mixing of high and low art[4]), and in identities in postmodern works.

Ultimately, the distinction between modernism and postmodernism may best be understood through the idea of epistemology. Epistemology is the theory of knowledge. As a philosophical idea, it is concerned with how we know what we know, how knowledge is constructed and construed, and the limitations of knowledge and thus of truth. As previously stated, modernism is concerned with Truth, with "master narratives." The postmodern moment is one of epistemological crisis as it questions the idea of Truth, argues for a situated knowledge (a more localized and partial knowledge), and rejects the idea of "master narratives."

The X-Files illustrates this quandary well. Mulder believes "the truth is out there," while Scully searches for a scientific "truth" to explain her experiential knowledge. The heroes are thus on a modernist quest, often impotent because of the larger forces working against them in a complex and chaotic reality. The show, however, is postmodern in that it problematizes the idea of truth and frustrates an audience expecting the truth to be revealed.[5]

Although we've been speaking in generalities, Marshall reminds us that "[t]he postmodern moment resists totalizations, absolute Identity, absolute Truths. It does, however, believe in the use-value of identit*ies* and local and contingent truths" (6, emphasis in original).

Karma often distinguishes between the Truth and truthiness when guiding students through postmodernism. Although Stephen Colbert[6] coined the term on the first episode of *The Colbert Report* in an attempt to satirize George W. Bush's belief that his gut instinct could constitute "truth," the idea that things can have inherent "truthiness" without being actually true (fictional accounts of war, for example) is useful. It can also stand in as a word meaning "situated truth" rather than "master Truth." As the American Dialect Society named "truthiness" the word of the year for 2005 (seconded by Merriam-Webster the following year), we find it a perfectly cromulent word.

Explications of how *The Simpsons* illustrates the postmodern moment will arise as we discuss other terms central to understanding this particular postmodern text: parody and pastiche; irony; self-reflexivity; refusal of an ending; intertextuality; high and low comedy (including many comedy terms the students should know). In addition, we will investigate satire and the role of reader-response/reception theory. Finally, we will turn our attention to the idea of zeitgeist, which will illustrate the ways in which *The Simpsons* embodies many of the central concerns of postmodernism.

Parody

Parody is a complex enough term to have spawned Linda Hutcheon's seminal text *A Theory of Parody: The Teachings of Twentieth-Century Art Forms*, as well as reactions (pro and con) to her definitions and examples. Most discussions of parody begin by discussing what parody is not. We will follow suit. Parody is often wrongly conflated with other terms: allusion, imitation, pastiche, and satire, among others.

We discussed allusions (references to other texts) at some length in Chapter 4. Allusions create intertextuality, which will be discussed below. In short, these references are usually brief, sometimes fleeting, while parody tends to be a more extended working-through of the original text within the new text.

Hutcheon distinguishes between the idea of imitation and parody in terms of history (that what we might now call parody was at one time called imitation) (10) and in her own definition of parody, which builds upon the idea of simple imitation: "Parody, therefore, is a form of imitation, but imitation characterized by ironic inversion, not always at the expense of the parodied text" (Hutcheon 6). Thus, a sense of irony marks parody, as Hutcheon explains "parody as a form of repetition with ironic critical distance, marking difference rather than similarity" (Hutcheon xii).

It is this idea of difference that distinguishes parody and pastiche for Hutcheon: "parody does seek differentiation in its relationship to its model; pastiche operates more by similarity and correspondence" (Hutcheon 38). Jonathan Gray, in *Watching with* The Simpsons: *Television, Parody, and Intertextuality*, similarly dismisses "uncritical pastiche" (5). Pastiche can actually be understood in two ways. The lesser-used definition means a work that comprises imitations of several other works. The more common definition of pastiche is a work that imitates the style of another work. In this way, it is often used interchangeably with homage, as pastiche is read as complimentary. Thus, Hutcheon and Gray are making a common distinction in highlighting parody as focusing on difference and critical irony rather than similarity and imitation.

However, different viewers will encounter works differently, which is why it is possible to have an argument (sometimes in class) about whether a given work is parody or pastiche. For example, many colleagues have dismissed all of "Weird Al" Yankovic's works as pastiche. Many of his works are, as he incorporates the styles of other musicians into his work, oftentimes as homage. Yet an argument can be made that some of his works imitate and criticize their source or that an homage to one artist can comprise an ironic commentary on the subject of the song (which is separate from the form/style).

"The Debarted," an episode that imitates the film *The Departed*, may be discussed in a similar way. The general plot of *The Departed* is borrowed for "The Debarted," while the setting changes to incorporate the *Simpsons* world, and the stakes change to incorporate a ten-year-old protagonist. The music, clothing, and even some "cinematography" signal the imitation as well. Overall, *The Simpsons* episode seems merely to be a tongue-in-cheek imitation. Yet the very last moment makes an ironic commentary on the original. *The Departed* ends with a rat crawling outside the "rat's" (the man who betrayed his department) apartment. "The Debarted" also ends with a rat. Ralph Wiggum then addresses the audience: "The rat symbolizes obviousness."

Having Ralph break the fourth wall is extreme, not only because the audience is rarely addressed directly, but also because Ralph's general obliviousness and stupidity comments on just how obvious (and arguably silly) *The Departed*'s ending metaphor was. We might then ask, does this last moment mean that the episode is parody rather than pastiche? Can we have room to say it is both? Isn't our distinction always on some level problematic because it relies on subjective determinations of intention and reception and results in reinforcing a dichotomy that privileges parody?

The same problems occur when distinguishing between parody and satire as the definitions shift. Even when working with a single definition, it is often the eye of the beholder that determines whether a text is parody or satire. Linda Hutcheon makes this distinction: "Both satire and parody imply critical distancing and therefore value judgments, but satire generally uses that distance to make a negative statement about that which is satirized" (Hutcheon 43–44). She states that parody cannot be so negative because "[a]ny real attack would be self-destructive" (Hutcheon 44). Gray's definitions pose problems in our understandings of all these terms: "Parody can be tributary and loving, serving as homage and flattery, but it can also take the ground in order to transgress and subvert" (45). Gray seems to be saying that parody can be what he has called "uncritical pastiche," while maintaining that it can also have the ironic commentary that distinguishes it from pastiche/imitation. He is also careful to point out that parody, which he believes seeks "to teach and correct" (4), is not satire: "Parody is often confused with satire or with pastiche, but neither of these forms shares parody's interest in a genre's form and conventions. Parody can be satiric, but pure satire bypasses concerns of form and aims straight at the content, whereas pastiche alludes to form and/or content, but with no critical comment on either" (47).

Satire, discussed below, is commonly called "corrective comedy." When Gray notes that parody can be critical and does seek to teach, he is right in saying that this kind of parody is satiric. Gray is interested in parody because his focus is on form, while satire does not depend solely on form make its critical point. Satire is more integral to *The Simpsons* than is parody. In fact, while parody is a common form on *The Simpsons*, parody is often taught as a tool of satire. Hutcheon, although also focused on parody, discusses it as an implement of satire: "It is [parody's] critical distance, however, that has always permitted satire to be so effectively deployed through the textual forms of parody. From Tony Kushner to "Weird Al" Yankovic, satirists continue to use the pointed and effective doubling of parody's voices as a vehicle to unmask the duplicities of modern society" (Hutcheon xiv).

One might well ask, how, then, we can explicate all of this to the students. We often use "Weird Al" Yankovic as a starting point. As stated previously, his work is often pastiche/homage of other artists. "Eat It" is an affectionate revision of "Beat It," and not quite ironic enough to be considered a parody, if we use Hutcheon's definitions.

We tend to use a more general definition of parody when introducing these concepts, although the students are warned that our definitions may not be replicated in the readings for the course and we explain that others distinguish between parody and pastiche in the above ways. Parody, as we explain it to the students, is imitation of form, style, content, or artistic conventions. Using this definition, "Eat It" parodies the style/form of Michael Jackson's song, though it may not be making any critical commentary. Parody as imitation is general enough to include homage, imitations that make fun of other works and ideas, or satire. Note that making fun of something does not constitute satire unless that which is made fun of can be considered a social problem (explained in the discussion of satire which follows).

In other words, in our classrooms, the distinction between parody and satire (noting that parodies can be satires) becomes more germane to the discussion than the distinction between parody and pastiche. Other instructors will use these definitions differently, reflecting their own biases and foci.

Returning to the "Weird Al" Yankovic example, some songs are satiric parodies. "Jerry Springer" is a parody of the Barenaked Ladies song "One Week." That is, the form/style of the song is from the Barenaked Ladies, while the content of the song has changed completely — the narrator of the song is singing about watching *The Jerry Springer Show* compulsively. Students are able to easily identify *The Jerry Springer Show* as a social problem being critiqued, and can be led to see that Yankovic's deeper criticism is of *viewers* of the show, as it is their complicity in viewing the show, even if they see themselves as "above" it, that enables production.

Similarly, *The Simpsons* enables a discussion of parody and satire. Jonathan Gray holds that parody "aims to destabilize the common sense of genre" (44). *The Simpsons* is a parody of the sitcom[7] and the sitcom's depiction of the suburban family (44), though a focus on genre like Gray's will necessarily be more interested in the former. Finally, as Gray notes,

"While *The Simpsons* is a show about a family, it is also a show about television. As the opening credit sequence ends, the Simpsons crowd around the television, and the final credits appear in the center of an animated television box, signaling that we are viewers watching television with the Simpsons and with *The Simpsons*" (7).

The form of the show is usually the sitcom, but other parody consists of parody of content. That is, the occasional episode will borrow form ("Behind the Laughter" parodies the form and the content of *Behind the Music*, and "24 Minutes" parodies the form and content of *24*. However, most parody retains the form of *The Simpsons* while using borrowed content. The show's parodies of various horror films in the "Treehouse of Horror" Halloween episodes are prime examples. "Nightmare on Evergreen Terrace" is a parody of the plot and content of the *Nightmare on Elm Street* movies, arguably without critical commentary (and thus relegated to the realm of pastiche by some critics). "Rosebud" is a parody of *Citizen Kane* (with some stylistic parodic elements as well), and arguably functions as satire if the episode is analyzed as critiquing greed and the corruption that comes with power.

The conventions of art forms are also parodied on *The Simpsons*. For example, the action-film conventions of car crashes and large explosions are parodied at every opportunity — even the smallest crash on *The Simpsons*, with the most innocuous ingredients (such as milk trucks), results in a large explosion. The repetition of this convention throughout the episodes (it has become a running gag) both critiques the convention and the prevalence of the convention.

When discussing parody's relation to postmodernism, one must remember that parody is an old form, though it existed as imitation throughout most existing written literature and art. Parody, at least parody created in the postmodern era, is associated with postmodernism when it incorporates ironic commentary/critique.

Hutcheon reminds us that parody has a paradox when it comes to its possibility for critique: "Parody is fundamentally double and divided; its ambivalence stems from the dual drives of conservative and revolutionary forces that are inherent in its nature as authorized transgression" (Hutcheon 26). Hutcheon recalls here the problems with transgression itself, as understood by theorists such as Mikhail Bakhtin and Michel Foucault. These theorists hold that hegemonic ideology is so pervasive that it even determines how people may resist and subvert it, ensuring that the ideology is not ultimately destabilized. Bakhtin discusses how ancient carnivals allowed people to reverse hierarchies for a day, allowing commoners to blow off steam and thus delaying revolution that might destroy the hierarchies completely. Similarly, Foucault notes that the forms our transgressions take are completely determined by our societies and thus are mostly ineffectual.

Hutcheon is thus acknowledging that parody, while transgressive, may not be as revolutionary as we may hope. Jonathan Gray shares this caveat, as he reminds us that *The Simpsons,* for all of its satiric parody of power, has helped the Murdoch media empire rise: "*The Simpsons* also brings television parody's central dilemma into tight focus: economic complicity" (9). Further, "its merchandising and advertising wing has made *The Simpsons* into exactly the type of brand that the show regularly derides" (9). This point is made self-reflexively in the show, such as the many occasions when T-shirts appear within the show featuring a member of the Simpson family ("The Springfield Files") and when Bart complains to Krusty about his camp, saying, "How could you, Krusty? I'd never lend my name to an inferior product" ("Kamp Krusty").

The other problem with parody is that it necessitates knowledge the audience may not have: "For parody to be recognized and interpreted, there must be certain codes shared between encoder and decoder" (Hutcheon 27). Some critics see parody as aligned with modernism, which also privileges canonical knowledge, although postmodern parody does not necessarily rely on the canon as its sole source. Postmodern parody is also distinctive in its sense of play, as opposed to a snobbish knowledge requirement (that is not to say that viewers do not get an elitist thrill from recognizing allusions and parody, nor that postmodernists are not sometimes snobs — of course we are). However, as Hutcheon reminds us, "[t]he potential for elitism in parody has frequently been pointed out, but little attention has been paid to the didactic value of parody in teaching or co-opting the art of the past by textual incorporation and ironic commentary" (Hutcheon 27).

Karma and her son enact the didactic value. Karma's son is well versed in anime, while Karma knows classic films. When they watch *The Simpsons* together, they often know that parody is happening, though they may not know the original text. Alexander will often say, "I know they're referring to something — what is it?" Karma will often see an old reference and ask, "Did you get that?" They will then teach each other about high and popular culture through viewing *The Simpsons*; "[m]utual codes are shared, even if we, as receivers of texts, have to be reminded of them" (Hutcheon 27).

The assignment that ends this chapter (writing a mini-script) forces the students to understand parody. Writing any content in *Simpsons* style is parodic by nature, but students often incorporate further parody (they might parody a horror film in *Simpsons* style for a Halloween short, for example). Some scripts even manage to incorporate self-reflexive parody, such as one student script, "Grumbling Abe Simpson and His Raging Grandson in 'The Return of the Curse of the Flying Hellfish *Returns* II.'"

Irony

Readers may hope that after the messy explanations of postmodernism and parody above, we have finally come to something we can all identify and understand. Yet Wayne Booth, in his *A Rhetoric of Irony*, claims, "Irony has come to stand for so many things that we are in danger of losing it as a useful term altogether" (2). Booth does hold, however, that literature provides moments of "stable irony." Stable irony is marked by four qualities — it is intended to be read as ironic; it is covert (that is, it does not mark itself self-reflexively as ironic); it is stable in that once it is understood, the reader does not usually deconstruct the ironic meaning; it is finite in that the range of possible meaning is very small (5–6). One should note that Booth is assuming a specific kind of reader with a specific kind of reading ability.

Further, Booth holds that irony is not "deliberate deception"; not "flattery and other hyperbole not designed to be seen through"; not "advertising euphemism [or] plain lies" (Booth 21). Sarcasm is not irony, though novices often confuse the two.[8] Booth explicates irony by giving clues to irony, handicaps to getting irony, and evaluation standards. He also posits that there are unstable ironies — ironies with unclear referents, with more open meanings than stable ironies have.

Students will likely have heard the term "irony," though they may not fully grasp what counts as such. If they've heard the Alanis Morissette song, they will probably completely misunderstand, as rain on your wedding day, while unfortunate, is not ironic. (Students may be instructed that the song is ironic in that none of the things listed are ironic, as we might think they would be, considering the title and the narrator deem them so.)

Irony is both a literary and a rhetorical device. In language, it means there is an incongruity between what someone says and the meaning intended or taken. The surface meaning and the actual meaning are never congruent. This is *verbal irony.* In one *Simpsons* episode, "Home Sweet Homediddly-Dum-Doodily," Marge must undergo a second drug test after a false positive. She proclaims, "The only thing I'm high on is love. Love for my son and daughters. Yes, a little LSD is all I need," unaware that she is making a drug reference.

Dramatic irony occurs when speech or action holds a meaning that the audience is aware of, while the speaker/character remains ignorant. A dark example comes at the end of "Simpsoncalifragilisticexpiala(Annoyed Grunt)cious," when Homer assures his children that they'll see their Mary Poppins–esque nanny again. As he's talking to the children, the audience sees the nanny, flying away with her umbrella, get sucked into a jet engine, thus making Homer's claim impossible.

Situational irony is what Morissette's song purports to describe. Although some claim situational irony is not irony at all, those who do describe it as when the expected result is not what happens, but in a situation-specific way. For example, Sideshow Bob points out that it is strange that he uses the television medium to announce his plans to ban television broadcasts from Springfield: "I'm aware of the irony of appearing on TV in order to decry it, so don't bother pointing that out" ("Sideshow Bob's Last Gleaming"). (Note that the verbal act of pointing it out isn't ironic.)

Cosmic irony falls under the situational irony category. It is when there is disparity between our wishes and the real world or when the universe/the gods seem to thwart us. For example, in "Mr. Plow," Homer and Barney join their plow businesses together and believe "not even God himself can stop us," but then God melts all of the snow.

Irony, like parody and satire, has the problem of being "accused of elitism." Booth counters: "There is a curious further point about this community of those who grasp any irony: it is often a larger community, with fewer outsiders, than would have been built by non-ironic statement" (Booth 29). Arguably, understanding these moments of irony in the show, along with catching allusions, parodic references, and other postmodern techniques, allows the audience to feel a bond with the show, the producers, and other fans. Obscure examples of the above may tempt viewers to say, along with Dr. Hibbert, after an intertextual moment at a concert, "I wonder if anyone else got that?" ("The Springfield Connection").

Self-Reflexivity

Simply put, self-reflexivity (self-reference, self-referentiality) is a facet of postmodern art in which the art acknowledges itself as a construction. Many can remember the first time they saw *Ferris Bueller's Day Off* in the theater. At the end of the credits, Ferris addresses the audience, telling them to go home.[9] Film audiences had been addressed before, in noir voice-overs, for example, but they had not been interpolated as an audience in a theater in quite that way.

The fourth wall in theater, film, and television[10] is often broken, but audience members are still rarely addressed as audience members. This address disturbs the suspension of disbelief necessary for engrossment in theater, film, and television. In many ways, this is part of postmodernism's sense of play — moments of self-reflexivity are winks to the audience. "Remember that you're watching us," they seem to say, "and we *know* that you're watching us."

Self-reflexivity may also be understood as part of the *alienation effect* (also known as the distancing effect, the *Verfremdungseffekt*). Bertolt Brecht coined this phrase as an explanation of his epic theater. Brecht believed that traditional theater, which often resulted in a sense of catharsis, relieved the audience of their responsibility to change their world for the better. That is, traditional tragedy might show a family in distress. At the end, the audience might weep for them, but then return to their lives and their homes without feeling the need to help actual families like the fictional ones they'd wept for.

Brecht wanted the audience's emotional response to the characters to be disrupted so that they would engage with the text on an intellectual level. He also wanted the audience to understand that tragic characters were determined by their materialist conditions (not in the sense of consumerist materialism, but in terms of power construction — by geographic location, class, sex, and so on), so that they might see failings not as necessarily related to an individual's tragic flaw, but as related to conditions that might be changed. Self-reflexivity was instrumental in disrupting the emotional response. Thus, Brecht did not allow his audience to forget that they were watching a play. He might, for example, have all of the actors seated on the stage, watching a few of the characters perform a scene. The audience would then have the opportunity to observe an actor get up and get into character as s/he joined the scene.

Self-reflexivity is integral to *metafiction*, which is also identified with postmodernism. Metafiction is concerned with fiction, it is fiction about fiction, a story about storytelling, a text about the creation/production/ publishing of a text. Metafiction often contains stories within stories and is concerned with the idea of fiction vs. nonfiction as questions of Truth/truth are raised.

The Simpsons often have metafictional ("metatelevision" might be a better term here) and self-reflexive moments. The episode guide in the Introduction lists many (but not all) of these moments. To take one episode as an example, we need only examine "The Front." In this episode, the Simpson children feel that their beloved *Itchy & Scratchy* is declining in quality (a criticism leveled against *The Simpsons* for almost two decades now). They write their own episode. When it's rejected because of their age, they resubmit under their grandfather's name. Their grandfather is hired as a writer; the episode eventually wins an award, and Grampa Simpson is horrified by the violence running under his name.

This cartoon episode is thus about cartoon viewing, writing, and production. It contains numerous references to actual *Simpsons* writers, and the *Itchy & Scratchy* writing staff is depicted as resembling *Simpsons* writers. Among other self-reflexive jokes, when the head of Itchy and Scratchy Studios takes the children on a tour, he says, "Sometimes, to save money, our animators will reuse the same backgrounds over and over and over again." They then walk in silence down a long hallway, past the same water cooler and cleaning woman many times. When Grampa goes up on stage to accept his award, the band plays *The Simpsons* theme rather than *Itchy & Scratchy* music, which would have been more "realistic." Grandpa's tirade against the cartoon producers draws attention to the issue of cartoon violence, morality in children's programming, and the fact that many in Grampa's generation believe *The Simpsons* to be a harbinger of America's decline.

Refusal of an Ending

Brenda K. Marshall reminds us that "[p]ostmodernism resists closure, but a physical text must end" (17). When Marshall discusses postmodern closure, she means:

Meanings and answers are both infinite and particular. Postmodernism resists closure in that it insists that we try to constantly keep our own subject positions, history, and motives in mind as we interpret, that we recognize how each interpretation (of a book, a law, a class, a life) is also a domination, a will to power. But only one among many. Postmodernism also recognizes, however, that we cannot live without trying to make sense. Neither innately positive nor negative, postmodernism is an opening, a space created for a particular awareness, interrogation [192–193].

Certainly, we can keep reinterpreting episodes of *The Simpsons*. In fact, one of the journal entries we assign to students asks them to think through the experience of rewatching an episode and to think about how they have changed and how their understanding of the episode has changed since the first viewing.

However, *The Simpsons* resists closure in another sense. Many of their episodes end in the typical sitcom way — the plot lines are wrapped up and equilibrium is reestablished. Yet some of the episodes undercut the "happy family" sensibility, even as order is restored. For example, at the end of "Simpsoncalifragilisticexpiala(Annoyed Grunt)cious," not only is the nanny killed, but the family has just sung a song that celebrates their dysfunction. The equilibrium of the nuclear family existing without the nanny, as well as the equilibrium of dysfunction, is reinstated, but our attention is drawn to the family's problems. Marge is "going bald from stress," Lisa is "getting used to never getting noticed," Homer "would rather drink a beer than win father of the year," but they're "happy just the way [they] are."

In fact, Jonathan Gray argues that the few genuinely happy endings exist only to serve the undercut happiness. That is, if every ending were one that undercut traditional sitcom values, the audience would grow too used to the convention (60).

A few episodes refuse to end conventionally at all, removing us from the security of the dysfunctional family setup at 742 Evergreen Terrace. "The Computer Wore Menace Shoes" (a parody of *The Prisoner*), for example, features Homer stumbling upon a plot to control people through flu shots. He is taken to a secret island where he is repeatedly drugged. After his escape, he returns home. The family welcomes him back, but then the family dog emits a gas. The family is next seen on the island, with Marge remarking, "Once you get used to the druggings, this isn't a bad place." Not only is the family far away from the television set in front of which they will gather in next week's credits, but a koala bear approaches the "camera" and gasses the audience.

Thus, while many of the episodes are modernist in their epistemological answers (tying things up neatly), there are moments of postmodernity, such as when Homer declares that they have wrapped things up nicely, "much quicker than usual," when in fact they haven't ("Homer and Apu").

Intertextuality

"Intertextuality" is often used interchangeably with allusion and parody, as parody and allusion sources are, by definition, intertexts. Linda Hutcheon holds that allusion and parody are often more useful terms in that they indicate an intention on the part of the author — that the author would have to intentionally allude to or parody another work.

Some use "intertextuality" to mean associations with any works that come into the readers' minds, whether the text intended an association or not. While we acknowledge that readers will make associations with other texts, we do not encourage the use of the term "intertextuality" in this way.

Instead, we see it as a larger umbrella term for *intended* reference, allusion, and parody. As Marshall notes, "Intertextuality is not simply a reference to earlier texts, but is a manipulation of those texts as well" (130). Further, "Intertextuality is precisely a momentary compendium of everything that has come before and is now. Intertextuality calls attention to prior texts in the sense that it acknowledges that no text can have meaning without those prior texts, it is a space where 'meanings' intersect" (128). Gray similarly defines intertextuality as "the fundamental and inescapable interdependence of all textual meaning upon the structures of meaning proposed by other texts" (3–4).

A discussion of the intended and unintended associations might use the term "hypertextuality," which refers to the interconnectedness of all works. This is especially useful when students commit a chronological fallacy. For example, they might watch a *Simpsons* parody of horror films and assume the parody refers to a specific movie, although *The Simpsons* episode appeared before the horror movie. The student can be instructed that they have not noticed an intertext, but their response is hypertextual.

Productive discussions can also be held around the process of viewing the show. The show has its own intertexts, yet we often experience the show with a set of intertexts the network creates. Jonathan Gray reminds us: "Program flows into ad, flows into program, flows into station identification, flows into next text so seamlessly" (73) and we must remember that the ads, the station identifications, and the shows surrounding any given show (on a singular station) are designed intentionally.

The Simpsons reference this many times. For example, in "Attack of the 50' Eyesores," from "Treehouse of Horror VI," advertisements come to life, threatening the citizenry. They are defeated in Springfield, but Kent Brockman warns that the next ads the audience sees may kill them. Homer then addresses the "camera" with "We'll be right back," making the show's audience potential victims of the ads that appear on Fox a second later.

High and Low Comedy (and Other Comedy Terms)

"High" and "low" comedy have been recognized as necessary and complementary components of comedy since time immemorial. Common understanding is that high comedy is largely a comedy of language, of allusion, of intellect, while low comedy is physical, farcical, and of the body. Great comedy combines both.

Farce often uses caricatures and exaggerated stereotypes, improbable situations, and sexual and physical humor. In many ways, *The Simpsons* could be said to embody this type of humor, although the main characters are generally more round than the flat characters of farce. For example, Lisa is a stereotypical precocious nerd in many ways, yet she exhibits other, competing desires more typical of an eight-year-old child. While some critics see this as an inconsistency, it in fact makes Lisa more realistic — very few of us can be pigeonholed as a "type" with no variance.

The Simpsons may also be seen as a comedy of manners, in that it allows us to question the etiquette rules involved in relationships (between acquaintances, co-workers, married couples, and so on). Traditionally, comedies of manners focused on the upper classes and relied on witty dialogue (as in *The Importance of Being Earnest*), but today we can observe this art form among other classes and forms (think *Seinfeld*).

High and low comedy can also be discussed in terms of characters. In *The Road to Mars*, one of Eric Idle's characters (a comedy theorist) makes a distinction between "Red Nose" and "White Face" characters:

There are two types of comedian ... both deriving from the circus, which I shall call the White Face and the Red Nose. Almost all comedians fall into one or the other of these two simple archetypes. In the circus, the White Face is the controlling clown with the deathly pale masklike face who never takes a pie; the Red Nose is the subversive clown with the yellow and red makeup who takes all the pies and the pratfalls and the buckets of water and the banana skins. The White Face represents the mind, reminding humanity of the constant mocking presence of death; the Red Nose represents the body, reminding mankind of its constant embarrassing vulgarities.... The emblem of the White Face is the skull, that of the Red Nose is the phallus. One stems from the plague, the other from the carnival. The bleakness of the funeral, the wildness of the orgy. The graveyard and the fiesta. The brain and the penis ... the White Face is the controlling neurotic and the Red Nose is the rude, rough Pan. The White Face compels your respect; the Red Nose begs for it. The Red Nose smiles and winks, and wants your love; the White Face rejects it. He never smiles; he is always deadly serious. Never more so than when doing comedy [6].

These terms are useful in discussing characters like Krusty the Clown, but also in understanding characters like Homer as comedic types.

Satire

As seen above, satire is both an important comedy term and a highly relevant term to Simpsonology. Satire is not directly interchangeable with parody, though satire sometimes uses parody as a method or tool. Satire is not just irony or sarcasm, although satire often has an ironic twist and poorly written satires often consist mostly of sarcasm.

Satire is often called "corrective comedy" because, aside from just making fun of something, satire seeks to illustrate a social problem or condition to its audience so that the audience might do something about the problem. The object of satirical critique may be as important as a war, as personal as your boss, or as common as snobbery. Satirists typically believe that audiences need to see a problem anew and thus they use exaggeration. "A Modest Proposal" by Jonathan Swift, for example, sees the narrator proposing a problematic solution to the problem of overcrowding and starvation. Swift's essay is meant to elicit the audience to proclaim that they would never eat babies, but then to ask themselves what the moral difference is between that and leaving them to starve.

The Simpsons is an example of *indirect satire*, as it is not a direct address from a first-person narrator. Students should be told that in *direct (formal) satire*, there is a first-person narrator. There can be several types of narrators, but if students work on their own satires in essay form (see assignment at the end of the chapter), they should be reminded that the narrative voice is necessarily different from the author's, as the narrator's surface argument serves the author's actual critique.[11]

There are several problems with the efficacy of satire as an instrument of social change. The first is that satire can be misunderstood. Marge, for example, when hearing a noncritical parody of a song, declares, "That's good satire — it doesn't hurt anyone" ("Large Marge"). The song is not satire — in fact, the absence of a satiric target should have been a clue, but Marge, like many audiences, is uncertain of exactly what satire is. It is also possible for people to read a satire and to be unaware that there's a difference between the narrator's argument and the author's argument. For example, many of our students have read "A Modest Proposal" and taken it at face value.

Satire is also criticized because it sometimes seems to be "preaching to the choir." That is, those who agree with the criticism will be more likely to "get" the satire. The objects of a satire (those whose behavior the satire critiques) will be less likely to understand the satire, to see their actions as its target (they might understand that the satire attacks racists, but not identify themselves that way), or to shut down when they realize their own values are being "made fun of." However, satire is still valuable in several ways. First, we should not discount anything that serves to be entertaining or to provoke laughter.[12] Second, the converted often need further consciousness-raising and community building and satire can fulfill these needs. Third, some (including us) maintain that satire like *The Simpsons* serves to create better viewers and consumers (Chapter 5 discusses this further).

It should be noted that we often make the last claim without any evidence to back it up because we are working on assumptions shared by most scholars of reader-response and reception theory, like Roland Barthes. As Barthes explains in *S/Z*, the *writerly text*[13] is one that "make[s] the reader no longer a consumer, but a producer of the text" (4). The *readerly text* is "what can be read, but not written" (4). The writerly text, then, creates the potential for active rather than passive reading, while the readerly text leaves the reader "with no more than the poor freedom to either accept or reject the text" (4).[14] *The Simpsons* is generally agreed to be a writerly text, inviting the audience to make connections, to recognize parody, and to understand the satiric commentary on the larger world. In our experience as teachers, we have found that while *The Simpsons* is in fact a writerly text, it does not *force* readers to become more active viewers. While super-fans tend to be more critical readers/viewers, it may be because as critical thinkers, they are drawn to the show.

The cause of the critical thinking must be seen to be a combination of many factors — their intelligence, their prior instruction, a range of texts they've encountered. In fact, in a limited empirical study Karma did on active readers, she found that the main determinant of which student would be an "active" reader as opposed to a "passive" reader was whether the student read on his/her own (that is, whether s/he read texts other than just skimming what was required by teachers). Active viewers vs. passive viewers may be understood in the same way — passive viewers watch, but don't necessarily engage. They are less likely to seek out shows which challenge them or which contain postmodern elements. (They may be more likely to seek out a course that focuses on *The Simpsons*, however, as they believe such a course will entail passive viewing.)

The good news is that passive viewers can become active viewers if trained to think about texts in a new way. Our favorite complaint from students is that we've ruined television and film for them — after they've been in our classes, they find it difficult to watch passively. One student in particular was irritated at Denise for "wrecking *Friends*" for her. She had previously enjoyed watching it as brain candy but couldn't anymore because it was "just too dumb."

The Simpsons is primarily a postmodern satiric sitcom. To list what is satirized through the shows would be too much to take on here (though it is often productive to have students brainstorm a list from a single episode as they attempt to grapple with satire). Sometimes it is helpful to orient students by considering the more overt examples of satire in the show.

Let us take, for example, politics. When discussing politics and satire, Karma distributes the following handout:

Simpsons, South Park, and Politics

[From Wikipedia, April 18, 2008]: "*South Park* Republican" is a term that was circulated in weblogs and articles on the Internet circa 2001 and 2002, to describe what some claimed as a "new wave" of young adults and teenagers who hold political beliefs that are, in general, aligned with those that seem to underpin gags and storylines in the popular television cartoon. The phrase was coined by commentator Andrew Sullivan in 2001. Sullivan identified himself as a *South Park* Republican after hearing that the show's creators had "outed" themselves as Republicans at an awards ceremony.

While *South Park* co-creator Matt Stone is a registered Republican, co-creator Trey Parker is actually a registered member of the Libertarian Party. As the show's co-creator, Matt Stone, sums it up: "I hate conservatives, but I really fucking hate liberals."

Creators' views

Both Parker and Stone have claimed that the "South Park Republican" tag was a "dumb notion." However, when Parker was asked to elaborate on what the term means to him, he claimed that he is getting "sick" of the fact that one must "either like Michael Moore or ... wanna fuckin' go overseas and shoot Iraqis." He goes on to stress the lack of a "middle ground," where they consider themselves.

Karma finds the term ironic, as an Emmy-winning *South Park* episode from 2005, "Best Friends Forever," has a demon declare that to win the fight, he'll bring in Satan's constant minions: the Republican Party. *South Park*, like many satires, satirizes the foibles of *all* sides. What's interesting is that most satires exaggerate the Republicans as being purely evil and the Democrats as being ineffective and naive. One of these seems a worse indictment than the other.

Vocabulary:

Libertarian: Usually means that you're socially liberal (keep your laws off my body) and fiscally conservative (keep your laws off my money).

Verbal irony: Statement in which the meaning that a speaker implies differs sharply from the meaning expressed.

Sarcasm: It is the taunting use of apparent praise for dispraise. It is sometimes referred to as irony, but actually is its cruder cousin.

Structural irony: When the writer incorporates a structural feature, such as a naive hero, that sustains ironic meaning throughout the text.

Examples of irony and political beliefs satirized in *The Simpsons*: [to be filled in by the students]

Students are usually able to have engaged conversations on the political position of the show (they should be encouraged to think about the show's position, as opposed to saying "the writers" or "the producers" in terms of beliefs). Students usually find that the show satirizes both sides of a position. For example, in "Weekend at Burnsie's," Homer is prescribed medical marijuana. Homer and many others petition for legalized marijuana (theoretically ascribing the show with that position), but then find that they have missed the election date because they were too stoned (problematizing the support for the drug).

Other episodes, however, seem to be more overt in their political leanings. In 2008, news reports revealed that Homer would be voting for Obama in the week before the election in "Treehouse of Horror XIX." Homer goes to vote for Obama, but the voting machine records his votes (he ends up voting several times in an attempt to correct the problem) as votes for "President McCain." At first glance, this would seem to be influencing voters. Of course, we might remember that Homer is rarely on the "right" side of politics (at the beginnings of episodes, he often takes the conservative side in an argument. Also, there are problems with using a noncritical thinker who succumbs to mob rule very easily as a voting guide).[15]

Homer voting for Obama may therefore be seen as an endorsement for McCain. However, before the viewer really has the chance to think this through, we see that the episode is less an endorsement about who to vote for as a satire of voting machines and the controversy both over their problems and over the fact that the owner of the voting machines is a well-known supporter of the Republican Party. We also learn that at least one of Homer's votes was for McCain, showing that while the Republican system and its candidates are shown as problematic, so is Homer as a voter.

A similar discussion of politics happens in "E Pluribus Wiggum," which skewers both Democrats and Republicans, the media that feeds the machine, the voters who don't seem to know any better than to let politicians and reporters influence them, and many of the most famous talking heads in contemporary politics.

In "Citizen Kang" ("Treehouse of Horror VII"), when Kang and Kodos (the Halloween episode resident aliens) take over the bodies of Bill Clinton and Bob Dole the week before the election (when the episode aired), many students see the satire initially as being about "politics" in general, or the parties, or the actual candidates. With a little bit of prompting, they discover that the actual butt of the joke is the voter. For example, when Marge hears "Clinton" say, "I am Clin-ton. As overlord, all will kneel trembling before me and obey my brutal commands," she responds, "Hmm, that's Slick Willie for you, always with the smooth talk," indicating that she is predisposed to hear what she expects to hear from a candidate, rather than keeping an open mind and open ears.

"Dole" receives a negative response when he says that no one should have abortions, but an equally negative response when he says that everyone should have them. The alien quickly learns about placating voters: "Abortions for some, miniature American flags for others!" When the candidates are exposed as monsters (a not-so-subtle metaphor for what often happens with political candidates), they remind the voters that America in effect operates with a two-party system. The voters' belief that this is so becomes self-fulfilling. Two parties then leave us with two very closely related candidates in many ways and we must vote for "the lesser of two evils," or opt out of the system, and then declare ourselves not culpable because we "voted for Kodos." Thus the voter, even while fulfilling the democratic duty, is still seen as culpable because s/he has literally done the minimum to ensure that the social contract is upheld — he or she has not demanded campaign reform or supported third-party candidates on a local level, for example. In this episode, the nation is enslaved and forced into building weapons for an intergalactic war — thus the wasteful, war-mongering administrations that use the taxes and labor of the masses of Americans at any given time are satirically exaggerated, as are the voters who are complicit in upholding the status quo.

Zeitgeist

Time magazine declared that *The Simpsons* was the 20th century's best television series (December 31, 1999). To a great extent, this is because the show so perfectly captured the zeitgeist of the latter part of the century. Zeitgeist means "spirit of the age." Thus, the zeitgeist of a time means the spirit or ethos of the dominant culture. It should be noted that "zeitgeist" refers to a specific place and that it may be used to describe subcultures as well. It is in fact this move against an ahistorical notion of spirit that marks zeitgeist as a postmodern understanding of spirit (that is, it is always situated).

Karma often uses *Shaun of the Dead* when discussing zeitgeist.[16] Monster films can be especially useful for thinking through zeitgeist, as what film monsters stand for is often determined by the zeitgeist of fear in any given place/time. *Shaun of the Dead* captures a passive populace, one who, even after confronted with great adversity, merely adapts and returns to passivity. Arguably, the same analysis may be applied to *The Simpsons*, as the sitcom format recapitulates the repetition, adaptivity, and ultimately inertia of our society.

Of course, there are things that change — Lisa's vegetarianism, her Buddhism (although actually it seems only that she's found the name for what she's been all along), some divorces of minor characters — but apart from some technologies the characters use, their basic lives do not change — even after the town is moved five miles down the road,[17] after it is almost destroyed by a comet,[18] and after it is domed off and almost completely destroyed in *The Simpsons Movie*.[19]

Any assignment that asked students to discuss zeitgeist in its entirety as represented by *The Simpsons* would simply be too much. Yet narrowing the subject can lead to fruitful discussions. In terms of gender, for instance, *The Simpsons* reflects contemporary expectations of gender and sexuality and the counters to them that mark our particular time/place. The nuclear family is not the only one represented on the show, although it is still held as the desired norm. The homemaker struggles with the expectations of her role, with sexism, with her own feminism, with the limitations of her power and influence. The man is supposed to be the head of the household, but family dynamics are not as clear-cut as the nuclear family model would have us believe. The children seek to define and redefine themselves.

The show exposes current attitudes on beauty, the focus on entertainment, and service as valued over production of goods. A change in the role of corporations in America is portrayed as corporations take more power while giving less protection to their workers (compared to the 1950s, at least). Mr. Burns refuses to give Christmas bonuses,[20] negotiates to take away health coverage,[21] and uses his employees as human chimney sweeps.[22] The social contract is still expected, and a good number of the citizens believe that their government, that the powers that rule them (including corporations), should uphold it. Yet there is voter apathy (though apparently not town-meeting apathy in Springfield), and the government cannot fulfill its contract (it is corrupt, stealing money, working with the mafia, bombing Springfield). The church fails when it sells out, when it refuses to accept all its citizens, and when Lovejoy ceases to care. The police can't or won't always help (though the same can't be said of the professional firefighters in the town). While many of these institutions are merely shown to be as imperfect as the citizens who comprise them, the critique of these institutions and of the people who do little to force them to uphold their end of the bargain is clear.

Cultural attitudes toward contemporary issues are revealed in *The Simpsons*, as episodes feature food ethics, immigration, gun rights and control, and so on. Students should be reminded that what is being debated at any given time tells us about values and assumptions in that time. For example, they should remember that in most of the history of the world and in many places in the world currently, vegetarianism is not an issue (due to animals being valued in different ways, the diet not being varied enough, or economic circumstances that make not eating meat irrelevant or impossible). While the show upholds vegetarianism as a moral choice, it also represents the sanctimonious way in which non-vegetarians often see vegetarians.

With an eye to zeitgeist, the show allows us to greet and to think through a host of modern issues and attitudes, as we examine American habits, values, recreation, working style, community systems, and stereotypes of other peoples, to name a few (Chapter 5 discusses many of these issues).

Discussion Questions

The following questions may be used to spur discussion, journal entries, or free-writes as the students work through *The Simpsons*.
- What examples of parody are operating in the text? Is the parody critical/satiric?
- What intertexts are at work here?
- Who or what is being satirized in the text? Does the satire take a definite side?
- Examine the text for zeitgeist. What is the cultural climate captured by the text?
- Do you find yourself emotionally involved with the characters or with the story?
- Is this an example of metafiction or of meta-television?
- Does this episode take the form of a traditional sitcom? In what way is the genre parodied here and in what ways is it reinforced?
- How does the text treat the audience of *The Simpsons*?

The Postmodern Simpsons *Classroom*

To teach postmodernism often recapitulates the problems of modernity. That is, it usually happens in elitist settings (colleges with tuition that is outside the bounds of most Americans, or at least a space that doesn't happen to be available for everyone. And while those who teach postmodernism sometimes do so with "low culture," such as television, the majority of the texts are high literature (Coetzee's *Foe*, Nabokov's *Pale Fire*) and high theory (Adorno, and his ilk). Using *The Simpsons* is a way to combat this (although those of us who don't consider the show "low" culture might rankle at this definition).

Thus, a successful postmodern classroom needs to at least be aware of its own limitations, constraints, and biases. The structuralist binary of teacher and student, even in the most student-centered classroom, still holds. We should acknowledge epistemological concerns both within our texts and within our classrooms. Marshall reminds us that "every act of interpretation is a domination. A will to control the knowledge of history through the transmission of language is also a will to power" (184).

As instructors think through how they will organize their class, what assignments they will use, how they will engage the students, and how student-centered the class will be, they are invited to consider that "[o]ne potential of the postmodern moment could be a refusal to recognize the barriers between theory and practice" (15).

Assignments

The following assignments are written with the student as the audience and can be duplicated verbatim as handouts.

Assignment #1: Understanding Satire
Length: 250–500 words

Every time is a time for comedy in a world of tension that would languish without it. —James Thurber

We'll be studying satire for two reasons. First, because it's an important American tradition. Second, it takes a higher level of reading skill to "get" satire. If you can read and write satire, you can read and write anything. First, some definitions. Satire is a form of humor. All humor involves some form of exaggeration designed to trigger laughter. Humor also involves an object — something that's being made fun of, such as a person, place, thing, idea, or experience. Satire is specialized. If you're satirizing something, you're not just doing it for the laugh. You're exaggerating something (making fun of it) to draw attention to it. What you're hoping is that by shocking the observers through your satire, you'll get them to think about some problem (and maybe find a way to fix it). Satire doesn't always evoke laughter; sometimes the "truth" uncovered by the satire won't allow it. Nevertheless, it should be clever. Satire is called "corrective comedy."

> *Power, money, persuasion, supplication, persecution — these can lift at a colossal humbug — push it a little — weaken it a little, century by century; but only laughter can blow it to rags and atoms at a blast. Against the assault of laughter nothing can stand.* —Mark Twain

The most studied satire in the Western world is Jonathan Swift's "A Modest Proposal." A few centuries ago, Ireland was wracked with famine and overpopulation. Swift proposed that one solution to both problems would be to eat babies. This would feed the poor, prevent overpopulation, and simultaneously prevent infanticide and the abuse of pregnant women. Swift was making an exaggerated point. His *surface argument* (we should eat babies) was designed to convey the *actual argument*. Swift was counting on his audience being horrified by the thought of killing babies and eating them. He was hoping to shock them into asking themselves why it was then okay to allow those same babies to starve to death simply because they were poor. Citizens of Ireland were complacent in allowing the population to starve; he needed to exaggerate the point to get them to realize what was happening was wrong.

> *Laughter is the sound you make when you are free.* —Regina Barreca

As we study satire, I'll be asking you to identify not only the surface arguments but also the deeper arguments (the serious ones).

Then you'll write one. Choose a problem, preferably one you know something about — something local. Write a satiric argument to get me to recognize the problem as a problem.

I would recommend doing outside research in terms of finding models for this assignment as we just aren't able to read enough of them together. The best satires on TV are *The Simpsons*, *The Colbert Report*, and *The Daily Show with Jon Stewart*. You can find satire online; start with theonion.com, comedycentral.com, and humorgazette.com. Satirical editorial cartoons can be found at http://eagle.slate.msn.com. When you go to these sites or others, my only caution is that most of these sites don't distinguish between humor and satire — remember, it's not enough to just make fun of something.

I want this assignment to be fun for you, so see me if this freaks you out and we'll talk about it. The best way to start is to make a list of things that bug the hell out of you — you'll have something to say about them.

> There's a tendency to think of satire as cute and clever. It's not as dangerous as it should be. I think the people you're satirizing should get pissed off.—Tim Robbins

There are things a satire cannot be — a satire is not just a rant. A satire is not just being sarcastic. The narrator of a piece of satire is often a naive narrator, wholly invested in arguing the opposite of what the author actually believes. The narrator isn't sarcastic; instead, she is sincere. The audience must be trusted to "get" that the narrative voice is different from the author. People who don't get satire often don't understand because the narrative voice seems so sincere.

Satire techniques:

naive narrator —a persona the author creates; the persona believes completely in the argument s/he is making, which is usually the opposite of what the actual author believes

intentional logical fallacies— the author has the narrator intentionally make mistakes to point out the fallacies in the argument

logic extension— the author/narrator takes the logic of the other side and applies it to its furthest implications

satire genres— you can find satire in movies, songs, television, essays, books, magazines, etc. If your essay isn't working as a straight essay, consider turning it into a fake news piece or vice versa.

Assignment #2: Creating a Parody
Length: will vary

Write a parody or imitation of one of the works we've encountered, including a 500-word explanation of your work. Be careful to avoid simply mocking someone else's work — a successful parody or imitation will include both the strengths and weaknesses of the original. Parody and imitation is considered one of the highest forms of compliment. (Another option for this assignment is to rewrite one of the works we've read in another author's style. It must be in another author's style, though, not just your own revision.)

Assignment #3: The Zeitgeist Essay[23]
Length: 1250–1750 words

Don't take any shit from the zeitgeist. — George Carlin

Look back over your notes on zeitgeist. Your assignment is to choose some specific example of media (a book, movie, television show, online text [LonelyGirl15], whatever) and to evaluate it as revealing the zeitgeist of its age. For example, Bill Maher has argued that *Forrest Gump* reveals contemporary America's desire to believe that achievement can come to anyone, regardless of hard work or intelligence.

How to go about this:

- Don't just focus on the plot of the text. Think through themes, values, assumptions, symbols, and other aspects.
- Narrow as much as possible. Your text is not discussing the zeitgeist of the whole 20th century. A depression-era comedy, *The Philadelphia Story*, for example, expresses the zeitgeist of early 1930s America in that it exposes both a desire to ridicule the upper class and to maintain the illusion that crossing into the upper class is possible and desirable. Ultimately, the film reifies class positions and stratifications, implying instead that success comes from a willingness to love and to forgive.
- Note that your essay will have to discuss the particular time and place you choose — you'll have to articulate that zeitgeist and show how the text propagates it.
- Don't forget that communities can be broken down by such categories as sex, race, nationality, sexuality, and class. Some texts will capture the zeitgeist of very specific communities, and these may be the easiest to talk about.
- There must be at least two items on your Works Cited page: the text and a review of the text. You may, of course, use other research as you choose. I don't care how you use the review — you may cite from it at length (if it's appropriate to do so), you may include just a clever phrase in your summary, or anything in-between. I am mandating, though, that you prove to me that you can do research, integrate quotations, and provide a Works Cited page in MLA style.
- Remember that your audience may not be familiar with your

text. You should provide just enough summary to help them follow your argument.

- If you write about literature, do so in present tense. Refer to characters by their names, not the actors' names.

Some things to be careful about:

- Oversimplifying — don't assume that any one show can perfectly capture the spirit of an entire community of varied individuals. Qualify your statements accordingly.
- Not narrowing appropriately
- Not engaging counter-argument
- If you pick a text that is set in another time, the zeitgeist the text reveals is that of the time of production, not of the past or future. Why did the 1970s produce a bunch of texts like *Grease*— what was their obsession with the 1950s about?
- Don't forget your Works Cited page in MLA format
- Do not assume that any sources (or reviews) you find will be about this particular point — your paper should be original, after all.

Alternate Zeitgeist Essay

This assignment entails explaining how certain films are restored and kept by the American Film Institute and invites students to nominate a film (or a particular *Simpsons* episode) to be protected in the same way. The students can be encouraged to envision a time capsule. If we could choose one *Simpsons* episode or film to represent us (as we are, not as we want to be), how would it illustrate the spirit of our age to others? A longer paper can try to analyze the episode in every detail, while a shorter one would have a very focused thesis: we should save "Lisa on Ice" to discuss the issue of children in sports and competition (rather than looking at absolutely every angle, such as sibling rivalry, gambling, community, mob rule, and so forth).

Sample Syllabus

What follows is a sample syllabus from Karma's two-unit, quarter-length course, taught at the University of California, Davis. This course was developed as part of the Freshman Seminar Program. Choosing themes and episodes can be difficult with as many choices as *The Simpsons* provides. The instructor is encouraged to choose themes that fit with the goals of the course. Organizing the course in a different way (more chronologically than thematically, for example) is also possible. While the syllabus provides themes for ten weeks, other thematic units have been developed. Karma is averse to teaching the same course twice. Some of her units have been on Halloween, parenting, ethics, consumerism, war, and contemporary argument (featuring single episodes on a topic such as gun control, marijuana legalization, vegetarianism, outsourcing, creationism, or ADHD medications). One class also saw the students propose and vote on a topic for one of the later weeks.

The Simpsons: *Satire and Postmodernism*

For all of The Simpsons' *darker strains of satire, ultimately it's a celebration of America and the American family in its exuberance and absurdity*—Matt Groening

This course will investigate the longest running sitcom in America — *The Simpsons.* As Duane Dudek of the *Milwaukee Journal Sentinel* maintains, "If television stirs primal memories of ancient communal campfires, then *The Simpsons* are the cave paintings for our times." We will be social anthropologists, exploring the cave paintings to understand what they reveal about our culture. We will pay special attention to how the show functions as a satire — how it serves as corrective comedy to issues such as consumerism, inequality, and political dysfunction. We will also discuss the show as an example of postmodern literature. Students will collaborate to produce a "mini script" of *The Simpsons* to demonstrate a mastery of the subject and to discover the intricacies of humor composition.

Outline of Assignments

Assignments and readings are due on the day listed.
Subject to change. TWO journal entries due each week
(except the first) at the beginning of class.

Class 1 Introduction: A Portrait of the Simpsonesque. View[24]: "Simpsons Roasting on an Open Fire" *(December 17th, 1989 Season 1.)*[25]

Class 2 *The Simpsons* & Religion: View: "Homer the Heretic" *(1992, Season 4)*; "Lisa the Skeptic" *(1997, Season 9)*; "Bart Gets an F" *(1990, Season 2)*; "Simpsons Bible Stories" *(1999, Season 10)*. Have read: Gerry's Bowler's "God and *The Simpsons*: The Religious Life of an Animated Sitcom"; Jamey Heit's "Reason's Revenge: Science Confronts Christianity in Springfield." (Recommended Home Viewing[26]: "Bart Sells His Soul" *(1995, Season 7)*; "She of Little Faith" *(2001, Season 13)*; "The Father, The Son

& The Holy Guest Star" *(2005, Season 16)* "Joy of Sect" *(1998, Season 9)*; "The Monkey Suit *(2006, Season 17)*; "Faith Off" *(2000, Season 11))*. Journal 1 & 2 due.

Class 3   *The Simpsons* & Politics: View: "Much Apu About Nothing" *(1996, Season 7)*; "Mr. Lisa Goes to Washington" *(1991, Season 3)*; "Citizen Kang" *(1996, Season 8)*; "Sideshow Bob Roberts" *(1994, Season 6)*. Have read: Aeon J. Skoble's "Lisa and American Anti-Intellectualism." (Recommended Home Viewing: "Bart-Mangled Banner" *(2004, Season 15)*; "Two Cars in Every Garage and Three Eyes on Every Fish" *(1989, Season 2)*. Journal 3 & 4 due.

Class 4   *The Simpsons* & the Road: View: "Thirty Minutes Over Tokyo" (1999, Season 10); "The City of New York vs. Homer Simpson" *(1997, Season 9)*; "The Crepes of Wrath" *(1990, Season 1)*; "Bart Vs. Australia" *(1995, Season 6)*. Have read: Kevin J.H. Dettmar's "Countercultural Literacy: Learning Irony with *The Simpsons*"; William Irwin and J.R. Lombardo's "*The Simpsons* and Allusion: 'Worst Essay Ever.'" (Recommended Home Viewing: "The Regina Monologues" *(2003, Season 15)*; "Blame it on Lisa" *(2002, Season 15))*. Journal 5 & 6 due.

Class 5   *The Simpsons* & "Infotainment": View: "Homer Badman" *(1994, Season 6)*; "Duffless" *(1993, Season 4)*; "Attack of the 50' Eyesores" *(1995, Season 7)*. Have read: Jonathan Gray's "Introduction," *Watching with The Simpsons: Television, Parody, and Intertextuality*; Gray's "The Logic of Television and Ad Parody"; Gray's "News Parody and the Public Sphere"; Sam Tingleff's "*The Simpsons* as a Critique of Consumer Culture." (Recommended Home Viewing: "You Kent Always Say What You Want" *(2007, Season 18))*. Journal 7 & 8 due.

Class 6   *The Simpsons* & Family: View: "Secrets of a Successful Marriage" *(1994, Season 5)*; "Home Sweet Homediddly-Dum-Doodily" *(1995, Season 7)*; "A Milhouse Divided" *(1996, Season 8)*; "Brother From the Same Planet" *(1993, Season 4)*. Have read Eliezer van Allen's "An Imperfect Ideal Family"; Linda Heath and Kathryn Brown's "Sex and Gender in Springfield." (Recommended Viewing: "A Streetcar Named Marge" *(1992, Season 4)*; "War of the Simpsons" *(1991, Season 2)*; "Lisa's First Word" *(1992, Season 4))*. Journal 9 & 10 due.

Class 7   *The Simpsons* & Sexuality: View: "Homer's Phobia" *(1997, Season 8)*; "Colonel Homer" *(1992, Season 3)*; "Natural Born Kissers" *(1998, Season 9)*; "Life on the Fast Lane" *(1990, Season 1)*. Have read: Karma Waltonen's "We're All Pigs"; Matthew Henry's "Looking for Amanda Hugginkiss: Gay Life on *The Simpsons*";

Denise Du Vernay's "Homer Simpson: Homophobic Hero?" (Recommended home viewing: "The Last Temptation of Homer" *(1993, Season 5)*; "Grampa Vs. Sexual Inadequacy" *(1994, Season 6)*; "Three Gays of the Condo" *(2003, Season 15)*; "There's Something About Marrying" *(2005, Season 16)*. Journal 11 & 12 due.

Class 8   *The Simpsons* & Education: View: "Homer Goes to College" *(1993, Season 5)*; "Separate Vocations" *(1992; Season 3)*; "Whacking Day" *(1993, Season 4)*; "The PTA Disbands" *(1995, Season 6)*. Have read Carla Meskill's "Through the Screen, Into the School." (Recommended home viewing: "Little Girl in the Big Ten" *(2002, Season 13)*; "Lisa's Substitute" *(1991, Season 2)*; "How the Test Was Won" *(2009, Season 20)*; "Girls Just Want to Have Sums" *(2006, Season 17)*; "The Secret War of Lisa Simpson" *(1997, Season 8)*). Journal 13 & 14 due.

Class 9   *The Simpsons* and Self-Referentiality: View: "Two Bad Neighbors" *(1996, Season 7)*; "Homer's Enemy" *(1997, Season 8)*; "Homer Cubed" *(1995, Season 7)*; "The Itchy and Scratchy and Poochie Show" *(1997, Season 8)*. Have read: Robert Sloane's "Who Wants Candy? Disenchantment in *The Simpsons*." (Recommended home viewing: "Itchy & Scratchy & Marge" *(1990, Season 2)*; "The Front" *(1993, Season 4)*; "Bart Gets Famous" *(1994, Season 5)*; "Behind the Laughter" *(2000, Season 11)*). Journal 15 & 16 due.

Class 10   Concluding Discussion; Scripts Due. View: "The Simpsons 138th Episode Spectacular" *(1995, Season 7)*; *The Simpsons Movie*. Journal 17 & 18 due.

Grading

The majority of the grade will be determined by a small group project. Members of the group will collaborate to produce an original "mini script" of *The Simpsons* (50%). The remainder of the course grade will be based on an informal reading journal (25%) and the frequency and quality of your participation in class (25%).[27] I expect to see everyone in my office hours **at least once.**

Journals: I expect at least **two entries per week.** One might respond to your work outside class, while the other might respond to the work we're doing in class, for example. While most of the entries will be self-directed, you can record daily questions, questions unanswered by the end of a class discussion, and the directed reflections I will sometimes require. Journals can be creative — incorporating pictures, drawings, creative work, etc. is fine. Most of your journals will be free topic — that is, you will chose what to write about. Occasionally, I will give you an idea to ponder for a specific journal entry. Here are some other directed journals:

Journal 1: Write about your history with *The Simpsons*.

Journal 3: Look up one of the following terms: parody, satire, postmodernism, irony, zeitgeist (look in several sources; do not settle for a one-line definition in a dictionary). Put the definition into your own words and then write about how *The Simpsons* relates to that word.

Journal 5: Jonathan Gray, in his analysis of *The Simpsons*, argues that they engage "in a rather high risk strategy[.] *The Simpsons* employs what we could call *hyper*-stereotypes. From Scottish Groundskeeper Willie and Kwik-E-Mart owner Apu, to the show's depictions of Japan, Australia, East Africa, Canada, and Brazil in family trip episodes, the show rounds up multiple stereotypes and jams them into one character or episode. The result, although admittedly this is a strategy that passes many by, and hence risks backfiring on itself, is to make the *process* of stereotyping the target, rather than the people themselves. Certainly, while many Australians were offended by a *Simpsons* episode set in Australia, for instance, the episode's key targets were American behavior overseas and smalltown American mindsets that view other countries in one-dimensional ways" (64). To what extent do you find this argument compelling?

Journal 7: As you're watching and rewatching episodes, are you catching jokes that you didn't see before? Are there jokes that you've grown into (jokes that you weren't old enough or knowledgeable enough to get before)?

Journal 9: Read a few of the fan scripts at snpp.com. Write up an evaluation. Are there scripts that are stronger than others? What makes the difference?

Journal 11: Find an article (analysis, not news) we're not reading together as a class (check the syllabus to make sure you haven't picked one that we're going to read in the next few weeks). Summarize the argument in a paragraph and then write at least a page response.

Journal 13: Write up an analysis of a theme or issue we aren't covering in the class: race, class, the military, literature, friendship, alcoholism, Halloween, nerds, the elderly, child rearing, sports, etc.

Journal 15: Answer an unanswerable question. Examples: Who is Homer's BEST friend? Where is Springfield? Make sure to acknowledge other valid viewpoints.

Journal 17: Look back over your relationship with *The Simpsons*. How has your view of the show changed after this class?

Journal 18: What was your experience in writing a mini-script?

All Journal Entries must be **a page, typed, and proofread.** Please note that *The Simpsons* should be underlined or italicized. Episode titles should be in quotation marks.

Telescript

Your assignment is to break up into groups to produce a short script (10–15 Pages). If you wish, you can work alone, but you will still have to produce the required amount. The short script should be self-contained, i.e., your work should have a beginning, middle, and end. Your story should have an identifiable plot. Use the format of the online transcripts when composing. Please remember that you will have to document sound effects and physical jokes. Your scriptwriting will take place outside of class. You are responsible for arranging times to meet with your groups and organizing your writing time accordingly. Don't expect to be able to throw something together hastily. This is harder than you think. Please remember to proofread. Check the spelling of characters' names. (When addressing another person, you separate his/her name with a comma. "Homer, please don't eat that.")

Your script should take several things into account.

1. The characters must stay in character.
2. The actions must be realistic (in the world of the show; it can be a Halloween special).
3. The jokes should be funny.

Chapter Notes

Introduction

1. Besides Denise's class (Writing about *The Simpsons*: Satire, Parody, and Pop Culture) and Karma's class (*The Simpsons*: Satire and Postmodernism), many other classes have been just about *The Simpsons* (as opposed to classes that integrate *The Simpsons*). Among them: *The Simpsons* as Satirical Authors of Humanist Culture, Columbia, Professor Deb Foote; *Simpsons and Philosophy*, UC Berkeley, Tyler Shores (student instructor) and Chris Nealon (faculty sponsor); and Sociology of *The Simpsons*, University College of the Fraser Valley, Professor Darren Blakeborough.

2. Elizabeth Freund's 1987 work *The Return of the Reader* gives a useful overview of the history and terminology of reader-response criticism. Reception studies, which is a related but separate field, is explained succinctly in Philip J. Hanes's article "The Advantages and Limitations of a Focus on Audience in Media Studies."

3. We have been using the term to describe ourselves for approximately 10 years. It is on our business cards, and our Twitter handle is "Simpsonology." Although we are aware of Tim Delaney's book *Simpsonology: There's a Little Bit of Springfield in All of Us* (2008), we are in no way affiliated. However, our review of the book is in this chapter.

4. Maggie actually said a few words in the Ullman shorts. After Taylor's performance in "Maggie's First Word," Maggie has spoken a few more times, notably in "Coming to Homerica," which is discussed in Chapter 3.

5. This episode has the beloved "Mr. Pinchy" storyline.

6. Season 10 featured three Catholic jokes — in "Sunday, Cruddy Sunday" as mentioned; in "Homer Simpson in: Kidney Trouble," Marge asks the Reverend Lovejoy if he's going to perform last rites on Grampa, and he responds, "That's Catholic, Marge. You might as well ask me to do a voodoo dance." Finally, in "Lisa Gets an *A*," Bart wants to turn Catholic for communion wafers, to which Marge says no because "three children is enough, thank you." See Karma's article "4 Simpsons Controversies That Didn't End in Lawsuits" for a discussion of the Catholic Church's response.

7. This is considered a meta-reference by many fans, some of whom had voiced disappointment with the writing on the show. Homer asks the crowd if they care about Comic Book Guy's opinion, and everyone says no. Comic Book Guy, it has been argued, is representative of critical fans everywhere. In addition, Comic Book Guy is wearing a T-shirt that reads "Worst Episode Ever," which is a reference to "The Itchy & Scratchy & Poochie Show."

8. In a wonderful self-referential joke, this episode ends with Homer watching a *Simpsons* episode in which it's declared, "The Simpsons are going to Delaware!" He announces that it will be the last season. The last episode in Season 12, "Simpsons Tall Tales," begins with the Simpsons winning a trip to Delaware, prompting the announcement, "The Simpsons are going to Delaware!"

9. The Albuquerque minor league baseball team changed its name to the Isotopes because of this episode.

10. "Barting Over" was the 302nd

episode in production, but advertised as the 300th, hence Marge's response that she swore it was the 302nd crazy thing.

11. This was the first episode to air after *The Simpsons Movie* was released, and Springfield shows evidence of destruction from the dome's collapse.

Chapter 1

1. Since this chapter serves as an annotated bibliography, the resources discussed here will not be listed in our works cited at the end of the book unless we refer to these authors in other sections of the text.

2. This change in usage from adjective to noun can be used to illustrate nominalization to students.

3. While various politicians, preachers, and organizations have objected to the show, we have not uncovered evidence of scholarly articles that do so.

4. Academic articles, whether they appear in print or online, are found here, while academic-minded websites and more general Internet sources are listed below.

5. *The Simpsons Archive* is described under Internet Resources. Academic articles (peer-reviewed and non-peer-reviewed) are found on the site by navigating to **miscellaneous > academic**.

6. At the time of this writing, it was possible to access many online syllabi of *Simpsons* classes, including that of Professor Thomas B. Gold's sociology course, "The Simpsons Global Mirror," at UC Berkeley.

Chapter 2

1. This trend is critiqued in the episode "How the Test Was Won."

2. See Chapter 3 for a discussion of Shakespeare in *The Simpsons*.

3. John Boe has perfected this assignment. For further information, see "The Degrees of the Lie."

4. An unrelated reading assignment that works well to discuss warrant as an unexpressed overlap of values between au-

thor and readers is Dan Savage's "Is No Adoption Really Better Than a Gay Adoption?," an op-ed that appeared in the *New York Times* on September 8, 2001. Savage is a gay married man who has an adopted son, but the essay firmly bases its warrant on the understanding that most people care about America's children and would rather see them in permanent homes than bounced around in foster care.

5. In addition to qualifiers, this thesis has been modified to include an actionable argument to avoid a "so what" thesis.

6. Dr. Kip Wheeler of Carson-Newman College has a thorough handout on logical fallacies on his website: http://web.cn.edu/kwheeler/fallacies_list.html.

7. Students respond well to a showing of George Carlin's "euphemisms" routine.

8. See George Orwell's work for definitions and discussions of doublespeak.

9. This episode is probably an homage to Shirley Jackson's story "The Lottery."

10. This episode seems to have been inspired by a statement of economist Lawrence Summers, a former Harvard University president, that men are stronger at science than women.

11. The *Our Favorite Family* books are explained in Chapter 1.

12. Some of these themes will be discussed in Chapter 6.

13. An exercise on counter-arguments is included later in this chapter.

14. In one of Denise's classes, a student wrote a terrific essay about gender identification in children's toys after watching this episode.

15. This type of activity is also useful in social science classes.

16. This note appears when Karma assigns this exercise: "Normally, you would not note a page break when quoting. I do so to check that you give the correct page citation."

17. Thank you to Tanya Jarvik, who kindly allowed us to adapt her handout.

18. Denise once received a student paper in which the word "contain" was used in every instance where a form of the verb "to have" was appropriate.

19. Thanks to Loy Durham, who shared this example.

Chapter 3

1. There are some differences in the phonetic symbols used in the North American (or NA) system.

2. The word's appearance in *The Wall Street Journal* online was discussed during *On the Media*'s September 18, 2009, show, although the commentators were unaware of its previous use on *The Simpsons*.

3. In *The Simpsons Movie*, the abbreviation EPA (Environmental Protection Agency) creates a mystery when Grampa keeps repeating "epa" as a word and not initials, and Marge struggles to figure out what he means.

4. The word "ridiculous" is undergoing an interesting amelioration. Our students will often say someone or something is ridiculous, meaning it in a positive way. It seems that a sentence like "LeBron James is ridiculously talented" has been shortened to "LeBron James is ridiculous."

5. Audiences of *The Simpsons Movie* found Marge's line "Somebody throw the goddamn bomb" hysterical for this reason; on the show, Marge would not normally speak that way.

6. Such as in the expression "You can bank on it," which is a particularly ironic statement considering the recent bank meltdowns.

7. In British English, "wanker" is a considered graphic and had to be changed when the episode aired in Britain, not unlike the word "shag" in the title for the film *Austin Powers: The Spy Who Shagged Me*. The differences in cuss words between the two countries may be an interesting (if slightly dangerous) topic for class discussion.

8. Psycholinguistics is not to be confused with neurolinguistics, which studies the parts of the brain related to language processing. The important regions of the brain related to language processes are in the left hemisphere, and include the Angular gyrus, Broca's area, and Wernicke's area.

9. We wonder if anyone has ever said "when the fit hits the shan" unintentionally.

10. For an interesting history of the phrase, see this article from the *Washington Post* by Paul Farhi called "Conception of a Question: Who's Your Daddy?" http://www.washingtonpost.com/wp-dyn/articles/A46032-2005Jan3.html.

11. Be warned that the latter is an "adult" word. This word (as opposed to the person) comes up high in Google search results, which can teach the students about the utility of such searches and about how quickly language changes.

Chapter 4

1. Coined by Julia Kristeva, this term was first meant to signal that texts have a heteroglossia (multiple meanings), many of which are influenced by allusions to other texts, which are decoded in various ways by the readers.

2. "The Boy Who Knew Too Much" features another reference to *Huckleberry Finn*, as Bart fantasizes about being the character when he is truant from school. Principal Skinner also reads *Huckleberry Finn* to some of his troubled students in "How the Test Was Won." The students enjoy the text and connect with their principal.

3. A detailed analysis of the differences between *The Simpsons* episode and Twain's text is available at http://etext.virginia.edu/railton/projects/tysse/SIMPSONSthings.htm.

4. *Heart of Darkness* is also referenced in "Kiss Kiss, Bang Bangalore" when Homer becomes a godlike figure in India.

5. The title is a parody of the book and film *Diary of a Mad Housewife*.

6. Publishers of romance novels give tip sheets to new writers, with suggestions for characterization based on suitable careers, drinking habits, age, and the like. These tip sheets are immensely entertaining.

7. When we taught the novella and film *Brokeback Mountain*, the students

found that the film version was clearer about one of the character's deaths. When we reminded them that the scene they remembered was clearly only what the other character imagined, they reported that they felt they had *seen* the actual death and that was what they remembered.

8. Zeitgeist means "spirit of the age"; *The Simpsons* is a perpetual exploration of zeitgeist.

9. Postcolonial criticism sometimes falls under this category, as it deals with identity and alterity; however, it is difficult to do postcolonial criticism with *The Simpsons*, as American literature is rarely considered "postcolonial," despite the nation's colonial history.

10. Karma's article, "4 *Simpsons* Controversies That Didn't End in Lawsuits," might be useful here: http://www.mentalfloss.com/blogs/archives/25661.

11. Poe's works are also referenced in "The Telltale Head" and "Lisa's Rival."

12. Jones voices a character in each of the vignettes in this episode.

13. Marge writes a poem for Homer in "One Fish, Two Fish, Blowfish, Blue Fish."

14. Watching *Simpsons* characters speaking Shakespeare's lines in "Do the Bard, Man" and "Four Great Women and a Manicure" allows for discussion of blank verse, rhyming couplet, and so on.

15. The fact that Homer shares a full name with the main character in Nathanael West's *The Day of the Locust* is purely coincidental.

16. The current connotation of "hero" is "the performer of a heroic deed; or a role model." The classical hero had to meet many more criteria. Although heroes typically had admirable traits, tempered with hubris, their personality was not a determinant. It was the events and circumstances of their life that defined them. E. B. Tylor, a 19th-century anthropologist, classified a three-point sequence: The hero is abandoned at birth, the hero is rescued by humans or animals, the hero finally becomes a national hero (like Romulus). Johann Georg von Hahn expanded Tylor's ideas to his life-template of the Aryan hero. In von

Hahn's pattern, the hero was a high-spirited son of a princess and a god. The father would abandon the child due to fear of being overthrown. The hero would be saved by animals and raised by shepherds. The hero would journey abroad and return in triumph, having killed his enemies, freed his mother, murdered his younger brother, and founded a city. He would die in an extraordinary way. Lord Raglan devised a list of 22 heroic "events," of which no hero has ever experienced all 22. The evolution of the understanding of the "hero's journey" can be traced from Otto Rank through Freud, Jung, and Joseph Campbell (and then to George Lucas).

17. In "Natural Born Kissers" and "Apocalypse Cow."

18. In "The Springfield Files."

19. In "Two Dozen and One Greyhounds."

20. *The Godfather* was most directly parodied in "The Mook, the Chef, the Wife and Her Homer," in which Fat Tony's son reluctantly enters his father's life of crime.

21. There was actually an action film titled *McBain* in 1991.

22. "Materialist" does not mean "consumerist" in this context. We are using the term to refer to materialist feminism, which maintains that power is a matrix. An individual's place within the matrix is determined by material position — class, race, sex, age, education, geographical location, and so forth.

23. *Thelma and Louise* was also directly mentioned in "Homer Alone," when Marge watches the film during a vacation away from her family.

24. *Paint Your Wagon* was originally a stage musical.

25. Many may be surprised to learn that the stage musical is one of the few art forms to originate from America. While opera and variety shows that incorporated musical numbers came from Europe, Americans developed theater in which the music was incorporated into a narrative, forwarding the plot and furthering character. *Show Boat* is cited as the first example of the form

(its use of music may be called circumstantial) and *Oklahoma!* is the recognized as the first modern musical.

26. "Annoyed Grunt" was the original script annotation for what became "D'oh," a word now featured in the OED.

27. This was also a stage play. Jack Lemmon, when discussing this film on *Inside the Actor's Studio*, admitted that he was a recovering alcoholic.

28. *Glengarry Glen Ross* is also a stage play; Gil is a reference to the film version, as he has Lemmon's character's mannerisms and voice.

29. "A Star Is Burns" is the one episode from which Matt Groening removed his name. He believed that the crossover of *The Simpsons* and *The Critic*, another Fox show, was just an ad for the latter.

30. Comparing Aristotle's hierarchy with our own expectations provides rich class discussions, especially when students realize how much "spectacle" has taken over popular media.

31. "Cape Feare" is an extended parody of *Cape Fear*.

32. Two other references are striking. The Simpsons eat Shakespeare's Fried Chicken, which they never directly remark upon. The episode "Much Apu about Nothing" could be read as broad allegory in that the episode presents a big problem that comes to nothing at the end.

33. In Shakespeare's time, people would go "hear" a play, hence the term "audience."

34. The saving machina in *Dodgeball*, a case of money, is actually labeled "Deus Ex Machina."

35. For example, Karma considers Benedick's line from *Much Ado about Nothing*, "I do love nothing in the world so well as you — is that not strange?" (IV.i.266–267) the touchstone, as it evokes loving, nothingness, and the strangeness of it all.

36. Ayn Rand's ideas are represented in a more positive light in "Four Great Women and a Manicure," in which Marge revises the story of *The Fountainhead*, with Maggie as "Maggie Roark," a gifted and unappreciated baby artist.

37. This assignment is routinely offered as an alternative to producing a traditional synthesis or compare/contrast essay.

38. This essay is easier if the students have been keeping a reading journal, as detailed in the preceding chapter.

39. This assignment routinely follows the argument about form and precedes a synthesis/compare and contrast essay in Karma's classes. The various definitions of literary criticism are given to students as detailed in this chapter.

Chapter 5

1. We should remember, though, that *The Simpsons* will not be available to those whom James Fallows describes as "the invisible poor" — the homeless, the indigent, etc. Nor would it be available to contemporary slaves. In 2000, the spread of slave labor was "estimated by the CIA to involve 700,000 to 2 million women and children a year" (Grey).

2. Most memorably, George Washington appeared in "Lisa the Iconoclast" and "I Love Lisa." Bart waits for the tooth fairy in "Fat Man and Little Boy." In "Selma's Choice," an animatronic Abe Lincoln hawks beer: "Four score and seven years ago we took the finest hops and barley to brew a refreshing, full-bodied lager." *The Simpsons* parodies *Hamlet* in the "Do the Bard, Man" segment of "Tales from the Public Domain."

3. The list of *K* words appears on pages 182–183 of Hirsch's text (1987 edition).

4. Examples of episodes for the humanities themes appear at the end of this chapter.

5. Examples of episodes for each topic and free-write prompts also appear at the end of this chapter.

6. We could think of no examples, so we put the question into the Twittersphere. *Soap, Mad about You*, and an episode of *Family Ties* in which Steven's brother announces he's leaving his wife for another woman were the only examples our Twitter followers could supply in which an affair is scripted into a sitcom.

7. We are using a simplified version of Judith Butler's notion of the "performativity of gender" from her 1990 book, *Gender Trouble*.

8. The phrase "girl on girl crime" is borrowed from the film *Mean Girls*. A scene towards the end features Tina Fey as a teacher talking to the high school girls about the dangers of these girl on girl crimes, including calling each other "sluts," which only opens the door for boys to do the same. Most students have seen this film, and it's an excellent example for discussion.

9. The word "slut" has been used very few times on the show, notably in the episode "Take My Wife, Sleaze," in which Marge is named "Cycle Slut of the Month" by *Outlaw Biker* magazine. In addition, a video game played by Bart called "Cat Fight" features two girls kicking each other and pulling each other's hair, while saying "slut, loser, skank." Leora Tanenbaum's *Slut! Growing Up Female with a Bad Reputation* gives an excellent history of the word, double standards, and the power of female on female abjection.

10. While this trend goes back to *The Honeymooners*, it has experienced a resurgence as of late, and we suspect it was restarted by Homer and Marge.

11. We've had interesting class discussions about the sitcom convention of narrative self-containment: everything wraps up nicely in the end. This is particularly interesting in "Bart Star," as the issue of overweight kids seems forgotten.

12. If you choose to tackle this topic in your classes, remind the students that discussing how the culture or a television show treats a topic requires no editorial from them regarding the topic. (Namely, they should be able to have a critical analysis without ever letting the rest of the class know how they personally feel about the topic).

13. GLAAD, the Gay & Lesbian Alliance Against Defamation, created this media award in 1990 to "recognize and honor media for their fair, accurate and inclusive representations of the lesbian, gay, bisexual and transgender (LGBT) community and the issues that affect their lives."

14. At the time of this writing, *American Idol* has announced that Ellen DeGeneres will be replacing Paula Abdul in the next season of the show, which is another sign that the general American public might be taking Apatow's message to heart.

15. Approximately five years later, Karma showed this episode in her class. One student accused her of being part of "the gay agenda" and complained about her showing "sexually explicit" material in class. The student believed that a character saying s/he was gay was "sexually explicit." When asked if a character announcing his or her heterosexuality would be "explicit," the student replied no, because heterosexuality was "normal." Karma maintains that the teaching moment this instigated was one of the most valuable of her career, both for herself and for the student.

16. This is not the only time Moe covers his self-hatred with vocalizations of intolerance. In "Much Apu about Nothing," he hosts the anti-immigrant factions in his bar and is seen protesting immigrants. He then takes the U.S. citizenship test while wearing a fake mustache.

17. "Homer's Phobia" also allows for a useful discussion of the reclamation of the word "queer."

18. This list was primarily compiled by Alexander Waltonen.

19. There are several sources that discuss religion in relation to *The Simpsons*; Chapter 1 outlines many of them. Many religion classes in schools and places of worship have used the show to stimulate discussion on issues of faith and morality. The Church of England even published a handbook for its youth counselors called *Mixing It Up with* The Simpsons.

20. According to the BBC, the city of Rio de Janeiro tourist board was upset by the unflattering depiction of Rio, especially the pictures of crime, slums, rats, and violence, which they feared would adversely affect American tourism. Authorities also expressed

anger that Rio was depicted as a jungle with monkeys, which has since become a running gag.

21. Of course, it should be noted that, like many Americans, Homer doesn't want a tax increase to fund the art, music, and gym curriculum. When Skinner asks him, Homer makes it clear that he won't accept a $1.23 tax hike to sustain the classes.

22. Sadly, this speech does not achieve its goal of turning the majority against the proposition, though it seems to work on a few community members.

23. Issues of addiction may well run in the family. While Homer's alcoholism is pervasively alluded to in the show, Marge's gambling goes largely ignored, except in the episode where it begins and in a few brief references elsewhere, such as in "The President Wore Pearls": "I have a problem with games of chance. I played Candyland with Maggie and ended up throwing vodka in her face."

24. See "The Simpsons Satire and Postmodernism" (Chapter 6) for definitions of these terms and for a larger conversation on how *The Simpsons* is a postmodern show.

25. Examples can be found in "Homer vs. the City of New York" and "Separate Vocations."

26. Yo-yos play a big role in "Bart the Lover."

27. MMORPGs, or massively multiplayer online role playing games, while very popular, were not new in 2007 when this episode first aired. For example, one of the inspirations for "Earthland Realms," "EverQuest," was born in 1999.

28. "Mypods and Broomsticks."

29. Turner's book is discussed in Chapter 1.

30. Full disclosure: Karma is on the editorial board of *The Journal of Popular Culture*.

31. The Popular Culture Association and American Culture Association hold joint conferences.

32. Some episodes are used more often than others. You may notice that many of the episodes we rely upon are from seasons 12 and earlier. This is simply because we

have been spoiled by having these episodes on DVD and now find VHS tapes to be cumbersome. Furthermore, we do not practice nor do we endorse downloading episodes illegally.

33. Ned sees Rachel again in the episode "I'm Goin' to Praiseland" but unfortunately, Ned is still not over Maude's death. Two seasons later, Ned falls for an actress in the episode "A Star Is Born-Again."

34. The use of *The Simpsons* to teach composition is described in detail in Chapter 2.

35. All of the sexuality/gender episodes are discussed at greater length earlier in the chapter with the exception of "Lisa vs. Malibu Stacy."

36. Marge's professor asks permission to kiss her, which satirizes the Date Safe Project, a trend on some college campuses wherein students were encouraged to ask the other person for permission before initiating any kind of sexual contact. Asking for permission is depicted as an exaggerated form of political correctness.

37. It makes Denise cry every time she sees it, and she doesn't mind you knowing that.

38. Any *Simpsons* episode will deal with family relationships to some degree, especially sibling issues and parenting, but here we have chosen three that affect all members of the family in one story.

39. Adapted from *The Art of Being Human* by Richard Paul Janaro and Thelma C. Altshuler.

40. This assignment is not only excellent for humanities courses, but could also be used in introductory anthropology courses, as ethnographies are anthropological works. When we use this assignment in composition courses, we tend to focus on the language elements of subcultures—namely, how members of the subculture are fluent in the dominant culture's language as well as in their subculture's specific lexicon and are able to code-shift with ease. We then discuss in class the various ways that we code-shift on a near constant basis, from texting to classroom discussions to

phone conversations with our parents and how we communicate at our jobs.

Chapter 6

1. While we generally favor Marshall's understanding of postmodernism, the reader is cautioned that Marshall is hardly the last word on the subject — she disagrees with aspects of other theorists' arguments. Thus, resist seeing her definitions as the Truth. Similar reservations may be held in regard to our own definitions and uses of definitions, however much "truthiness" they may contain.

2. For an accessible introduction to these ideas, you might consult Catherine Belsey's *Poststructuralism: A Very Short Introduction.*

3. Showing a few scenes from Charlie Chaplin's *Modern Times* can be useful, as he literalizes this concept.

4. The episode "Mom and Pop Art" might be used to discuss modernism and postmodernism, as it incorporates not only modernist and postmodernist visual art but also mixes high and low art, and exemplifies genre/parodic concerns.

5. "Jose Chung's *From Outer Space,*" an episode of *The X-Files*, is a perfect example of a postmodern text in that it incorporates the ideas of alienation, refusal of an ending, intertextuality, self-referentiality, situated knowledge/multiple voices, and epistemological quandaries.

6. Stephen Colbert has, of course, been on *The Simpsons* in "He Loves to Fly and He D'ohs."

7. Students often need to be reminded that "sitcom" is short for "situation comedy." The form, which necessitates a return to opening equilibrium after the "situation" is threatened, should be explicated before the students can understand how *The Simpsons* deconstructs/parodies it.

8. Sarcasm may be seen in *The Simpsons* in the following exchange from "Flaming Moe's":

Marge: Well, Homer, maybe you can take some consolation in the fact that something you created is making so many people happy.

Homer: Ooh, look at me! I'm making people happy! I'm the magical man from happy land, in a gumdrop house on Lollipop Lane. [leaves, slams door, then sticks his head back in the room] Oh, by the way, I was being sarcastic.

Marge: Well, duh.

9. It is ironic that one year after *Ferris Bueller*, Tracey Ullman routinely ended her television program with the same sentiment.

10. The fourth wall in television is perhaps most often broken in children's educational programming, as the characters attempt to engage the viewers in learning activities.

11. Once again, *The Colbert Report* may be useful. Colbert addresses his audience as a first-person narrator, but his on-screen persona is at odds with Colbert the man.

12. As Lord Byron wrote, "And if I laugh at any mortal thing, 'tis that I may not weep."

13. Stanley Fish makes a similar distinction, but uses the terms "rhetorical" for readerly and "dialectical" for writerly.

14. We should note the problem with this structuralist assumption of two distinct kinds of texts, especially as we find that even the most readerly of texts sometimes leaves gaps that allow the text to be read in a new way.

15. Of course, this is exactly what some viewers were initially worried about when the show débuted — that other viewers would be influenced to use Homer and Bart as their models for behavior.

16. *Shaun of the Dead* is also useful in teaching narrative economy.

17. "Trash of the Titans."

18. "Bart's Comet."

19. In fact, the next episode to premiere after the movie had a slightly different opening sequence, one in which Springfield is being rebuilt after the doming destruction ("He Loves to Fly and He D'ohs").

20. "Simpsons Roasting on an Open Fire."

21. In "Last Exit to Springfield," Burns is temporarily successful in nixing the employee dental plan, and in "Midnight Rx," Burns eliminates the prescription plan, prompting Homer to acquire reasonably priced Canadian drugs.

22. "Burns's Heir."

23. Some instructors routinely assign students to choose a text (movie) from the year of the student's birth.

24. Typically, Karma uses the first day to collect information about the students, to introduce the history of the show, to do a lesson on satire, postmodernism, parody, zeitgeist, and comedy terms, and to allow the students to get to know one another by asking each other *Simpsons* trivia questions from the cards that come with the Simpsons Trivia game. She sometimes shows "Some Enchanted Evening" instead of "Simpsons Roasting on an Open Fire." While the latter was the first full-length episode shown, the former was the first episode produced. Viewing the *Tracey Ullman* shorts that appear on the DVDs can also be useful, as most students' history with the show does not extend back to the 1980s.

25. Class viewing typically centers on older episodes for two reasons. First, students are more likely to have watched recent episodes and thus need to brush up on older works. Second, using older episodes allows use of the DVDs and avoidance of the dreaded VCR and the many, many tapes amassed over the years. Relying on streaming from Internet sites is a possibility, but should be avoided due to the potential for clunky buffering and user guilt.

26. Students are expected to be able to view at least one episode of *The Simpsons* outside of class per week. Karma also often makes the first *Favorite Family* guide a required text.

27. During some quarters, Karma has also had a portion of the grade determined by group presentations on various topics. Past topics have included Literature/Parody, Race/Nationality, Social Class, Consumerism, News Media, Work, and Crime.

Bibliography

Abrams, M. H. *A Glossary of Literary Terms*. Florence, Ky.: Wadsworth, 2008.

Aitchison, Jean. *Teach Yourself Linguistics*. London: Hodder Headline, 2003.

Apatow, Judd. Interview. *Fresh Air*. NPR. WHYY, Philadelphia. July 22, 2009.

Aristotle. *Poetics*. New York: Penguin Classics, 1997.

Atwood, Margaret. *Second Words: Selected Critical Prose*. Toronto: Anansi, 1982.

Bakhtin, Mikhail. *Rabelais and His World*. Bloomington: Indiana University Press, 1984.

Barthes, Roland. *S/Z*. Trans. Richard Miller. New York: Hill and Wang, 1974.

Belsey, Catherine. *Poststructuralism: A Very Short Introduction*. New York: Oxford University Press, 2002.

Boe, John. "The Degrees of the Lie." *Teaching Writing Creatively*. Ed. David Starkey. Portsmouth, N.H.: Boynton/Cook, 1998, pp. 86–101.

Booth, Wayne. *A Rhetoric of Irony*. Chicago: University of Chicago Press, 1974.

Brecht, Bertolt. *Brecht on Theatre: The Development of an Aesthetic*. Trans. John Willet. New York: Hill and Wang, 1977.

Butler, Judith. *Gender Trouble: Feminism and the Subversion of Identity*. New York: Routledge, 1990.

Campbell, Lyle. *Historical Linguistics: An Introduction*. 2nd ed. Cambridge, Mass.: MIT Press, 2004.

Cromulent Shakespeare Company. 2009. About Cromulent Shakespeare Company. http://www.cromulentshakespeare.org (accessed October 1, 2009).

Dolan, Jill. *The Feminist Spectator as Critic*. Ann Arbor: UMI Research Press, 1988.

Donkin, Annemarie. "*The Simpsons* Songsmith Hits 400: The Maestro of D'oh-re-mi Composes a New Simpsons Score Every Week." The Signal of Santa Clarita Valley. August 26, 2007. http://oldsite.the-signal.com/?module=displaystory&story_id=50309&format=html (accessed October 1, 2009).

Dudek, Duane. "Mmmm, *The Simpsons*: Series Feeds Need to Laugh at Our Foibles." *Milwaukee Journal Sentinel*, July 27, 2007.

Eagleton, Terry. *Literary Theory: An Introduction*. Minneapolis: University of Minnesota Press, 1983.

Elder, Sean. "Is TV the Coolest Invention Ever Invented? Subversive Cartoonist Matt Groening Goes Prime Time. *The Jetsons* Was Never Like This." *Mother Jones* (December 1989): 28–31.

Fallows, James. "The Invisible Poor." *The New York Times Magazine*. March 19, 2000. http://www.nytimes.com/library/magazine/home/20000319mag-poverty.html (accessed September 26, 2009).

Farhi, Paul. "Conception of a Question: Who's Your Daddy?" *The Washington*

Post. January 4, 2005. http://www.wa shingtonpost.com/wp-dyn/articles/A4 6032-2005Jan3.html (accessed October 1, 2009).

Foucault, Michel, and Raul Rabinow. *The Foucault Reader*. New York: Pantheon, 1984.

Freund, Elizabeth. *The Return of the Reader: Reader-response Criticism*. London: Methuen, 1987.

Gay and Lesbian Alliance Against Defamation. GLAAD Media Awards 2009. http://www.glaad.org/mediaawards (accessed October 1, 2009).

Gray, Jonathan. "Imagining America: The Simpsons Go Global." *Popular Communication* 5.2 (2007): 129–148.

_____. *Watching with* The Simpsons: *Television, Parody, and Intertextuality*. London: Routledge, 2006.

Grey, Barry. "Leaked CIA Report Says 50,000 Sold into Slavery in US Every Year." World Socialist Web Site. http://wsws.org. April 3, 2000. http://www. wsws.org/articles/2000/apr2000/slav-a03.shtml (accessed September 28, 2009).

Groening, Matt. The Simpsons: *A Complete Guide to Our Favorite Family*. New York: HarperPerennial, 1997.

_____. The Simpsons *Beyond Forever!: A Complete Guide to Our Favorite Family ... Still Continued*. New York: HarperPerennial, 2002.

_____. The Simpsons *Forever! A Complete Guide to Our Favorite Family ... Continued*. New York: HarperPerennial, 1999.

_____. The Simpsons *One Step Beyond Forever!: A Complete Guide to Our Favorite Family ... Continued Yet Again*. New York: Harper Paperbacks, 2005.

Gunning, Tom. "An Aesthetic of Astonishment: Early Film and the (In)Credulous Spectator." *Film Theory and Criticism: Introductory Readings*. Eds. Leo

Braudy and Marshall Cohen. New York: Oxford University Press, 1999, pp. 862–876.

Halpern, Paul. *What's Science Ever Done for Us? What the Simpsons Can Teach Us About Physics, Robots, Life and the Universe*. Hoboken, N.J.: John Wiley & Sons, 2007.

Hanes, Philip J. "The Advantages and Limitations of a Focus on Audience in Media Studies." April 11, 2005. http:// www.aber.ac.uk/media/Students/pph9 701.html (accessed November 10, 2009).

"Hannibal, MO: Meet Springfield, USA." Mark Twain in Our Times: Twain, Television, and Pop Culture. September 26, 2009. http://etext.virginia.edu/ railton/projects/tysse/SIMPSONS things.htm (accessed November 10, 2009).

Heit, Jamey. *The Springfield Reformation: The Simpsons, Christianity, and American Culture*. New York: Continuum, 2008.

Hirsch, E. D., Jr. *Cultural Literacy: What Every American Needs to Know*. Boston: Houghton Mifflin, 1987.

Hutcheon, Linda. *A Theory of Parody: The Teachings of Twentieth-Century Art Forms*. Urbana: University of Illinois Press, 2000.

Idle, Eric. *The Road to Mars: A Post-Modern Novel*. New York: Pantheon Books, 1999.

Janaro, Richard Paul, and Thelma C. Altshuler. *The Art of Being Human: The Humanities as a Technique for Living*. 9th ed. New York: Pearson, 2009.

Johnson, Steven. *Everything Bad Is Good for You: How Today's Popular Culture Is Actually Making Us Smarter*. New York: Riverhead Books, 2005.

Keslowitz, Steven. *The World According to* The Simpsons: *What Our Favorite TV Family Says About Life, Love, and the*

Pursuit of the Perfect Donut. Naperville, Ill.: Sourcebooks, Inc.: 2006.

Levitin, Daniel J. *This Is Your Brain on Music: The Science of a Human Obsession.* New York: Penguin, 2006.

Mantsios, Gregory. "Class in America: Myths and Realities." *Rereading America.* 7th ed. Eds. Gary Columbo, Robert Cullen, and Bonnie Lisle. Boston: Bedford/St. Martin's, 2007, pp. 318–333.

Marshall, Brenda K. *Teaching the Postmodern: Fiction and Theory.* New York: Routledge, 1992.

Morrison, Gavin, and Alan Britton. "Images of the Teacher in *The Simpsons*: Subversive, Superficial, or Sentimental?" Presented at "The Teacher: Image, Icon, Identity." Glasgow, 2008.

Mulvey, Laura. "Visual Pleasure and Narrative Cinema." *Multicultural Dimensions of Film: A Reader.* 3rd ed. Eds. Mark Garrett Cooper and Maricarmen Martinez. New York: McGraw-Hill, 1999, pp. 274–281.

O'Grady, William, et al. *Contemporary Linguistics: An Introduction.* 6th ed. Boston: Bedford/St. Martin's, 2010.

Pinker, Steven. *The Stuff of Thought: Language as a Window into Human Nature.* New York: Penguin, 2007.

Pinsky, Mark I. *The Gospel According to The Simpsons.* Louisville: Westminster John Knox Press, 2001.

Plutarch. *Moralia, Book V,* "Isis and Osiris," (De Iside et Osiride). Trans. F. C. Babbitt. Cambridge, Mass.: Harvard University Press, 1993.

Postman, Neil. *Amusing Ourselves to Death: Public Discourse in the Age of Show Business.* New York: Penguin Books, 1985.

Ross, Alec. Personal communication, August 26, 2009.

_____. "Pop Goes Academe." *Queen's Alumni Review* 2 (2005).

Savage, William J., Jr. "'So Television's

Responsible!': Oppositionality and the Interpretive Logic of Satire and Censorship in *The Simpsons* and *South Park*." *Leaving Springfield: The Simpsons and the Possibility of Oppositional Culture.* Ed. John Alberti. Detroit: Wayne State University Press, 2004, pp. 197–224.

Shakespeare, William. *Hamlet.* New York: Washington Square Press, 1970.

_____. *Much Ado about Nothing.* Walton-on-Thames, U.K.: Arden Shakespeare, 1981.

"Simpsons Apologise to Rio." BBC News. April 15, 2002. http://news.bbc.co.uk/2/hi/entertainment/1931551.stm (accessed November 10, 2009).

Sloane, Robert. "Who Wants Candy?: Disenchantment in *The Simpsons.*" *Leaving Springfield: The Simpsons and the Possibility of Oppositional Culture.* Ed. John Alberti. Detroit: Wayne State University Press, 2004, pp. 137–171.

Smith, Owen. *Mixing It Up with The Simpsons: 12 Sessions on Faith for 9-13s.* London: Church House, 2007.

Steinmetz, Sol, and Barbara Ann Kipfer. *The Life of Language.* New York: Random House, 2006.

Sung, Daniel. "Embiggen Your iPod to 240GB and 48,000 Tracks." *Tech Digest.* May1, 2009. http://www.techdigest.tv/2009/05/embiggen_your_i.html (accessed October 1, 2009).

Tanenbaum, Leora. *Slut! Growing Up Female with a Bad Reputation.* New York: Perennial, 2000.

Thomsen, Helle Klem, and Jacob David Eichler. "Preface." *What's Fun Got to Do with It? An Anthology of American Humor.* Eds. Helle Klem Thompson and Jacob David Eichler. Copenhagen: Copenhagen Business School Press, 1999, pp. 7–12.

Turner, Chris. *Planet Simpson: How a Cartoon Masterpiece Defined a Genera-*

tion. Cambridge, Mass.: Da Capo, 2004.

Urrea, Luis Alberto. *The Devil's Highway*. New York: Back Bay Books, 2004.

Waltonen, Karma. "4 *Simpsons* Controversies That Didn't End in Lawsuits." *Mental Floss*. May 18, 2009. http://www.mentalfloss.com/blogs/archives/25661 (accessed September 26, 2009).

Williams, Tennessee. *A Streetcar Named Desire*. New York: Signet Books, 1947. Reprint, New York: New American Library, 1984.

Wolfe, Susan. Personal communication, July 25, 2009.

Yankovic, Al. "Weasel Stomping Day." *Straight Outta Lynwood*. Compact disk, Volcano, 2006.

Index

All fictional character names are listed alphabetically
by the way the character is best known, usually by first name.

317